How to Sell Computer Services to Government Agencies

How to Sell Computer Services to Government Agencies

Herman Holtz

Chapman and Hall
New York   London

First published 1985
by Chapman and Hall
29 West 35th Street, New York NY 10001

© 1985 Herman Holtz

Printed in the United States of America

Library of Congress Cataloging in Publication Data

Holtz, Herman.
How to sell computer services to government agencies.

Bibliography: p.
Includes index.
1. Government purchasing—United States. 2. Selling—Computers. I.
Title.
JK1671.H638 1985   353.0071'2   85-6651
ISBN 0-412-00701-0

Preface

There are today several million customers, buying well over $500 *billion* annually (that's more than $500,000,000,000), in the "government market" in the United States. The U.S. Census Bureau identifies nearly 80,000 "governmental units," including over 3,000 counties; over 18,000 cities, towns, and townships; and nearly 60,000 school districts and special districts which function with almost the autonomy of local governments. (The Bureau also points to approximately 125 major urban or metropolitan centers in the country.) But there are still other mind-boggling statistics to consider.

The federal government alone employs 130,000 people full time in purchasing and procurement functions, and operates at least 15,000 purchasing offices throughout the United States, spending about $170 billion per year at current rates. And all but the smallest of those many thousands of state and local governments include hundreds of agencies, bureaus, offices, and institutions which do at least some of their buying independently, although most of those governments have central purchasing and supply organizations also.

To some degree at least this reflects a continuing trend. Over the years, and particularly since the Second World War, administration of all governments—federal, state, and local—has become more and more complex and difficult. In modern times all governments have grown steadily and at rates of increase that many find alarming. These are numerous. For this, citizens demand more services from government, for one thing, but other factors are at work also. The growing population and increasing complexity of society create demands for greater government control and regulation. Moreover, the increasing technological sophistication has created pressures on government too.

The effect on government has been to bring about a great increase in government spending at all levels, and this has in turn brought about huge increases in "contracting out," because governments are dependent on the private sector for much of their needed services, as well as for the goods produced by industry. But governments were unprepared for the revolutionary changes that began soon after World War II had ended and have been accelerating ever since. And to this day, many governments are still struggling to adjust to these new and different conditions, although most are on the same track, pursuing the same broad goals. For example, the federal government did not have an organized procurement system or even a formal set of procurement regulations before 1947—the federal government itself did not, in fact, even have a centralized purchasing and supply organization before that year. And only quite recently, and partly as a result of the 1969 Commission on Government Procurement, have the myriad sets of procurement regulations begun to be replaced by a single, uniform set of regulations effective for the entire U.S. Government. But the federal government was not alone in this: Even now, many state and local governments are still struggling to organize efficient purchasing organizations.

- Pasco County, Florida, eliminated its old decentralized, non-competitive bidding procedures with a formal system that requires formal, sealed-bid procedures (with public bid openings) for all procurements over $3,000.
- San Bernardino, California, now uses contractor services for snow removal, using competitive bidding.
- Orange County, California, has gotten 25 cities, 31 school districts, and 11 special districts in the county to purchase cooperatively, with the county acting as purchasing agent and administrator, achieving the benefits of large volume buying and more efficient paperwork.
- Rockingham County, Virginia, has established a centralized purchasing and accounting system so that all departments use the same set of numbers for control and reference.

Meanwhile, other forces have been at work, attempting to achieve the same goals. The American Bar Association launched a project to develop a Model Procurement Code for state and local governments, as a joint effort by the ABA Sections of Public Contract Law and Urban, State, and Local Government Law in early 1974.

In general, the Code endorses competitive sealed bidding as the preferred method of procurement but allows for other methods, as required by situations which preclude sealed bidding as a viable method. The Code also recognizes the necessity for and provides for small-purchase procedures, sole-source procurement, emergency procurement, and other special, negotiated procurements, particularly for certain types of services. Various types of contracts are acceptable under the Code but cost-plus-a-percentage-of-cost contracts are expressly prohibited. Meanwhile various articles in the Code cover such matters as architect-engineer and related services, construction, cost principles, accounting systems, supply management, contract terminations, and other relevant matters.

More and more jurisdictions are adopting the Code or at least using it as a model upon which to base their own procurement systems. The result is that most governments in the U.S. today utilize similar principles in their public purchasing, and the differences tend to be somewhat superficial, rather than fundamental. That is, the differences are most often those of degree, rather than of kind, with different jurisdictions using different size standards to define such things as small purchases and small business, while agreeing to recognize that there are requirements to define these things.

The federal and state governments have recognized that government purchasing has become a major economic force in our society, and that governments should feel morally compelled to employ this great economic force for both economic and social reforms. The result has been a plethora of programs, starting with the establishment of the U.S. Small Business

Administration more than three decades ago, but still proceeding, so that today there are literally hundreds of programs for small business, minority enterprise, women-owned businesses, handicapped entrepreneurs, and others at both federal and state levels of government. (And even at local-government levels in many cases.)

Ironically, only a relative handful have benefited from these great outreach programs. The vaunted SBA 8(a) program for minority entrepreneurs, for example, while delivering huge benefits to many of the fortunate few who were favored by and able to take advantage of it, has never had more than approximately 1,600 beneficiaries at any given time, and the "graduation" or turnover rate has been virtually nonexistent, at least until recently. So the benefited minority entrepreneurs were little more than a token, with useful political fallout for more than one Administration, but with little or nothing for most of that vast population for whom it was intended.

On the other hand, even those who neither are entitled to nor seek any special programs but who win substantial business from governments on a purely competitive, business basis are relatively few in number. There are between 13 and 15 million businesses in the United States (the number depends on whose estimates you accept), and less than 10 percent of those do business consistently with government agencies. (For example, only about 250,000 firms are consistent suppliers and contractors to the federal agencies, and that is only about 2 percent of all businesses, at best.)

The reason is simple enough: The governments do an extremely poor job of helping vendors learn about government needs, government purchasing, and government programs. Even those government needs that are advertised in newspapers represent a tiny fraction of all government procurement, and the federal government has its own publication for advertising its needs and bidding opportunities. Unless you happen to know about that publication, which at most lists only about 10 percent of all federal purchasing, in any case, you are not likely ever to learn about government needs and sales opportunities.

That is the reason for this book. It is addressed to a need that is growing as rapidly in the federal establishment as it is in the private sector, a need for computers, with all the related equipment, supplies, and services. This book can put your feet on the road to success in that enormous market—that enormous *set* of markets, that is. It is my sincere hope that it will do so.

Herman Holtz
Silver Spring, Maryland
May, 1985

Contents

Chapter 1

UNDERSTANDING THE GOVERNMENTS

Government at all levels in the United States follows the same general structure, in both organization and in procurement practices. The differences are more of degree than of kind, in most cases.

What Does "Government" Mean?

In the United States, when we speak of "the government," we are most frequently referring to the federal government, that organization with its headquarters in Washington, DC, but with thousands of facilities and offices scattered throughout the United States and, for that matter, in many other countries as well. When we wish to refer to other, lower-level governments, we tend to call those governments "the State," "the City," or "the County." For our purposes in this book, it is necessary to remind ourselves that these are all governments, some 38,777 governments, even if we count only those which are actually the governments of states, counties, cities, towns, and townships, in addition to the federal government.

Actually, there are even more than that large number, if we count governments the way the U.S. Census Bureau does. In fact, the Census Bureau reports that the United States includes 79,913 "governmental units," as the Bureau expresses it. And the Bureau supports that number by offering the following breakdowns of units and their numbers:

Federal Government	1
State governments	50
Counties	3,042
Municipalities	18,862
Townships	16,822
Local school districts	15,174
Special districts	25,962
Total:	79,913

What All Governments Have in Common

All governments in the United States have certain things in common, which are of interest to us in connection with marketing to government agencies. Like the federal government, other governments have a governing official—governor, mayor, or county executive—a legislative body, and a complex of supporting departments, offices, and other agencies. Most states have departments structured generally along the lines of the federal government; typically, there are in all state governments a governor, a lieutenant governor, a secretary of state, an attorney general, a supreme court or chief justice, and other departments corresponding generally to federal agencies and federal government structure. And whereas the federal government has a General Services Administration, which has at least nominal responsibility for federal procurement, most states have a purchasing office, although sometimes it is a full-fledged department of the state government, and sometimes it is only an office within a finance or administrative services department.

Our own federal government, for example, has 13 or 16 full departments (13 if you count the Department of Defense as a single department, 16 if you count each of the military departments, Army, Navy, and Air Force, as additional departments, since each bears the official title "Department"). But in addition to that, there are some 60 independent agencies—offices, administrations, commissions, authorities, etc. The General Services Administration (GSA) is a housekeeping and purchasing organization for the rest of the government, civilian and military, but since it spends only a tiny percentage of the total procurement budget (less than 1 percent for fiscal year 1983), it is quite obvious that the other agencies do not rely heavily on GSA for procurement support but do the bulk of their own purchasing via their own resources. (This will be found to have its counterpart in most state and local government procurement practices.)

Typical Government Organization

To illustrate typical state government organizations, and to show how much they resemble each other and the federal government structure, the chief offices and agencies of two extremes—a large western state, California, and a small eastern state, Delaware—are compared here:

California	*Delaware*
Secretary of State	Secretary of State
Attorney General	Attorney General
Supreme Court	Supreme Court
General Services Department	Division of Purchasing / Administrative Services Department
Food & Agriculture Department	Agriculture Department
Economic Development Commission	Commerce Department
Insurance Department	Insurance Commission

Labor Department
Controller Office
Transportation Department
Conservation Department

Public utilities Commission
Consumer Affairs Department
Arts Council
Department of Corrections

Labor Department
Treasurer
Transportation Department
Natural Resources &
  Environmental Control Department
Division of Public Utilities Control
Consumer Affairs
State Arts Council
Department of Correction

Department Missions and Needs

Except for military and diplomatic functions, state governments tend to have the same kinds of missions to carry out, the same kinds of problems to solve, and the same kinds of functions and needs as the federal agencies. State and local governments at all levels—county, township, town, and city—must generally provide and maintain most of such services and functions as these:

Executive system
Legislative system
Judicial system
Law enforcement (police)
Fire fighting (fire departments)
Health services
Social services
Public school systems
Community Colleges
City/state colleges and/or universities
Prison systems
Hospitals
Public cemeteries
Medical examiners
Tax collections
Utilities regulation
Insurance regulation
Purchasing
Highway construction and maintenance
Other public works construction and maintenance
Conservation of natural resources
Administration of all these functions

Obviously, there are wide variations, according to size and local conditions. A desert state, such as Arizona or Nevada, has a somewhat different economy and different needs than a heavily forested state, such as California or Washington, for example, and a state with a subtropical climate, such as Florida or Hawaii, would have some needs quite different from those of a far-northern state, such as Alaska or North Dakota. All, however, make some use of computers, and the usage of computers and computer services is increasing steadily in government agencies, as it is in society at large. In that respect, the chief difference between the various governments is primarily one of degree and application, rather than of kind. That is, a large and populous state or city, such as California or Chicago, would necessarily spend more money for computers and services than would a small or sparsely populated state or small city, such as New Mexico or Akron, although buying generally the same kinds of equipment, supplies, and services. And the applications would necessarily vary, too. California, for example, would have a rather large department of agriculture and would also have some organization analogous to the federal government's Forest Service. But Arizona and Nevada would have far less need for a forestry service, or at least they would need a much smaller forestry organization. This difference would be reflected in each state's computer applications as well as in other matters.

Of course, the size of the government overall is very much a factor, too. California, for example, is comparable in its size and in its public budget to many small countries. In fact, the California procurement system and its list of standard commodities and services purchased bear a striking resemblance to those of our federal government.

Governments as Customers

Governments, like other organizations, are also customers and represent markets for businesses. In this case, the total purchasing represented by this set of 79,913 purchasing entities—which should probably be called markets, rather than customers, for they represent a great many more customers than 79,913—is well in excess of $600 billion annually. That number is pretty hard for us to grasp. Perhaps it is easier to grasp this as representing a spending rate of $68,681,318 per hour or $1,144,688 per minute! And that's based on a 7-day week and 24-hour day. Were we to calculate the spending rate on the basis of the standard 5-day business week and 8-hour working day, the rates of spending would be about quadruple what they are shown here to be.

The federal government alone accounts for at least $175 billion annually. The total announced for fiscal year 1983 was $168,197,501,000, but the true figure is somewhat higher than that because the Postal Service, the Pension Benefit Guaranty Corporation, and several other government agencies are not required to report their procurement figures, and seven of the smaller Boards and Commissions were listed with the notation "Failed to Report," where the column would normally have shown the figures representing their purchasing totals. Of course procurement budgets have also been climbing steadily, partly as a result of inflation, but also as a result of new programs and increased buying by the governments, and federal procurement is likely to reach $200 billion or more annually by the time you read these words.

Governments as Markets

Government purchasing is the mainstay, the chief source of business, for at least some million-plus businesses in the United States. For a great many other enterprises, government procurement is at least one important source of business, one upon which they depend for a significant portion of their income. And there are few business enterprises in the United States which do not get some of their business, directly or indirectly, as a result of government buying.

What Government Buys

The public at large sees government procurement primarily in terms of guns, tanks, airplanes, and naval vessels. Other items of government procurement do not offer the drama of military procurement or the huge multi-billion-dollar awards. And it is true that in the federal procurement budget, by far the bulk of the dollars are spent by the Pentagon and its many military organizations and establishments. But in the overall governmental purchasing of hundreds of thousands of customers represented by the many offices and branches of all the government agencies and institutions, military procurement is a much smaller and hence much less significant number. In fact, the governments buy just about every kind of goods and service you can name and are, in many cases, the *only* buyers for some goods and services. (That is, some goods and services exist only to satisfy government's wants and have little or no commercial market elsewhere.)

A Focus on Federal Procurement

In exploring these markets in the pages ahead—and our interest is primarily the government markets for computer products and services—we will appear to be giving priority to the federal government markets, although the federal government, despite its huge size and huge expenditures, still represents less than one-third of all government purchasing in the United States. There are several reasons for this pronounced focus on federal government procurement:

1. The federal government makes far more information available than do other governments about its procurement needs, practices, and actions, making it possible to supply far more detailed and specific information than would otherwise be the case.
2. The federal government represents some kinds of important markets, such as military and scientific, which are represented sparsely or not at all by state and local governments.
3. Much of state and local government buying is based on and closely resembles federal procurement practices, regulations, and procedures. If you understand how the federal government does its buying, you will have a good understanding, in principle at least, of how the other governments buy.

4. Without federal government purchasing, the computer industry would probably not yet have reached its present technological state, and the industry's development might well have been retarded for many years. It is helpful to remember this and to understand some government attitudes with respect to computer services.

Early Federal Support of the Computer Industry

In the early days of computers, when they were massive and costly behemoths, few other than the largest and most heavily budgeted government agencies could afford such equipment. In fact, it was largely government willingness to support this infant industry, despite the cost and the relatively primitive systems, that made its survival and development possible. And over the years, government has continued to support the computer industry as a customer for both hardware and software, and it is probably the major customer for custom development of software and other computer R&D, even today.

The Expanding Market Today

The revolution wrought in computer technology by microcircuitry—chips, printed wiring, and all the related technological breakthroughs that have made possible the inexpensive personal or desktop computer—has resulted as much in a spurt in government purchasing of computers and computer services as it has in computer marketing generally. Hardly a day passes now that the federal government alone does not list 50 to 100 computer and computer-services bid opportunities in its *Commerce Business Daily* (CBD), the publication in which federal agencies announce their wants (bid opportunities) every day. Daily, many of the thousands of government offices solicit bids, quotations, and proposals for computer equipment, software, and services of many kinds. There are single purchases, indefinite-quantity purchases, term contracts, ordering agreements, time and material or hour-labor contracts, fixed-price buys and cost-reimbursement contracts. The buyers are military installations, regional offices and field offices of the major government departments and "independent" agencies, purchasing offices of state and local governments, and the many other agencies of all the state and local governments—prison systems, government-run colleges and universities, public school systems, police and fire departments, public libraries, and other such public agencies. And since so many of these units are in turn subdivided into many departments, branches, and other organizational units, the number of potential customers runs into well over six figures.

The Peculiar Needs of Government

Government agencies, and especially federal agencies, are outstanding customers for computers and computer services in several ways. One advantage is, of course, the sheer size of government agencies as a market: In general, it is often possible to get far larger orders from government agencies than from private-sector organizations. However, as noted earlier, frequently government agencies have needs that are peculiar to their missions and functions and different from any encountered elsewhere. That is itself an advantage to resourceful contractors who are willing to undertake highly specialized projects calling for great imagination and creativity.

In general, then, government agencies tend to buy far more custom work—to have services and goods designed especially for them—than do private-sector buyers. In the private sector, customers tend to search out what is available on the shelf, as standard or proprietary items, and select those which come closest to satisfying their needs. Rather than pay the usually much higher cost of having custom work done for them, they will make small compromises, as long as they can achieve most of their essential needs. Not so government agencies: as a rule, they tend to perceive their needs as unique and capable of being completely satisfied only by custom services.

In fact, they are not wrong: many government needs are unique. The Environmental Protection Agency (EPA), for example, has many unique needs, one of which is the requirement for pesticide registration. This is a massive program, which has cost the EPA many millions of dollars and much anxiety because it is a difficult and troublesome program and EPA is still issuing contracts to private-sector organizations for computer services and much other related support, in its efforts to satisfy the goals of this program.

This is a typical situation, in which legislators have created law and handed over to an existing agency the often-difficult and sometimes-impossible requirements resulting from the legislation. And sometimes the legislation creates new agencies, as in the case of EPA, the Pension Benefit Guaranty Corporation, the Consumer Product Safety Commission, the Department of Transportation, and most of the other government agencies which have come into existence over the 200-odd years of our history.

Of course, these agencies are faced with immediate problems, and they must almost always turn to the private sector for succor. A new agency is generally formed from a thin cadre of personnel borrowed from other, older agencies and reinforced with numerous consultants and contractors. However, many agencies, older, established ones as well as new ones, have far more work to do than their personnel can handle. Often, they have only enough personnel to do basic planning and managing of projects which have been contracted out. And frequently the agency must contract out many of its functions and services on a permanent basis. (Often the new agency hires as many of the consultants as it can, but rarely does a busy agency have enough in-house staff to handle everything that needs doing.)

Of course legislators are not the only creators of difficult requirements, calling for extraordinary efforts by agencies. Other circumstances and influences compel such efforts also. Simple technological advances, for one, often compel our military organizations to mount new programs which require outside help. When the Navy found it necessary to standardize its teleprinters, for example, it was necessary to turn to industry to do so. Had they decided to have the Navy's own technological staffs design a standard teleprinter, they might or might not have been blessed with the latest and most advanced teleprinter technology and the most advantageous design. By going out to industry at large and soliciting proposals, they gained many studies by industrial organizations, which enabled their own experts to make comparative analyses and evaluations and judge which appeared to be the best design to adopt.

While most of the government agencies have their own technical specialists on staff and can also turn to other, sister agencies for help, they can never be sure that their in-house experts are totally up-to-date on everything, especially in technological areas. Moreover, even if their own experts are completely up-to-date on the state of the art, there is always the possibility that some company in the industry has some special or proprietary ideas or capability that offers advantages. Government agencies are aware of this possibility and of the desirability of inviting as many ideas as possible.

Military needs and military competition—including rivalry among the various U.S. military services but, more pointedly, competition with the Soviet Union—absolutely compels many contracts. The Soviet Union, like the United States and other Western nations, is busily developing missiles and space systems, and computers are playing key roles in related R&D, deployment, and operation of such systems. We are therefore forced to push our own technological R&D and related work as rapidly and as energetically as possible. Our intelligence services make the utmost effort to learn where the Soviets are technologically, and our military organizations make the utmost effort to push our own basic research and R&D to keep us ahead of the Soviets. These efforts are in themselves the font of many contracts.

Kinds of Computer Services Government Agencies Buy

Aside from these special causes and sources of government's perceived needs that lead to contracts, there are some general considerations that apply to virtually all cases, even those of civilian agencies buying somewhat mundane goods and services. In doing business with government agencies, it is necessary to understand why and under what circumstances generally these agencies turn to the private sector for help. For while there are many different specific circumstances (such as a few we have already described), all fall into only two general classifications: Government agencies need help of two kinds or, perhaps it is more accurate to say, because of two different kinds of circumstances. In one case the agency needs help in doing things it is itself unable to do (e.g., solving a specific problem) because it lacks adequate know-how or because it is not sure that its know-how is adequate, and it therefore wants to gain the advantage of as much know-how as the private sector appears able to offer. In the other case, the agency needs help in doing things it cannot do simply because it does not have enough "hands and feet" —it lacks enough in-house staff to do the work.

To pursue government contracts successfully, it is important to understand this and to make the proper distinctions, as you will see later, when we probe more deeply into the specifics of pursuing and winning government contracts. But here are just a few of the kinds of the computer and computer-related services government agencies buy:

Basic computer (hardware) R&D
Basic computer (software) R&D
Design and development of hardware systems
Design and development of software systems
Operation of computer installations
Hardware maintenance
Software maintenance
Documentation
Forms design
Data collection
Teleprocessing
Leasing systems
Purchase of equipment
Purchase of supplies

Related Services

Frequently, government projects require services not directly related to computers and their operation or systems and yet essential elements of what is basically computer-related or computer-based projects. The EPA pesticides registration is a case in point: One major contract and a number of smaller ones have been let to software service firms to assist EPA in satisfying this requirement, but at least one of these contracts included requirements for the services of individuals who would have nothing to do with the computer work. These were experts in the substances—toxicological experts, chemists, microbiologists, and other specialists in some aspect of pesticides.

This is a common situation in many government projects, resulting from their complexity and from the government's tendency to let major prime contracts, where the prime contractor will have to let a number of subcontracts. This relieves the government of the necessity of managing a great many contracts because the prime contractor is thus made responsible for all the indirectly related work, which may be handled by the contractor's own staff or subcontracted out. Either way, the government's burden of contractor monitoring and management is thus lessened. But there is still another consideration that encourages a practice of letting major, prime contracts. In today's sophisticated and complex technological environment, a great deal of federal procurement is of systems, rather than of equipment. A missile, for example, requires a rather huge complex of launching equipment and ground support equipment, all functioning as a system. While each of the many pieces of equipment requires sets of drawings, maintenance procedures, operating manuals, training materials, and other such items, the system also requires all of this *at the system level*. Moreover, someone must supervise and coordinate all of this development, which usually involves a number of contractors. (The Ballistic Missile Early Warning System [BMEWS], for example, involved over 300 subcontracts.) The prime contractor must handle all of this "system coordination" and other documentation and general management of the entire system.

This again is a job the government agency does not normally wish to handle and is usually not at all equipped to handle. Hence the common practice of letting a prime contract for the entire system.

The Navy is something of an exception to this and often contracts for a system by letting a large number of individual contracts. However, the Navy is under the same burden of other departments of not having enough staff to monitor and manage all the contracts and do all the staff work necessary for system coordination. The Navy solves this problem by letting a contract to handle all that system coordination work, so that the Navy staff has little more than a nominal responsibility for management of all the complex of individual contracts.

Some Revealing Statistics

Not all federal procurement is competitive, and in many cases less than one-half of an agency's purchases are made competitively. That is unavoidable simply because of the nature of the procurement, in the majority of cases. Take the case of an aircraft manufacturer who has developed a new plane for the Air Force or Navy, for example, and has millions of dollars worth of tooling and other investment already made. (Actually this is often the property of the government already because it was purchased for the government's account under cost-plus contracts.) It would be a foolish economy to go competitive for follow-on production contracts, for it would cost the government many additional millions, probably even billions, to do so. But there are many other situations in which it is impractical or at least excessively costly to go competitive for the purchase; hence the large proportion of noncompetitive contracts. (Of course, you may yourself become the beneficiary of noncompetitive procurement, happily!)

Still, the portion that is competitive is quite staggering in size. In one recent year for which figures are available, approximately $59 billion, roughly 39 percent of the total budget, was expended in competitive procurements, 52 percent noncompetitively, and 9 percent by "other methods."

The Federal Procurement Data Center, an arm of the Office of Federal Procurement Policy (itself an arm of the Office of Management and Budget), issues reports with extensive breakdowns of federal procurement activity. One of those breakdowns reports federal procurement totals by type of contractor, type of contract, and other such indicators which help contractors get a more intimate view of how the federal government buys and how to position themselves to take advantage of these factors. Table 1-1 offers an indication of how federal procurement dollars are expended by listing several of the most significant of these items, to help you in defining and designing your marketing stance vis-à-vis the federal agencies.

Table 1-1   Selected Figures on Fiscal-year Federal Procurement

Item	No. Procurement Actions	Dollars $(000)
Type Contractor		
Business concerns	374,231	138,005,665
Procurement Method		
Negotiated	348,676	133,308,923
Small Business		
Prime contracts	165,524	20,940,367
Total setaside	57,755	7,296,466
Type of Contract		
Fixed price	336,932	105,755,734
Product/Service		
R&D	32,997	21,632,176
ADP services	8,213	1,412,362
ADP equipment, purchase/lease	19,075	2,218,723
Consultant services	1,491	119,282

The figures are somewhat misleading, however, if you take them literally, because although the official government reports list such items as "Automatic Data Processing Services" and "Consultant Services," these reflect only those contracts that cite such services by those names. In fact, a great many consulting services, data processing services, and sundry other computer and computer-related services are procured under other designations and descriptions of the services. Some may be procured, in fact, as Architect-Engineer (A&E) services, government-owned, contractor-operated (GOCO) facilities, as abstracting services, and many other identifications. Therefore, the figures cited in the table are only a most general indication.

However, using the "ADP Services" as a kind of weather vane, at least, for whatever it is worth, some of the leading users who report their procurement of services so described are listed in Table 1-2.

Table 1-2   Comparisons of ADP-services procurement

Agency	No. Purchases	Dollar Value $(000)
Department of Defense	2,566	566,359
NASA	2,538	199,554
EPA	468	33,420
Department of Interior	243	250,547
Department of Health and Human Services	225	30,762
Department of Labor	208	26,435
Department of Energy	171	37,310
Department of Commerce	151	26,976
Tennessee Valley Authority	151	9,872
Department of Housing and Urban Development	118	14,842
Department of Treasury	78	11,574

You will note that while the agencies are listed in descending order of the number of "ADP services" purchases they report, the magnitude of dollars represented by these purchases does not "track" with the number of procurement actions. Obviously, some agencies tend to negotiate frequent small contracts for these services (e.g., NASA), whereas other agencies contract for such services less frequently but tend to award many large contracts (e.g., the Department of the Interior). Of course, this means that you have a better chance of winning contracts at NASA than at Interior, but they are likely to be smaller contracts than you might win at Interior.

There are trade-offs here, as there are in all things. The effort required to win, the number of competitors you will encounter, and the risk of losing the competition are almost always in proportion to the size of the contract. Therefore, if you are new to government contracting, you will probably do better to pursue the smaller contracts first and so have a better chance to win, while you begin to learn how you can best fit into the government's procurement patterns.

Chapter 2

GOVERNMENT PROCUREMENT SYSTEMS IN GENERAL

Just as government structures at all levels have many factors in common, so do government purchasing regulations and procedures have many common principles.

First Principle: It's Taxpayers' Money

One basic similarity among all governments, as far as purchasing is concerned, is that all are spending public money, taxpayers' money, and are therefore accountable to the taxpayers. That means, in more practical terms, that all spending of public money is under statutory control, and the basic statutes governing procurement are quite similar in principle, and variations are far more a matter of degree than of kind. There are several specific principles underlying all public procurement.

Basic Procurement Regulations and Procedures

An underlying philosophy of all purchasing with public money is that purchasing must be on a competitive basis. There are at least three fundamental reasons for this:

1. Competition tends to keep the suppliers working with "sharp pencils"—calculating costs and markups closely and therefore charging the lowest possible prices, so that the taxpayers stand the best chance of getting their money's worth.
2. It is fundamental in our representative form of government that everyone is entitled to the same opportunity to pursue business in the public sector, that is, business resulting from purchasing with public funds, with our own taxes. Competition, the *right* to compete, is inherent in that concept.

3. The standing requirement for open competition as the standard for purchasing, with noncompetitive procurement the exception, requiring special justification, tends to keep both seller and buyer honest by making it difficult to be otherwise without being detected.

There is really a fourth principle involved, one that is logically an extension of the third item. It is this: In our system, all government actions are supposed to be subject to the "sunshine" principle—conducted openly, in the light of day, exposed to public scrutiny—with only those exceptions justified as in the public interest vis-à-vis national security or to protect an individual's privacy and right to privacy.

These are goals, and it is true that these goals are not always realized in practice because no system is perfect. But it is true, also, that competition means something more than rivalry to induce the lowest bid. There are other kinds of competition than price or bid competition because there are many situations in which price is not the most important consideration. In many circumstances quality, durability, maintainability, and other considerations are more important than price. This is especially the case under such circumstances as these:

- When the product or service must be custom designed and there are no known specifications, but the government must make a judgment as to which prospective contractor will produce the most satisfactory result.
- When the quality—maintainability, dependability, etc.—is of critical importance, such as in the case of a military aircraft, weapons system, communications system, or other such end-item. (That is, where a low bid, if price were the only decisive factor, would be highly likely to result in an inferior product or service, resulting from typical cost- and corner-cutting.)
- When the government is seeking basic research or even applied research (R&D) and no one can predict what the end results are likely to be. In such circumstances the government must make a judgment as to which contractor has made the best case in its proposal and is thus likely to be the most productive contractor.

Procurement regulations take these situations into account, and provide other means and criteria than the lowest bid price for selecting an awardee for the contract. (That is still competition, but of a different type: it is competition based on technical/professional considerations, as well as price, which becomes only one of several evaluative criteria.)

Despite the many reasons for employing competition as a basis for most procurement, there are also some drawbacks to competitive methods in that competitive purchasing methods necessarily require more time to consummate a purchase and also entail much more procurement expense. Therefore, public purchasing statutes normally include exceptions, where the purchase is so small that competitive methods would be prohibitively high, compared with the size of the procurement, and/or where an emergency exists or for some other reason delay cannot be tolerated and the procurement must be facilitated.

An Exception to the Rule

If it is true that an exception proves the rule, we have an excellent example near at hand. In the mid-1980s *The Washington Post* ran a series on government procurement by the city of Washington, DC, which, the series alleges, is paying far more for various items than are procurement officials in surrounding jurisdictions. Even "small purchases" are set at not more than $10,000, while most jurisdictions set it at somewhat less than that—$500 to perhaps $2,500, in most cases tending to the lower side of that range. The District of Columbia, however, follows the federal lead and uses the $10,000 figure. And whereas most jurisdictions do the bulk of their purchasing via a centralized purchasing system and permit the various agencies to make only small purchases of not more than a few hundred dollars independently, the District of Columbia allows its agencies to make independent purchases up to $10,000. Only above that amount does the District require that a central city bureau, the Materials Management Administration, manage the purchase. And to further amplify the potential for abuse, the story charges, whereas most jurisdictions specifically prohibit breaking a large purchase into individual (small purchase) fragments so as to defeat the purpose of limiting the size of excepted and noncompetitive procurements, this particular evasion is widely practiced by the District government.

Some Typical Procurement Budgets

In preparing this series, the newspaper reports an annual procurement budget for the city of $2.5 billion and compares that with several others in the surrounding areas:

Arlington County, Virginia	$246 million
Fairfax County, Virginia	$1.1 billion
Montgomery County, Maryland	$883 million
Prince George's County, Maryland	$645 million
Alexandria City, Virginia	$215 million
Baltimore City, Maryland	$1.3 billion

These are rather typical and representative figures. Multiply such figures as these by 3,042 counties and 35,684 incorporated cities and towns not to mention 50 state governments and 41,136 school and special districts exercising considerable spending power of their own—and you can begin to see where those hundreds of billions in annual government purchasing originate. And consider further that each jurisdiction has many agencies—50 to 100 apiece, as a conservative estimate of the average—and you should begin to appreciate the potential of these many markets.

The Many Customers

It may occur to you now that there is something of an anomaly here. On the one hand, I speak of the central purchasing authority for all but very small purchases, and on the other hand I point to a huge number of potential buyers, well beyond the numbers represented by those central purchasing authorities, potential buyers who cannot buy independently, that is.

In fact, this is not an anomaly. While most of the agencies and individual employees in most jurisdictions cannot spend more than a few hundred dollars independently (or a few thousand dollars, for employees and offices of federal agencies), they can *request* specific purchases and, under the right circumstances, even arrange to direct that contract or purchase order to a chosen vendor—you, for example. The purchases are then made by and through the central purchasing authority for the individual agency or office you enlisted as your customer. So at least part of your marketing effort must be directed to the end user, as your actual customer, as well as to the purchasing officials of whatever centralized purchasing authority and organization with which you must contract.

Two Basic Procurement Systems

Since there are two kinds of competition—price competition and technical/quality competition—it follows logically that there are also two basic procurement systems, one for each kind of competition. The two systems are known generally in federal procurement regulations and procedures as *advertised* procurement (also referred to as "formally advertised" procurement) and as *negotiated* procurement. And the basic difference philosophically is the one just discussed; that is the difference between making awards to the lowest bidder and making awards to the bidder judged to be best qualified for the contract. Later, we'll be returning to this subject again and again, especially to the subject of negotiated procurement, but for now we'll look briefly at the federal systems as reasonably representative of those employed in most jurisdictions.

Advertised Procurement

Although the federal government publishes the *Commerce Business Daily* (CBD) six days a week and lists thousands of requirements in it every week, *advertised* does not refer to listing a solicitation therein. For purposes of legality, the requirement that the government "advertise" a bid solicitation is satisfied when the procurement office mails out several solicitations to prospective bidders on its bidders list. In practice, procurement offices do much more than mail out copies of the solicitation to some portion of their bidders lists. They generally also announce the solicitation in the CBD in a synopsis of the requirement (see Figure 2-1) and they post the solicitation in their offices somewhere. (If the procurement office is a large and busy one, it will probably have a "bid room" also, and then the notice will probably be posted on a bulletin board. If the office is small and not busy enough to boast a bulletin board, much less a bid room, the solicitation will be in some kind of a binder, available for inspection by anyone who wishes to take the trouble to visit and ask to see the current crop of solicitations.)

H Expert and Consultant Services

Health Resources and Services

USDA, Agricultural Research Service, Acquisition and Assistance Division, Contracting and Procurement Operations Branch, Service Contracts Section, 4th Floor, NAL Building, Beltsville, M 20705
H – MODIFY THE FLAMINGO COMMERCIAL SOFTWARE PROGRAM to treat specific conditions of soil and water processes including seepage face boundaries, infiltration and water extraction by roots; software shall be tested and documented on six government-owned computer

Armament Division, Deputy for Contracting and Manufacturing, Attn: Jackie L. Leitzel 904/882-4400, AD/PMY-I, Eglin AFB FL 32542
A – COMPUTER SIMULATION AND TECHNICAL SUPPORT
F08635-84-C-0219—14 May 84—$189,200. Street, LaJolla CA 92070
DEVELOP A COMPUTERIZED DATA BASE ON THE AIR LEAKAGE CHARACTERISTICS OF BUILDINGS AND THEIR COMPONENTS. The Data Base will include information on the leakage characteristics of the building and its components, building type, construction and material type, age, date of recent weatherization, location and prevailing climate code. The Data Base will include information on leakage characteristics of buildings. The contract will comprise a two year effort. No facility security clearance will be req
shoul   Ballistic Missile Defense Systems Command, Contracts Office,
This   BMDSC-CRS, Attn: Beverly L. Danner, 205/895-3880, P. O. Box 1500, Huntsville, AL 35807
H – ADVANCED SOFTWARE ENGINEERING FOR DISTRIBUTED COMPUTING SYSTEMS—RFP DASG60-84-R-0147—RFP to be issued approx 26 Sep 84 with sol closing date 30 days after issuance—Noncompetitive negotiations to be conducted with the Regents of the University of California, Berkeley—See Note 22. (266)

Harry Diamond Laboratories, Contracts Branch (Vint Hill)DELHD-PR-CV (D. Wood 703/347-6312) Vint Hill Farms Station, Warrenton, VA 22186-5120.
H – SOFTWARE ENGINEERING TECHNICAL ASSISTANCE—Intent to exercise Second Year Option from 30 September 1984 through 30 September 1985, Contract DAAK21-83-D-0100—The BDM Corporation, 7915 Jones Branch Drive, McLean, VA 22102—See Note 22. (266)

Director, Cash Management and Disbursing Div. Banking and Cash Management Branch (Code NAFC-432). Navy Accounting

USGPO, Regional Printing and Procurement Office Building 53, Room D 1010, P.O. Box 25347, Denver Federal Center, Denver, Colorado 80225.
T – LASER PRINTING AND COMPUTER SERVICES. Program 2862 S, Denver Colorado area, single Award Term Contract, January 1, 1985 to December 31, 1985. GPO Procurement for the Department of the Interior. Contractor must pickup, deliver and mail. approx 17,000 copies per job, sizes to 8-1/2 x 11. Black ink. F.O.B. Denver Regional

Office of Adm. Mgmt Services, Small Purchasing Section, National Library of Medicine, 8600 Rockville Pike, Bldg. 38A, Room B2N08, Bethesda, MD 20209, Attn: Zetherine L. Gore, Purchasing Agent
H – CONDUCT CONFERENCE ON THE EXECUTIVE MANAGEMENT OF COMPUTER RESOURCES IN THE ACADEMIC HEALTH CENTERS to be held in Washington, DC. Intent to provide partial support to the Assn of Academic Health Centers. The purpose of the conference is to explore in greater detail the concept of academic health center wide computerized info and communications networks, and the fiscal and management resources needed for planning and implementing them. This is a notice of intent, not a RFP. No sol pkg will be available. (300)

U.S. Army Electronics Command, Fort Monmouth, NJ 07703
* U – COMPUTER MAINTENANCE TRAINING COURSE The United States Army Communications-Electronics Command proposes to exercise an option under Contract No. DAAB07-84-C-E611 for the acquisition of a Computer Maintenance Training Course to Elmer Corporation, Neptune, NJ. This notice is for information made on the basis

US Department of Education, Assistance Management and Procurement Services, ADPAC Branch, Room 3674, ROB #3, 400 Maryland Ave., SW, Washington, DC 20202
H – SYSTEM MAINTENANCE AND DATA ANALYSIS—Award of 63 modification 63 to contract HEW 100-79-0103 Planning Research Dr, McLean, VA 22102. Amount of increase is $39,000.
H – COLLECTION ACTIVITY UNDER THE CUBAN STUDENT LOAN, LAW ENFORCEMENT EDUCATION, AND PELL GRANT PROGRAMS—The Department of Education has awarded contract 300-84-0145 to Corliss Credit Services, 580 Burnside Ave., E Hartford, CT 06108. The amont is $49,000. (175)

70 General Purpose ADP Equipment Software, Supplies and Support Equipment, incl Leasing

Naval Regional Contracting Center, Philadelphia, PA 19112
70 – MAINTENANCE DEC ADPE The Naval Regional Contracting Center, PA. intends to place a renewal order for maintenance of equipment listed below under Digital Equip. The equipment is

John F. Kennedy Space Center NASA, Kennedy Space Center, FL 32899
H – SDRC SOFTWARE MAINTENANCE, ENHANCEMENTS AND SUPPORT AGREEMENT (ME&S) for mechanical design software system P/N CAE 100 (CO30402) to include: (A) Correction of documentation and/or software codes arising from any variance between computer program function and user manuals. (B) System updates which operate under new releases of the VAX 11/780 operating system. (C) Documentation updates. (D) Documentation updates. (E) Impact of enhancement program enhancements. (F) Hotline telephone service to assist users with the design software system. Provision for three, one-year options—RFP 10-3-ed to company—PI to close on or after Oct. 25, 1984—Interested firms may obtain RFP N00173-84 referencing Synopsis 2456 within 15 days of the date of this notice. (258)

Supply Center, Naval Research Laboratory, Washington, D.C. 20375
70 – WORD PROCESSOR SERVICES—Planned procurement for the 12-month lease and maintenance of nine A. B. Dick Magna/SL word processing systems currently installed in NRL Bldg. 208. Interested firms may obtain RFQ N00173-84-Q ten request to Code 2414H, referencing Synopsis 2461 notice. (258)

National Institutes of Health, Procurement Branch, DAS, Bldg. 31, Room 3C-25, Bethesda, MD 20205, Ms. Helen G. Kelly, 301/496-4281
● T – GRANTS RECORDS MAINTENANCE SERVICES RFP 263-85-P(68)-0006 is available for a contract for one year with four hard and one-year options to create and maintain official updatable microfiche grants recordes masterfiles, provide duplicate updatable microfiche grants records to users of such records, create and maintain up-to-date individual paper based applications and grants records files, assure security for all

Social Security Administration, Division of Contracts and Grants Management, Post Office Box 7696, Baltimore, Maryland 21207 Attn: Elizabeth Clark
H – SOFTWARE ENGINEERING SUPPORT The Social Security Administration (SSA) will be installing a new Data Communications Network (DCU) in the near future. This new network will require extensive software modification prior to implementation SSA is searching for ADP software vendors with highly technical Contractors are needed
of the intercomm telephone
tractor must have an int
contractor to have access

Contracting Officer, (90C), VA Medical Center, 1601 Brenner Ave., Salisbury, NC 28144, J.D. Wood, 704/636-2351, ext 346
● H – WORD PROCESSING SERVICE To provide centralized correspondence preparation to all activities of the Veterans Administration Regional Office. Winston-Salem, NC. Processing involves transcription of dictation from cassette tapes, worksheets and source documents. Word processing operation requires extensive knowledge of medical, legal and realty terminology plus the formats of approximately 105 form letters. Estimated annual number of typed lines range from 3,000,000 to 3,500,000, may very depending on workload. Finished product must be proofread and verified as error free. Correction of the contractor to correct at no charge to the VA. tractor error is the responsibility

Figure 2-1 Some typical notices in the *Commerce Business Daily*

Note in Figure 2-1 that some of these notices appear under different CBD headings (supply categories). Computer services and/or products might be found under a number of CBD headings, including all of these:

A Experimental Development, Test and Research Work (research includes both basic and applied research)
H Expert and Consultant Services
J Maintenance and/or Repair of Equipment
K Modification, Alteration, and/or Rebuilding of Equipment
L Technical Representative Services
M Operation and/or Maintenance of Government Owned Facility
T Photographic, Mapping, Printing, and Publication Services
U Training Services
X Miscellaneous
69 Training Aids and Devices
70 General Purpose ADP Equipment Software, Supplies and Support Equipment, incl. Leasing

The federal government uses a Standard Form 33 (see Figure 2-2), and checks off a box labeled *Advertised (IFB)* (Information for Bid and Award). This advises the reader immediately that the award will go to the lowest bidder. Technically, it is to go to the lowest *qualified* bidder, but in practice it is difficult legally to disqualify a bidder who has gone through all the proper steps in bidding, so it rarely happens that a bidder is disqualified; almost without exception, the lowest bidder wins the contract. And that is in itself sometimes a contracting problem, one which enables an unqualified bidder to bid unrealistically low and win a contract he or she cannot perform acceptably on, to everyone's loss. For that reason, government agencies tend to negotiated procurement, in many cases, where such an eventuality is to be feared.

In advertised procurement, the usual practice is to request bidders to furnish price(s) only, after examining the specifications for the item(s) and/or service(s) described. (The solicitation may well include a "laundry list" of items and therefore require a list of prices.) Occasionally, the solicitation will ask also for textual materials describing the bidder's qualifications. However, that is virtually meaningless, as we have already seen, and is probably employed primarily in the hope of discouraging anyone not fully qualified from bidding at all.

The solicitation specifies a date, time, and place of opening, which is also the deadline for submission of the bids. The bid opening is public: anyone may attend, and most bid openings are attended by many, if not all, of those who have submitted bids. They sit, usually around a table, and record the bids, as they are opened and read aloud by the contracting official. As the contracting official opens the bids, he or she verifies that the bidder has signed the bid form in the proper place and made all the required entries.

It is soon obvious who has submitted the apparent low bid—apparent because many such bids have unit prices and quantities, requiring extensions, and all the arithmetic must be checked before a low bidder can be firmly identified. Where, as can happen, the bidder has made a mistake in making extensions, the unit price prevails. So the bidder with the apparent

SOLICITATION, OFFER AND AWARD	1. CERTIFIED FOR NATIONAL DEFENSE UNDER BDSA REG. 2 AND/OR DMS REG. 1 ▶	RATING	PAGE OF 1 | 33 PAGES

| 2. CONTRACT NO. | 3. SOLICITATION NO. DAAG60-84-B-6023 | 4. TYPE OF SOLICITATION [X] ADVERTISED (IFB) [ ] NEGOTIATED (RFP) | 5. DATE ISSUED 84 Oct 04 | 6. REQUISITION/PURCHASE NO. W96MK14222-5001 |

7. ISSUED BY   CODE
Contracting Office
Bldg 667-A, USMA
West Point, NY 10996-1594

8. ADDRESS OFFER TO (If other than Item 7)

NOTE: In advertised solicitations "offer" and "offeror" mean "bid" and "bidder"

SOLICITATION

9. Sealed offers in original and __01__ copies for furnishing the supplies or services in the Schedule will be received at the place specified in Item 8, or if handcarried, in the depository listed in Bldg 667A, 3rd. Floor, Room 4 until 2:00 local time 24 Oct 1984 (Hour) (Date)

CAUTION — LATE Submissions, Modifications, and Withdrawals: See Section I, Provision No. 52.214-7 or 52.215-10. All offers are subject to all terms and conditions contained in this solicitation.

| 10. FOR INFORMATION CALL: ▶ | A. NAME Bob Murphy | B. TELEPHONE NO. (Include area code) (NO COLLECT CALLS) 914-938-2473 |

11. TABLE OF CONTENTS

(✓)	SEC.	DESCRIPTION	PAGE(S)	(✓)	SEC.	DESCRIPTION	PAGE(S)
		PART I — THE SCHEDULE				PART II — CONTRACT CLAUSES	
	A	SOLICITATION/CONTRACT FORM			I	CONTRACT CLAUSES	
	B	SUPPLIES OR SERVICES AND PRICES/COSTS				PART III — LIST OF DOCUMENTS, EXHIBITS AND OTHER ATTACH.	
	C	DESCRIPTION/SPECS./WORK STATEMENT			J	LIST OF ATTACHMENTS	
	D	PACKAGING AND MARKING				PART IV — REPRESENTATIONS AND INSTRUCTIONS	
	E	INSPECTION AND ACCEPTANCE			K	REPRESENTATIONS, CERTIFICATIONS AND OTHER STATEMENTS OF OFFERORS	
	F	DELIVERIES OR PERFORMANCE					
	G	CONTRACT ADMINISTRATION DATA			L	INSTRS., CONDS., AND NOTICES TO OFFER	
	H	SPECIAL CONTRACT REQUIREMENTS			M	EVALUATION FACTORS FOR AWARD	

OFFER (Must be fully completed by offeror)

NOTE: Item 12 does not apply if the solicitation includes the provisions at 52.214-16, Minimum Bid Acceptance Period.

12. In compliance with the above, the undersigned agrees, if this offer is accepted within _____ calendar days (60 calendar days unless a different period is inserted by the offeror) from the date for receipt of offers specified above, to furnish any or all items upon which prices are offered at the price set opposite each item, delivered at the designated point(s), within the time specified in the schedule.

| 13. DISCOUNT FOR PROMPT PAYMENT (See Section I, Clause No. 52-232-8) ▶ | 10 CALENDAR DAYS % | 20 CALENDAR DAYS % | 30 CALENDAR DAYS % | CALENDAR DAYS % |

| 14. ACKNOWLEDGMENT OF AMENDMENTS (The offeror acknowledges receipt of amendments to the SOLICITATION for offerors and related documents numbered and dated: | AMENDMENT NO. | DATE | AMENDMENT NO. | DATE |

| 15A. NAME AND ADDRESS OF OFFEROR | CODE | FACILITY | | 16. NAME AND TITLE OF PERSON AUTHORIZED TO SIGN OFFER (Type or print) |
| | DUNS NO. | | | |

| 15B. TELEPHONE NO. (Include area code) | 15C. CHECK IF REMITTANCE ADDRESS IS DIFFERENT FROM ABOVE - ENTER SUCH ADDRESS IN SCHEDULE. | 17. SIGNATURE | 18. OFFER DATE |

AWARD (To be completed by Government)

| 19. ACCEPTED AS TO ITEMS NUMBERED | 20. AMOUNT | 21. ACCOUNTING AND APPROPRIATION 2152020 17-6725 P810000 2521 S30145 814721.15100 ZA41 |

| 22. SUBMIT INVOICES TO ADDRESS SHOWN IN (4 copies unless otherwise specified) ▶ | ITEM 25 | 23. NEGOTIATED PURSUANT TO [ ] 10 U.S.C. 2304(a) ( ) [ ] 41 U.S.C. 252(c) ( ) |

| 24. ADMINISTERED BY (If other than Item 7) CODE | 25. PAYMENT WILL BE MADE BY CODE Finance Office ATTN: Commercial Accounts, Bldg 632 West Point, NY 10996-1996 |

| 26. NAME OF CONTRACTING OFFICER (Type or print) | 27. UNITED STATES OF AMERICA (Signature of Contracting Officer) | 28. AWARD DATE |

IMPORTANT — Award will be made on this Form, or on Standard Form 26, or by other authorized official written notice.

NSN 7540-01-152-8064
PREVIOUS EDITION NOT USABLE   33-132   STANDARD FORM 33 (REV. 10-83)
Prescribed by GSA
FAR (48 CFR) 53.214(c)

Figure 2-2   Federal Standard Form 33, used for solicitations

low bid—the price on the bottom line—is sometimes not the low bidder, after all.

For this reason, the awards are not made officially until some time later, after the contracting official has verified the arithmetic and the eligibility of the bidder. For occasionally a bidder is blacklisted for some period of time, as a penalty for some earlier contracting infringement, and is therefore not eligible to bid until that period has elapsed.

Negotiated Procurement

The Standard Form 33 may have the *Negotiated (RFP)* box checked. RFP means Request for Proposals, which signals the reader that the procurement process will be quite different from the one just described. The solicitation package will include a Statement of Work, usually, although occasionally an RFP may be issued for a proprietary equipment "or equivalent," in which case the specification will actually be an item description, although it may still be called a work statement.

The work statement will describe what the customer feels a need for and wants to buy, but usually does not include highly detailed specifications. The inability to specify in detail what is needed is the reason normally for going to negotiated procurement and requesting proposals. It is on the basis of what the proposal states that the government will reach a decision on who is to be invited to sit down and negotiate the contract. The price quoted in the proposal is not necessarily binding. The government may and often does choose to actually conduct negotiations, trying to get better terms, on the basis of using that quoted price and whatever representations the proposal makes as the starting points. Or perhaps the terms offered are totally unacceptable, but the government likes the proposal enough to want to make an effort to reach agreement on better terms. This is fairly common when the proposer is in what the government refers to as "the competitive range," which means close enough to what the government wants to make it reasonable to expect to reach agreement in negotiation. (Some contracting officials make it a matter of policy to negotiate every contract that is to be over some minimum amount with the expectation that it is almost always possible to save the government at least some money, and some contractors write every proposal with the expectation that they will be required to negotiate before they are awarded a contract.)

If unsuccessful in reaching agreement, the government may turn to the next most highly rated proposer and attempt to reach agreement with that proposer through negotiation. Or the government may opt to simply abandon the procurement entirely. (This has happened.) Negotiation affords both the government and the bidder such flexibility of response and reactions.

Actually, the proposer submits two proposals, a technical proposal and a cost proposal. The evaluators then award the technical proposal a score on the basis of the merits of the proposer's plans, personnel, facilities, experience, and other resources and qualifications.

That technical rating is to be a major factor, with cost another factor, of course. Later, we will probe this subject much more deeply, as it is a critically important key to winning government contracts.

Some Statistical Data on Relevant Federal Contracting

For fiscal year 1983, the Office of Federal Procurement Policy reported 21,189,144 "actions" (individual purchases) totaling that $168,200,000,000 reported earlier. Some 85 percent of these purchases were made via advertised procurement—sealed bids. But some 85 percent of the *dollars* were spent in negotiated procurements—awards made as a result of proposal competitions. Some significant comparisons between fiscal years 1982 and 1983 can be made. In terms of major product and/or service, here are a few figures relevant to computer services:

	FY82	FY83
Supplies and Equipment:	$83.0 billion	$82.3 billion
R&D	20.1 billion	21.6 billion
ADP	1.1 billion	1.4 billion

Of course, we have no way of knowing from these figures how much of computer supplies and equipment and of computer R&D services were purchased under those first two categories because the report does not break those categories down that far. We can see, however, that identified ADP services totaled $1 billion in 1982 and grew to $1.4 billion in 1983. And that is only *major* procurement actions.

In another report, federal agencies were shown to have procured in fiscal year 1983 $1,584,535,000 worth of General Purpose ADP Equipment, Software, Supplies and Supporting services (category 70) alone. That, of course, does not account for computer equipment and services purchased under all those other categories listed earlier. However, still another report from the Office of Federal Procurement Policy's computer, the Federal Procurement Data System, reports these figures for fiscal year 1983:

Automatic Data Processing Services:	8,213 actions	$1,412,363,000
ADP Equipment, Purchase and Lease:	19,075 actions	$2,218,723,000
Totals:	27,288 actions	$3,631,085,000

Even that does not account for all the federal business in this area because it does not break out all the purchases of goods and services under those other procurement and commodity categories, but it begins to give us an idea of the magnitude of this federal government market alone.

Types of Contracts

There are a number of types of contracts, which have nothing to do with whether they were awarded under advertised or negotiated procurement. They are simply different types for different situations and purposes. First of all, they all fall into two broad categories, fixed price and cost reimbursement. Fixed-price contracts are agreements to deliver a specified product or service for a specified price. Cost-reimbursement contracts provide for billing within some agreed-upon limits, based upon some variable factors. There are a few variants of each and a type or two that might be considered to be hybrids.

Fixed-Price Contracts   There are two general types of fixed-price contracts. One is the simple, "for the job" contract, which generally involves a project calling for the delivery of some product or service, with flat payment of the agreed-upon price when the job is done. One variant is a fixed-price contract that calls for delivery of more than one product or service, especially when they are spaced out over some period of time, but when the deliveries and quantities are clearly specified and agreed upon. In such case, generally the customer is billed and payments are made after each delivery. In the federal system, the Federal Supply Service and other centralized federal supply services, such as those of the Department of Defense (the Defense Logistics Agency), the Postal Service, and the Veterans Administration, often use these kinds of supply contracts. They are often referred to as "term" contracts, especially by state and local government purchasing offices, who tend to favor them in purchasing supplies of commodities and even services.

The other type is the indefinite-quantity fixed-price contract, where the prices are clear, but the government cannot specify exactly how much of each item or when deliveries of the items will be required. But it is still fixed price because the unit prices are fixed, although the total value of the contract is not fixed, of course, because the total quantities are not fixed. The term contracts referred to in the preceding paragraph are far more likely to be of the indefinite-quantity type than for definite quantities, since they are generally entered into for a single year, and it is usually quite difficult to predict what agencies will use over the course of a year. In fact, such contracts are generally used to maintain warehouse stocks, rather than to fill specific, individual orders.

Contracts of this type may be used for services, however, as well as for goods to be stocked in warehouses and supply depots, especially when the services are of a more or less routine nature, the need for which may be easily anticipated, even if the time and quantity cannot be accurately predicted. Maintenance services are a good example of this, but are by no means the only example. Government agencies contract for services to handle a wide variety of services on a more or less ongoing or routine basis. There are, for example, many contracts of a type referred to as "basic ordering agreements" or "call contracts," under which the contractor signs an agreement to supply certain, specified classes of labor and perform certain kinds of tasks as specified rates, supplying the services whenever the government "calls" for them by issuing requests or task orders. (There are a number of variants of this basic concept, but all are along these general lines, despite dissimilarities in many specific provisions.)

A great many computer services are purchased in exactly this manner, even to the extent that in many cases the government has the contractor supply staff to work on the government's own premises, writing programs, and sometimes even operating the government's computer and computer-based systems in something called a "facilities management" contract. (Many government computer systems are programmed and managed by contractors, in this manner.) It is against federal regulations for contractors to work on government premises, ordinarily, and exceptions must be justified to be permitted legally. Therefore, "on-site" contracts must be justified by the agency as covering requirements that are of such a nature that they can be handled only by having the contractor personnel working on the government's premises. Such would be the case in operating government equipment and facilities, for example, or in doing work requiring access to government property that for one reason or another cannot be removed from government premises.

Socioeconomic Programs

Many programs have been initiated over the past few decades in attempts to right what pressure groups and legislators believe are social and economic inequities that call for adjustment through government programs. Several programs have been instituted to utilize government buying power as a weapon or tool in these efforts. These programs have taken different forms. Some are pure and simple set-asides of government contracts for certain classes of bidders, permitting no one else to bid, while others give certain kinds of preference to privileged classes of bidders. There are three general classes of bidders addressed in these programs: Small business generally, minority-owned enterprises, and businesses owned by women.

The leading programs are those offered by the federal government, which took the lead in such efforts, and it is on those that the following reports are made. However, many state governments have been influenced by the federal example and have emulated the federal examples by enacting similar programs in their own procurement programs. (These will be reported in more detail later.)

Set-Aside Procurements

Legislation requires that whenever possible contracts are to be set aside for small business. That means that only those qualifying as small businesses are permitted to compete for those awards. And the standards by which businesses do or do not qualify are set by the U.S. Small Business Administration (SBA).

The rationale for a set-aside is a simple one: If the procurement official determines that the government can get adequate competition for the contract, despite restricting the bidding to small businesses, the award is to be so restricted. And each agency is required to have a small business representative. In those agencies where the procurement offices do a great deal of purchasing, that small business representative may well be an individual devoting full time to that work, but in offices where the volume of procurement does not justify such a full-time position, someone wears the small-business representative's "hat," in addition to other duties. Not surprisingly, that person is usually the contracting official of the organization.

The size standards for small business vary from industry to industry, and may be based on annual sales, number of employees, or other quantifiable factors. In many cases, firms employing fewer than 500 employees qualify; in others, it is firms whose annual receipts are not more than $2 million, $5 million, or $8 million. But there are other standards than these also, according to the nature of the industry. (In the refining industry, for example, the size standard is in terms of barrels-per-day plant capacity.)

In fact, a relatively small number of such set-asides are made. For fiscal year 1983 the government reported $28.6 billion in small business set-asides, which was 18.735 percent of total procurement dollars. In terms of percentage of all awards made, 54.186 percent of the awards were made to small business. (This may seem a substantial percentage, but the SBA reports that 97 percent of American firms qualify as small business, so the percentage figure must be considered in that frame of reference.)

There are also minority-enterprise set-asides, awards set aside to be made to firms qualifying as "8a" firms. (These are firms certified by the SBA as minority owned and entitled to compete for these special set-asides. The competition, however, is purely technical, not cost, because the contract is actually awarded to the SBA, which subcontracts it to the 8a firm, generally for more than SBA is being paid, so that SBA subsidizes the minority firms by absorbing the losses.) For firms so certified and other minority and disadvantaged firms (classed as "large minority" and "small minority" firms) 4.964 percent of all procurement actions were made to them, totaling $3,085,967,000 or 2.026 percent of all procurement dollars.

Firms owned by women get some degree of preference in competition for some contracts, although not privileged with actual set-asides (unless they happen to be also members of a minority and certified as 8a firms, as is often the case). Women-owned firms won $567,550,000 (0.373 percent) with 1.590 percent of all procurement awards made.

Bidders to whom awards will mean some jobs in areas of exceptionally high unemployment (areas declared by the Labor Department to be labor-surplus areas) are given some preferences in certain procurements, and some awards are set aside for such areas. The fiscal year 1983 reports, however, show only $1,638,678,000 (1.076 percent) in awards so made.

Finally, the reports show that over 69 percent of the year's purchasing was made by fixed-price contracts, nearly 30 percent by some types of cost-reimbursement contracts, and the remainder scattered over several other types of contracting.

Chapter 3

PRINCIPLES OF MARKETING TO GOVERNMENT AGENCIES

Knowing how governments buy (the mechanics of typical government purchasing) is not the same as knowing how to sell to governments—the art of marketing effectively. You need to know both, in fact, to succeed in these markets.

Even Government Buyers Must be Persuaded

On the one hand, it is necessary to know how governments buy—their methods, rules, and procedures—to do business with them. On the other hand, it is a mistake to believe that knowledge of how governments buy is all that is needed to sell to them, or that such knowledge will result automatically in winning government business. For while there are some fundamental differences between doing business in the private sector and doing business in the public sector, the usual sales/marketing skills and efforts are just as necessary to success in selling to governments as they are to success in selling to customers in the private sector of the economy. In neither case can you afford to abandon good marketing and sales principles.

The Chief Difference

If there is one major difference between the two markets, it is that in the private sector, customers are free to do business with anyone at any time and make whatever buying decisions they wish. Private-sector customers may decide what to buy and from whom to buy, on the basis of logic, whim, friendship, bias, or any other basis. They do not have to shop for price, permit sellers to compete directly with each other, or listen to sales arguments. In the public sector, however, there are governing statutes—purchasing regulations which are either formal law or have the same authority—which control to a great extent what, how, and from whom the government agency may buy and, for that matter, most of the specific procedures which must be followed. That is the significant difference between the two sectors because from it flow other factors, in particular the marketing strategies that apply to doing business in the public sector. Since the law dictates how government agencies must buy, logic dictates that the marketer must know the law and understand how it works in practice.

Federal versus State and Local Governments

One way to gain a good understanding of all government markets and government procurement is to compare federal government purchasing with typical state and local government purchasing. For while the two are quite similar in principle, as already noted in an earlier chapter, they are quite different in many specific procedures and methods. And to make these comparisons it is necessary to examine at least the following aspects, concerns, and procedures of government procurement:

- Purchasing organizations
- Bidders lists: how they are developed, how to get on them
- Announcements: how governments advise of needs and bid opportunities
- Major procurements versus small purchases
- The degree of centralization versus decentralization of purchasing
- The exceptions to normal practices and procedures

Purchasing Organizations

Most state governments make a concerted effort to centralize the bulk of their purchasing by establishing a centralized purchasing organization in the state capital, and having that organization handle as much of the purchasing as possible. In general, the variation between the states lies in the degree to which the central purchasing organization controls purchasing by the state government and its many agencies and institutions. A few states exercise very tight control, so that with only rare exceptions, all agencies and institutions that are part of the state government place all purchase requisitions with the purchasing division. Others permit a few or a great many of the agencies and institutions to buy nonroutine supplies, equipment, and services independently.

The State of Alabama, for example, operates its Purchase and Stores Division as part of the state's Finance Department in the Capitol Building in Montgomery. That division does all purchasing, except for a few specified exceptions. There are 11 buyers in the division, responsible for the procurement of a wide variety of goods and services, with each buyer assigned certain specific items. A single buyer, for example, is responsible for buying computer equipment, tapes, disks, and consultant services, among other items. The purchase of electronic test equipment, on the other hand, is assigned to another of the buyers. The purchasing division of Ala-bama, like most other state purchasing organizations, encourages, even urges, vendors to visit the division's offices and meet the appropriate buyers, as an important early step in doing business with the state.

This is reasonably representative of the other state and local govern-ments. Purchasing organizations are found within various state agencies—administrative departments, finance divisions, general services divisions, and others.

Federal Government Purchasing Organizations

The federal government of the United States operates several centralized purchasing and supply organizations but only rarely mandates that the various agencies utilize these for purchasing. So while a great deal of the government's needs are satisfied through these agencies, the bulk of federal procurement dollars, especially for technical and professional services and major items of equipment, are used to make purchases through the indivi-dual purchasing offices within the operating agencies. And in some cases those purchasing offices are quite large.

The centralized purchasing and supply organizations of the federal government include these:

General Services Administration
Defense Logistics Agency
Veterans Administration supply service
Postal Service supply service

The General Services Administration (GSA) operates the Federal Supply Service (FSS), which buys a variety of commodities and services for repur-chase by the other agencies. But GSA also operates, among its subordinate organizations, the Automated Data and Telecommunications Service (ADTS), which serves the government generally as technical expert and sometimes as standards setter for data and communications equipment and supplies.

The Defense Logistics Agency (DLA) is part of the Department of Defense and buys for the military organizations, although they each do a great deal of their own buying also.

Military Procurement

Official figures reveal quite clearly that while all major agencies of the federal government spend heavily to sustain their operations, none begins to approach the procurement budgets of the Department of Defense (DOD), which is over 80 percent of all federal procurement. Even the com-bined spending of all other federal agencies is only a fraction of DOD's budget. Obviously, a serious marketer cannot afford to neglect that sector of the market.

At the same time, it must be recognized that the huge DOD purchasing is not carried out solely by the Defense Logistics Agency and the other DOD offices and organizations, but is actually the sum total of purchasing and procurement by thousands of individual organizations in the several military departments—Air Force, Army, and Navy (and the Marine Corps, which is part of the Navy). Each of these has its own centralized procurement and supply organization, but still the various units within each military department also have their own budgets and do much of their own buying. The Navy, for instance, does a great deal of its purchasing via its own Naval Supply Service and operates a number of busy procurement offices in various locations.

For example, each military base—Army camp, Air force base, and Naval installation—has a procurement officer and in some cases an entire procurement organization. To market to the DOD effectively, it is necessary to address your marketing efforts to a number of these organizations, many of which are quite substantial customers, spending many millions of dollars every year.

Many of these functional units, organizations, and purchasing offices are listed in a later portion of this book, which is given over to such directories.

The Veterans Administration satisfies a great many of its own needs through its own purchasing and supply organization, as does the Veterans Administration, although they and the DLA can turn to GSA for purchasing and supply support, too.

There are at least 15,000 purchasing offices within the federal establishment, housing some 130,000 procurement specialists. The largest agencies have extensive procurement offices and staffs. The National Aeronautics and Space Administration (NASA), for example, operates a number of bases around the country, each of which does extensive buying and therefore maintains a busy procurement staff. Many of the larger military bases also do a great deal of independent purchasing, as do the Department of Agriculture and the Labor Department, among others.

Bidders Lists

All purchasing organizations establish and maintain bidders lists for those goods and services they buy regularly. The federal government supplies applicants with a Standard Form 129 (see Figure 3-1), which will add the applicant's name to the agencies' bidders lists for the appropriate items. The state purchasing offices have equivalent forms (see Figures 3-2 and 3-3).

In some states the form used is more than an application to be placed on a bidders list; it is a vendor-registration form, and is a prerequisite to contracting with the state. In fact, in some cases the vendor will not qualify to submit a bid unless the vendor has such a form on file with the state's purchasing organization. And whereas the federal government makes no charge to submit a Bidder's List Application and most states do not, some do require the vendor to pay a (usually small) registration fee.

Filling out such application and registration forms, however, does not guarantee that you will receive all solicitations of interest. For one thing, there are frequently more names on the list than the purchasing office wishes to solicit, so they rotate the names, and you may receive only one out

BIDDER'S MAILING LIST APPLICATION	INITIAL APPLICATION	FORM APPROVED OMB NO.
	REVISION	29–R0069

Fill in all spaces. Insert "NA" in blocks not applicable. Type or print all entries. See reverse for instructions.

TO (*Enter name and address of Federal agency to which form is submitted. Include ZIP Code*) | DATE

1. APPLICANT'S NAME AND ADDRESS (*Include county and ZIP Code*)

2. ADDRESS (*Include county and ZIP Code*) TO WHICH SOLICITATIONS ARE TO BE MAILED (*If different from item 1*)

3. TYPE OF ORGANIZATION (*Check one*)

INDIVIDUAL | PARTNERSHIP | NON-PROFIT ORGANIZATION

CORPORATION, INCORPORATED UNDER THE LAWS OF THE STATE OF

4. HOW LONG IN PRESENT BUSINESS

5. NAMES OF OFFICERS, OWNERS, OR PARTNERS

PRESIDENT | VICE PRESIDENT | SECRETARY

TREASURER | OWNERS OR PARTNERS

6. AFFILIATES OF APPLICANT (*Names, locations and nature of affiliation. See definition on reverse*)

7. PERSONS AUTHORIZED TO SIGN BIDS, OFFERS, AND CONTRACTS IN YOUR NAME (*Indicate if agent*)

NAME | OFFICIAL CAPACITY | TEL. NO. (*Incl. area code*)

8. IDENTIFY EQUIPMENT, SUPPLIES, MATERIALS, AND/OR SERVICES ON WHICH YOU DESIRE TO BID (*See attached Federal agency's supplemental listing and instructions, if any*)

9. TYPE OF OWNERSHIP (*See definitions on reverse*)

MINORITY BUSINESS ENTERPRISE | OTHER THAN MINORITY BUSINESS ENTERPRISE

10. TYPE OF BUSINESS (*See definitions on reverse*)

MANUFACTURER OR PRODUCER | REGULAR DEALER (*Type 1*) | REGULAR DEALER (*Type 2*)

SERVICE ESTABLISHMENT | CONSTRUCTION CONCERN | RESEARCH AND DEVELOPMENT FIRM

☐ SURPLUS DEALER (*Check this box if you are also a dealer in surplus goods*)

11. SIZE OF BUSINESS (*See definitions on reverse*)

SMALL BUSINESS CONCERN* | OTHER THAN SMALL BUSINESS CONCERN

*If you are a small business concern, fill in (a) and (b): | (a) AVERAGE NUMBER OF EMPLOYEES (*Including affiliates*) FOR FOUR PRECEDING CALENDAR QUARTERS | (b) AVERAGE ANNUAL SALES OR RECEIPTS FOR PRECEDING THREE FISCAL YEARS

12. FLOOR SPACE (*Square feet*)

MANUFACTURING | WAREHOUSE

13. NET WORTH

DATE | AMOUNT

14. SECURITY CLEARANCE (*If applicable, check highest clearance authorized*)

FOR | TOP SECRET | SECRET | CONFIDENTIAL | NAMES OF AGENCIES WHICH GRANTED SECURITY CLEARANCES (*Include dates*)

KEY PERSONNEL

PLANT ONLY

THIS SPACE FOR USE BY THE GOVERNMENT

CERTIFICATION

I certify that information supplied herein (*Including all pages attached*) is correct and that neither the applicant nor any person (*Or concern*) in any connection with the applicant as a principal or officer, so far as is known, is now debarred or otherwise declared ineligible by any agency of the Federal Government from bidding for furnishing materials, supplies, or services to the Government or any agency thereof.

SIGNATURE

NAME AND TITLE OF PERSON AUTHORIZED TO SIGN (*Type or print*)

STANDARD FORM 129 (REV. 2–77)
Prescribed by GSA, FPR (41 CFR) 1–16.802

129–105

Figure 3-1   Federal government's bidders list application

INFORMATION AND INSTRUCTIONS

Persons or concerns wishing to be added to a particular agency's bidder's mailing list for supplies or services shall file this properly completed and certified Bidder's Mailing List Application, together with such other lists as may be attached to this application form, with each procurement office of the Federal agency with which they desire to do business. If a Federal agency has attached a Supplemental Commodity List with instructions, complete the application as instructed. Otherwise, identify in item 8 the equipment, supplies and/or services on which you desire to bid. The application shall be submitted and signed by the principal as distinguished from an agent, however constituted.

After placement on the bidder's mailing list of an agency, a supplier's failure to respond (submission of bid, or notice in writing, that you are unable to bid on that particular transaction but wish to remain on the active bidder's mailing list for that particular item) to Invitations for Bids will be understood by the agency to indicate lack of interest and concurrence in the removal of the supplier's name from the purchasing activity's bidder's mailing list for the items concerned.

DEFINITION RELATING TO TYPE OF OWNERSHIP
(See item 9)

Minority business enterprise. A minority business enterprise is defined as a "business, at least 50 percent of which is owned by minority group members or, in case of publicly owned businesses, at least 51 percent of the stock of which is owned by minority group members." For the purpose of this definition, minority group members are Negroes, Spanish-speaking Americans, American-Orientals, American-Indians, American-Eskimos, and American-Aleuts.

TYPE OF BUSINESS DEFINITIONS
(See item 10)

a. Manufacturer or producer—means a person (or concern) owning, operating, or maintaining a store, warehouse, or other establishment that produces, on the premises, the materials, supplies, articles, or equipment of the general character of those listed in item 8, or in the Federal Agency's Supplemental Commodity List, if attached.

b. Regular dealer—means a person (or concern) who owns, operates, or maintains a store, warehouse, or other establishment in which the materials, supplies, articles, or equipment of the general character listed in item 8 or in the Federal Agency's Supplemental Commodity List, if attached, are bought, kept in stock, and sold to the public in the usual course of business.

c. Regular dealer (Type 2)—in the case of supplies of particular kinds (at present, petroleum, lumber and timber products, machine tools, raw cotton, green coffee, hay, grain, feed, or straw, agricultural liming materials, tea, raw or unmanufactured cotton linters). Regular dealer—means a person (or concern) satisfying the requirements of the regulations (Code of Federal Regulations, Title 41, 50–201.101(b)) as amended from time to time, prescribed by the Secretary of Labor under the Walsh-Healey Public Contracts Act (Title 41 U.S. Code 35–45). For coal dealers see Code of Federal Regulations, Title 41, 50–201.604(a).

d. Service establishment—means a concern (or person) which owns, operates, or maintains any type of business which is principally engaged in the furnishing of nonpersonal services, such as (but not limited to) repairing, cleaning, redecorating, or rental of personal property, including the furnishing of necessary repair parts or other supplies as part of the services performed.

e. Construction concern—means a concern (or person) engaged in construction, alteration or repair (including dredging, excavating, and painting) of buildings, structures, and other real property.

DEFINITIONS RELATING TO SIZE OF BUSINESS
(See item 11)

a. Small business concern—A small business concern for the purpose of Government procurement is a concern, including its affiliates, which is independently owned and operated, is not dominant in the field of operation in which it is bidding on Government contracts and can further qualify under the criteria concerning number of employees, average annual receipts, or other criteria, as prescribed by the Small Business Administration. (See Code of Federal Regulations, Title 13, Part 121, as amended, which contains detailed industry definitions and related procedures.)

b. Affiliates—Business concerns are affiliates of each other when either directly or indirectly (i) one concern controls or has the power to control the other, or (ii) a third party controls or has the power to control both. In determining whether concerns are independently owned and operated and whether or not affiliation exists, consideration is given to all appropriate factors including common ownership, common management, and contractual relationship. (See items 6 and 11.)

c. Number of employees—In connection with the determination of small business status, "number of employees" means the average employment of any concern, including the employees of its domestic and foreign affiliates, based on the number of persons employed on a full-time, part-time, temporary, or other basis during each of the pay periods of the preceding 12 months. If a concern has not been in existence for 12 months, "number of employees" means the average employment of such concern and its affiliates during the period that such concern has been in existence based on the number of persons employed during each of the pay periods of the period that such concern has been in business. (See item 11.)

● **COMMERCE BUSINESS DAILY**—The Commerce Business Daily, published by the Department of Commerce, contains information concerning proposed procurements, sales, and contract awards. For further information concerning this publication, contact your local Commerce Field Office.

Figure 3-1   Federal government's bidders list application

BIDDER LIST APPLICATION

FORM DMB 219 Rev. 1-81

RETURN COMPLETED FORM TO:

STATE OF MICHIGAN
PURCHASING DIVISION
DEPARTMENT OF MANAGEMENT AND BUDGET
STEVENS T. MASON BUILDING, SECOND FLOOR
P.O. BOX 30026, LANSING, MICHIGAN 48909

1. BUSINESS NAME AND MAILING ADDRESS (INCLUDING ZIP CODE)	2. TYPE OF BUSINESS	3. CHECK ONE OR MORE BELOW. IF APPLICABLE. SEE DEFINITIONS ON REVERSE.
	☐ CONTRACTOR/CONSULTANT (C) ☐ DISTRIBUTOR (D) ☐ FACTORY REP. (F) ☐ MANUFACTURER (M) ☐ RETAIL DEALER (R) ☐ SHELTERED WORKSHOP (S) ☐ WHOLESALER (W) ☐ OTHER (O) _____	☐ WOMAN OWNED BUSINESS ☐ MINORITY OWNED BUSINESS ☐ BLACK (B) ☐ HISPANIC (H) ☐ ORIENTAL (O) ☐ ESKIMO (E) ☐ AMERICAN INDIAN (I)

TELEPHONE NUMBER:

4. FEDERAL I.D. NO. OR SOCIAL SECURITY NO. IF INDIVIDUAL	5. NUMBER OF YEARS IN BUSINESS

6. NO. OF EMPLOYEES WORKING IN MICHIGAN	7. NO. OF EMPLOYEES IN ENTIRE COMPANY

8. PARENT COMPANY NAME AND ADDRESS AND ADDITIONAL OFFICE LOCATIONS IN MICHIGAN

9. COMMODITIES AND/OR SERVICES OFFERED

10. INDICATE LOCATIONS YOU WISH TO SUPPLY ☐ ENTIRE STATE ☐ AREA(S) DESCRIBED BELOW ONLY

11. BANK REFERENCES: Include complete mailing address and phone number for each reference.

12. CUSTOMER REFERENCES (PREFERABLY GOVERNMENT AGENCIES AT THE FEDERAL, STATE, OR LARGE MUNICIPALITY LEVEL): For each reference, include complete mailing address, phone number, and name of person to contact.

THIS APPLICATION must be signed by a ranking official of the company. If an agent, application must be endorsed by the principal. Show additional principals separately. The undersigned certifies that information provided on this application is correct and complete. Submittal of false information will be grounds for cancellation of any contract without penalty to the State of Michigan and for removal from all Bidder Lists.

PRINCIPAL: AGENT:

NAME _____   NAME _____

TITLE _____   TITLE _____

SIGNATURE _____ DATE _____   SIGNATURE _____ DATE _____

THIS SECTION NOT TO BE FILLED IN BY VENDOR

UNIT NUMBER(S) _____   BUYER(S) _____

DATE APPROVED _____   DIRECTOR _____

BIDDER LIST NUMBER(S)

If additional Bidder List Numbers are needed, check here ☐ and record numbers on reverse at bottom of form.

Figure 3-2 Michigan state bidders list application

BIDDER LIST APPLICATION

STATE OF MICHIGAN
(Reverse)

FORM DMB-219 Rev. 1-81

Pursuant to Act No. 428 of the Public Acts of 1981, minority owned business and woman owned business are defined as follows:

MINORITY OWNED BUSINESS means a business enterprise of which more than 50% of the voting shares or interest in the business is owned, controlled, and operated by individuals who are members of a minority and with respect to which more than 50% of the net profit or loss attributable to the business accrues to shareholders who are members of a minority. MINORITY means a person who is black, hispanic, oriental, eskimo, or an American Indian who is not less than ¼ quantum Indian blood as certified by the person's tribal association and verified by the Indian affairs commission.

WOMAN OWNED BUSINESS means a business of which more than 50% of the voting shares or interest in the business is owned, controlled, and operated by women and with respect to which more than 50% of the net profit or loss attributable to the business accrues to the women shareholders.

CONTROLLED means exercising the power to make policy decisions in a business.

OPERATED means the activity of being involved in the day to day management of a business.

THIS SECTION NOT TO BE FILLED IN BY VENDOR

History of any suspension or debarment from Bidder List, including reason for disqualification:

Figure 3-2   Michigan state bidders list application

ADM 3283 (Rev. 1/3/74)
Formerly DF 563

STATE OF OHIO
DEPT. OF ADMINISTRATIVE SERVICES
STATE PURCHASING
BOX 16523
COLUMBUS, OHIO 43216

VENDORS APPLICATION FOR REGISTRATION
(Attach Additional Sheets if Necessary)

1. E.I. ±

All information submitted on this application, except items 2, 3, 5 and 6, is confidential.

2. Name of Company

4. Address of Main Business Office   Phone No.

3. Address to which Bid Invitations are to be mailed   Phone No.
Street
City & State   Zip

5. Class and Item Numbers on which you wish to Bid

Class Number	Item Number	Class Number	Item Number

6. Circle District Numbers in which you desire to Bid (See attached Map and List)

1 2 3 4 5 6 7 8 9 10 11   For all districts — circle 20

Figure 3-3 Ohio state vendor's registration form

7. Location of Principal Factory	8. Location of Principal Warehouse	9. Location of Principal Shipping Point

10. Name and Addresses of three Largest Customers	
NAME	ADDRESS

11. Applicant's Comments

12. Length of time in Present Business: ___ years	14. Type of Organization ☐ Individual	15. If incorporated, when and in what state?	16. Type of Organization (See definitions on other side)
	☐ Partnership		☐ Manufacturer ☐ Retail Dealer
13. Number of Persons now Employed	☐ Corporation	Year of Incorporation State	☐ Authorized Distributor ☐ Manufacturer's Agent

*17. **IMPORTANT:** THE FEDERAL SOCIAL SECURITY IDENTIFICATION NUMBER OF THE BIDDER (THE NUMBER USED ON THE EMPLOYER'S QUARTERLY FEDERAL TAX RETURN, U. S. TREASURY DEPARTMENT, FORM 941) MUST BE ENTERED ON FACE OF APPLICATION, ABOVE THE NAME OF COMPANY. QUESTION =1.

18. Signature	Name and Title	Date

THE STATE OF OHIO RESERVES THE RIGHT TO REQUEST INFORMATION CONCERNING THE FINANCIAL STATUS OF APPLICANT AND TO REQUEST THE FURNISHING OF REFERENCES.	SEND APPLICATION TO:

DEFINITIONS

MANUFACTURER — A manufacturer is one who operates and maintains a factory or establishment that produces on the premises the materials, supplies or equipment for which application to bid is made.

AUTHORIZED DISTRIBUTOR — An authorized distributor is one who operates and maintains a store, warehouse or other establishment in which the materials, supplies or equipment for which application to bid is made, are either bought or held on consignment, stocked and regularly sold to the public in the usual course of business, a regular license or authorization to do so having been granted by the manufacturer.

MANUFACTURER'S AGENT — A factory representative or agent is one who is authorized by the manufacturer as his exclusive representative within a designated area for sales of the materials, supplies or equipment for which application to bid is made. Bids when made by a factory representative or agent shall be as binding on the manufacturer as if made by the manufacturer himself.

Figure 3-3 Ohio state vendor's registration form

of three or four, or even fewer solicitations, as a result. In addition, the purchasing staff must interpret what you have written on your form and may not judge accurately what solicitations will interest you. So you cannot depend entirely on these forms to result in your receiving all solicitations that are of interest to you. To market effectively, you must take other, additional measures: you must somehow keep abreast of the governments' announcements and specifically request copies of the various solicitations, even if you have already submitted your name and information to that office.

How Governments Announce Their Needs

Earlier, you read that the federal government publishes its purchasing needs and bid opportunities in its daily publication, the *Commerce Business Daily* (CBD). Unfortunately, only about 10 to 15 percent of the procurements are so listed, despite the law requiring the announcements. (Exceptions are justified, technically, and some 85 to 90 percent of the procurements are "exceptions.") So it is necessary to file the applications and get on appropriate bid lists, read the CBD, but also visit procurement offices as often as possible and inspect bulletin boards, where copies of current solicitations are displayed. (Or ask to see them, in small offices, where such bulletin boards do not exist and the display or public-information copies of current solicitations are made available in a bound volume.)

State and local governments do not have an equivalent of the CBD, although some state governments (Maryland, for example) publish their bid opportunities in the state's *Register*, a state counterpart of the federal government's *Federal Register*. But state and local governments typically announce their needs in newspaper advertisements, usually the classified columns, under "Bids & Proposals," but often in display advertising. (See Figure 3-4.)

Effective marketing to governments requires continuous monitoring of all such avenues of information to expose the maximum number of bidding opportunities. Learning of *bidding opportunities*, and that term refers to opportunities to submit proposals, as well as bids per se, is at least half the battle in marketing to governments.

Marketing Analysis

Identification of bidding opportunities is only one reason for monitoring all sources of information on government procurement. It is necessary to understand the markets, and while these pages will furnish a great deal of general and specific information about government markets for computer equipment, supplies, and services, government markets are at least as fluid as commercial markets. For example, suppose that some legislation creates a new agency or causes an existing agency to expand with some large new program. There is an excellent possibility that this event will create a great many market opportunities. On the other hand, such events do not always create such opportunities or do not create them immediately. Monitoring

Figure 3-4 Newspaper announcements of bidding opportunities

the solicitation announcements is one way to gain insight into procurement trends, particularly when some event results in such opportunities only after a lengthy lag. For example, the creation of the Office of Economic Opportunity (OEO) and the Job Corps, created many marketing opportunities for Job Corps contracts almost at once, but many of the other programs of the OEO resulted in substantial marketing opportunities only many months later. Likewise, the conversion of the old Post Office Department to the U.S. Postal Service, a corporation, created billion-dollar markets in training and other opportunities—mechanization of postal work, especially—but only after a long hiatus caused by reorganization.

The reverse is also true: frequently an agency that has been an excellent market declines as a market, when conditions change and old programs or missions fade into insignificance as new programs replace them. Or as new programs—the EPA's pesticide-registration program, for example—prove troublesome and the agency goes in search of help. Here again the Postal Service furnishes an excellent example. For several years its training facilities in Bethesda, Maryland, and Norman, Oklahoma, were continuous and substantial purchasers of training materials, supplies, and services. But ultimately their originally generous budgets were sharply reduced, and they are today compelled to do most of their work in-house, with relatively little contracting for services from the private sector.

Of course, technology itself brings about changes in markets, government as well as commercial. The federal government, once the major purchaser of mainframe computers, has responded to the development and proliferation of personal computers and is today a mass purchaser of these machines and related supplies and services, GSA having awarded major contracts in connection with such purchasing. Moreover, as in the private sector, government agencies and offices that are too small to have enjoyed the services of mainframe computers or even minicomputers can now have their own computers, and personal computers, particularly (although not exclusively) for use in word processing. Such offices are proliferating in all governments as they are in the commercial world.

The new market has not been confined to the personal computers themselves, however, but has necessarily created other needs, as new developments usually do. Concomitant with this trend to personal computers and word processors has been a trend to necessary training of personnel in operation and application of personal computers to various functions. Those who were alert and farsighted enough to anticipate this companion need moved swiftly to take advantage of this new market.

Chapter 4

MAIN CUSTOMERS IN
FEDERAL SYSTEM

It is not easy to understand the complex structure of the
federal government, but it is necessary if one is to market
to the federal agencies effectively.

The Government and Change

Only a few years ago it would have been comparatively easy to point to the
main customers in the federal government for computer equipment, supplies, and services. It would have been those federal agencies whose needs
and budgets were big enough to support the purchase and maintenance of
one or more of those big and costly computers. It would have been also
those agencies peopled with those bold enough to venture into new fields
and/or those whose basic missions compelled them to such ventures. The
Department of Defense (DOD), under intense pressure to develop ever
more sophisticated and deadly weapons systems, and the National
Aeronautics and Space Administration (NASA), under intense pressure to
press on with Buck Rogersish space projects, were undoubtedly in the forefront of those agencies, although there were others under similar pressures.
(The NASA/Goddard Space Flight Center held the world's record for
number of computers in one location, with over 200 mainframe computers
at their Greenbelt, Maryland, site.)

Things have changed in recent years, partly as a result of technological
advances which have made small and inexpensive computers readily available (inexpensive in both acquisition costs and maintenance costs), and
partly as a result of trends which make it all but unthinkable to operate a
busy office without computer support.

One other factor is at work, change, and change, in the case of government, almost always means growth. The government changes primarily by
growing new facilities and new organizations or reorganizing and expanding existing organizations. The federal government of today is not the
federal government of only a few years ago. Almost every Administration

adds to the structure. Since World War II, for example, there have been added the General Services Administration, the Departments of Transportation, Health and Human Services, Education, and Energy; the Environmental Protection Agency, the Consumer Product Safety Commission, and the Pension Benefit Guaranty Corporation, to name only a few.

This means more federal organizations and physical facilities, but it also means that most federal agencies grow in size, as time goes on. The National Aeronautics and Space Administration, for example, was an obscure little group concerned with aviation before President Eisenhower decided that the United States needed a civilian agency to carry out our space programs, and assigned the job (along with a colossal budget) to this quite small agency, the existence of which was hardly known to anyone not connected with it. And the Department of Transportation was not entirely a new entity, since it was made up principally of several smaller agencies, assembled and organized into a department.

And it means also that the government grows as a market, of course. And that has some direct relationship to government growth in general.

In Government, Growth Need Not Mean More People

There is always political pressure to keep the number of federal employees to a minimum. Hardly any Administration of either party comes to Washington without launching an initial campaign to reduce the number of federal employees, as well as the size of the government generally. So the number of federal employees has remained fairly constant for some years at about 2.8 million, despite mammoth increases in government spending and in government size. In fact, because the former Post Office Department became a quasi-independent government corporation, the U.S. Postal Service, postal employees are often dropped from recognition as federal employees, and some official documents claim federal employment of only slightly over 2 million, as a result.

But government organizations do not need to increase their staffs and payrolls to grow. Government organizations grow by "contracting out," and a few years ago several members of Congress and a few prominent journalists "discovered" this, to their alleged shock and horror. They professed dismay that for every federal employee actually on federal payrolls, there were several contractor employees who were virtually on federal payrolls, although not literally so. Many, in fact, even work directly on government premises, and their employers actually bill the employees' salaries to the government, suitably marked up to provide reimbursement of overhead and a profit. In this way, these innocents learned, there are many millions who are on the federal payrolls, in a practical sense, probably as many as 11 or 12 million.

This explains how the government has managed to grow steadily, despite the relative stability in the size of the federal payrolls. This is a measure of the government market size: It keeps many millions busily at work directly on government contracts, while many millions more are supported indirectly by government procurement.

Federal Purchasing

There is, of course, no question but that among federal agencies, DOD dominates the procurement budget, spending 81 percent of all the procurement dollars in making 70 percent of the purchases ($135,462,268,000 for 14,763,361 purchases) in FY83. Other federal agencies leading in procurement—purchases and dollars—include these:

Agency	No. Purchases	$(000)
Dept. Health and Human Services	704,968	$12,226,146
NASA	132,800	6,262,409
Veterans Administration	1,933,666	2,634,464
Dept. of Agriculture	739,003	1,785,389
Dept. of Interior	613,664	1,672,984
General Services Administration	754,702	1,652,433
Dept. of Transportation	281,647	1,099,605

You can see quite readily that the number of purchases and the number of dollars spent have nothing in common because some agencies tend to large purchases, while others tend to small ones, and the agencies spending the greatest amounts of money on procurement are not the ones with the busiest procurement offices.

In terms of computer usage, especially in using mainframe systems, DOD and NASA undoubtedly head the list. And they use their computers primarily for technical purposes, rather than for administrative ones. In the case of DOD, computers are integral to many of the modern weapons systems, since they are, in fact, often control subsystems for those systems, one of which may employ several computers. And in the case of NASA, computers are employed for various technical and scientific purposes, largely in direct connection with designing and operating satellites, developing space technologies, and other space projects. Even this, however, fails to paint the market picture accurately, due to the way the federal government is organized and the way it buys. Understanding of that organization is necessary to succeed in the government markets.

Government Decentralization

Organizationally, the first level down in the Executive Branch of government, under the President, are the departments, each of which is represented by a head who is a member of the President's cabinet. Thus the DOD is headed by a cabinet officer. However, within DOD there are three military agencies, the Army, the Navy, and the Air Force, each of which is also called "Department of" (the Army, the Navy, and the Air Force), although none of these rates a cabinet officer at its head. (The U.S. Marine Corps is part of the Navy, of course, and the U.S. Coast Guard is part of the DOT, although it reverts to the Navy in time of war.)

The DOD procurement expenditures reported by the Federal Procurement Data System and cited in part here are for all military procurement, but only a small fraction of that procurement is made in Washington and/or by DOD itself. By far the bulk of the purchasing is done by the military units, and not at department levels, either, but directly by the military bases and organizations. Witness the following sampling (not the full listing) of military purchasers of computers and computer-related supplies and services listed in only one day's issue of the CBD (selected entirely at random):

Army Electronics activity at Vint Hill, Virginia
Naval Supply Center at San Diego, California
Navy office at Washington Navy Yard
Army Aviation Systems Command at St. Louis, Missouri
Army Information Systems Command at Fort Huachuca, Arizona
Army Corps of Engineers at Vicksburg, Mississippi
Air Force at Kirtland AFB, New Mexico
Naval Station overseas (c/o Miami, Florida FPO)
Air Force at Offutt AFB, Nebraska
Army at Fort McPherson, Georgia
Army Corps of Engineers at Norfolk, Virginia
Air Force at Wright-Patterson AFB, Ohio

None of these are at the top levels of their departments, but are field commands. Each of the services has some centralized procurement, also. (The Navy, for example, maintains extensive centralized headquarters offices in the Virginia suburbs of Washington, and does much of its major procurements there, although the other two military departments do their procurement on a far more decentralized basis.) And DOD has its own centralized procurement in the Defense Logistics Agency and other DOD support agencies.

What is true here for the various units of the military is equally true for all other government departments and agencies, virtually all of which have a number of offices and installations scattered throughout the United States and even in foreign countries. Here are some more listings of federal procurements to illustrate that point, also a partial listing from that same one day's listings from which the military examples were cited:

Department of Agriculture, Washington, DC
Department of Commerce, Boulder, Colorado
Department of Energy, Morgantown, West Virginia
Department of Agriculture, Soil Conservation Service, Honolulu, Hawaii
Department of the Interior, Menlo Park, California
Forest Service, Atlanta, Georgia
NASA Johnson Space Center, Houston, Texas
NASA Marshall Space Flight Center, Huntsville, Alabama
NASA Goddard Space Flight Center, Greenbelt, Maryland

Whether all of this is the most efficient way to organize a government bureaucracy and/or to procure needed goods and services is moot, but this is the way it is done, for whatever reasons, and it offers the advantages of diversity and, probably, far greater opportunities for small businesses, consultants, and other entrepreneurs.

The Basic Structure

The federal government today includes these departments:

Department of Agriculture
Department of Commerce
Department of Defense
   Department of the Air Force
   Department of the Army
   Department of the Navy
Department of Education
Department of Energy
Department of Health and Human Services
Department of the Interior
Department of Labor
Department of Transportation

All of these have regional offices, and most have numerous subordinate "offices of," "administrations," and other subordinate organizations, some of which have their own regional offices and field offices, laboratories, bases, and other physical facilities. The result is that many of these departments actually represent large and complex networks of organizations and facilities. But they still represent only part of the federal establishment, which also supports some 60 "independent agencies" of the federal government, some of them as large as the larger departments, others rather small. Some of these are also large complexes of subordinate organizations, offices, and facilities, every bit as imposing as are the departments. These are the ones which are significant in size and purchasing power—that is, as potential markets (although this is not to say that some of those small agencies not listed here may not be occasional customers too):

Agency for International Development
Environmental Protection Agency
Equal Employment Opportunity Commission
Federal Communications Commission
Federal Emergency Management Agency
Federal Trade Commission
General Services Administration
NASA
National Science Foundation
Nuclear Regulatory Commission
Office of Personnel Management
Peace Corps
Tennessee Valley Authority
U.S. Information Agency
Veterans Administration

Wheels within Wheels

Many well-known agencies are not on this list because they are part of some department. In fact, often the subordinate agency is better known than is the department to which it belongs. The Occupational Safety and Health Administration (OSHA) is probably one of those. Relatively few people not concerned directly with OSHA in some manner are aware that it is part of the Labor Department.

The following are some of the more well-known and important (from the marketing viewpoint) agencies within departments and major independent agencies (note, however, that in most cases these are not all the agencies within the departments and other major agencies):

Department of Agriculture:
  Forest Service, Soil Conservation Services, Farmers Home Administration
Department of Commerce:
  Maritime Administration, Minority Business Development Agency, National Bureau of Standards, National Oceanic and Atmospheric Administration, National Technical Information Services, Bureau of the Census, Office of Telecommunications, United States Travel Service
Department of Defense:
  Defense Advanced Research Projects Agency, Defense Communications Agency, Defense Intelligence Agency, Defense Logistics Agency, Defense Contract Administrative Services, National Security Agency, Department of the Air Force, Department of the Army, Department of the Navy. (Note: each military department has a number of commands, generally for training, systems development and management, electronics, matériel, supply services, personnel, communications, and whatever major weapons systems—aircraft, tanks, ships, etc.—are peculiar to that military service.)
Department of Health and Human Services:
  Public Health Service; Alcohol, Drug Abuse, and Mental Health Administration; Food and Drug Administration; National Institutes of Health
Department of the Interior:
  National Park Service, Bureau of Geological Survey, Bureau of Indian Affairs, Bureau of Land Management
Department of Labor:
  Employment and Training Administration, Employment Standards Administration, Occupational Safety and Health Administration
Department of Transportation:
  Coast Guard, Federal Aviation Administration, Federal Highway Administration, Federal Railroad Administration, National Highway Traffic Safety Administration, Urban Mass Transportation Administration
General Services Administration:
  Automated Data and Telecommunications Service, Federal Supply

Service, Public Buildings Service, National Archives and Records Service

What the Agencies Need

Probably no buyer in the entire world is quite as diversified in what it buys as is the federal government. Even in the more restricted terms of computer equipment, supplies, and services, government requirements are highly diverse. And the diversity occurs along more than one line: First of all, there is enormous diversity in the sizes and locations of the thousands of government agencies that buy computers and computer-related goods and services. The diversity also extends to the missions of these many agencies and the uses to which the computers are to be put. To illustrate that, we turn again to the CBD as a reliable source of information—since it does present the agencies' own words in describing what they are seeking—to review some of the items for which the agencies solicit bids and proposals. Here are the headlines of the various synopses describing the agencies' wants:

Data General ADPE (automatic data processing equipment)
IBM ADPE
Courier ADPE
ROLM ADPE
Renewal of Maintenance ADP Equipment
Renewal of Lease/Maintenance of ADP Equipment
Analysis, Design Development, Test and Support of System Software for HIS 6000, Datanet 355, and Level VI Computer Systems
Numerical Method Computer Model and Several Engineering Studies of a Dustpan Style Dredging (Suction) System
Data Entry Services
ADP Systems Development
Daily Data Processing Keypunch Services
Digital Equipment Corp ADP Equipment
Wang Word Processing Systems or Equal
    System Support, Preventive and Remedial Maintenance Software
Computer Terminal
Telephone Directory Assistance Systems with CPU
Local Area Network Equipment
Basic Image Analysis System
Printers
Lease of Word Processing Equipment
Software Packages
Modification: Circuit Boards
Computer Operations
Data Reduction and Analysis of Data from Interplanetary Monitoring Platform
AN/UYK-43 Tactical Embedded Computer Development
ADP Support Services
General Purpose ADP Software Training Manuals

Teleprocessing Services
Logical Data Base Design
Financial Data Base
Vocabulary Development
Hardware and Software for a Word Processing Center
Workstations
Software Services
Software Design and Implementation
Development of Interface Simulation System
Computer Processing of Military Payroll
Machine Readable Records
Cost Comparison Study at Word Processing Center (operate and
    manage government facility)
Programming Training
B/5000/6000/7000/COBOL 74 Differences Course
Word Processing Services
Support for War Gaming Software
Course Entitled IAPX 86, 88, 186 Microprocessor Workshop
Consultant to Work in the Areas of EDP Technical Services
Conduct Lectures, Seminars, Conferences; Review Research and
    Related Products; and Provide Technical Publications and Reports
    as Part of the Computing Associates Program
Develop Data Base Management System
Analysis and Design of Initial Data Base
Development of a Handbook for Managing the Acquisition of Mission
    Critical Computer Resources

Facilities Management and On-Site Contracts

Only one of the project requirements listed here called for operating and
management of a government facility. These are projects let as term contracts, normally, usually rather large projects and usually for two or three
years, with yearly options, so such requirements do not appear every day in
the CBD. For example, NASA's Scientific and Technical Information Facility is operated by a contractor, although NASA owns the facility and the
millions of dollars' worth of computers, printing equipment, microfilming
cameras, and other equipment and furniture. The contractor operates the
facility for NASA, with a staff of several hundred computer people, abstrac-
tors, indexers, writers, printers, and sundry other specialists. Periodically,
the contract changes hands, as a new bidder happens along and wins the
contract away from the incumbent by submitting a better proposal. But this
is only one of many such contracts. A great many of the government's
major computer installations are operated by contractors because such
facilities require many "hands and feet" to operate, and there is usually
strong opposition in the government to expanding the government's own
staffs of employees.

Many contracts do not necessarily require that the contractor literally
manage the entire facility per se, but only that the personnel be assigned to

work on the government's site. This is an obvious necessity when the nature of the work is to operate government equipment that is fixed and cannot very well be moved or is a functional part of the facility's daily operation. In such cases, the contractor must manage the contract staff, because it is illegal for civil service personnel to give orders to contractor personnel—that is, contractor personnel cannot report to civil service personnel. However, the government's project manager must give the contractor "technical direction." The contractor's project manager must then translate that technical direction into such procedures, policies, organization, and marching orders as enables the contractor to comply with the requirement, which is to manage the work. The "facility" which the contractor is obliged to manage may therefore be merely some corner of a set of offices or a building in which the computer is installed, rather than the entire building.

There are many such projects and on-site contracts. The National Aeronautics and Space Administration, for example, has virtual battalions of computer programmers and analysts at Goddard Space Flight Center and other of its major centers, as do many other agencies. The Environmental Protection Agency's Pesticides Registration program is run by a contractor, as another example, who supplies an assortment of experts in computer technologies, chemistry, biochemistry, and other fields of interest in the program, in addition to the computer programmers, analysts, coding clerks, and other such personnel.

Quite often, operating a computer facility or providing some set of computer-related services on-site is only part of a larger task, as it is in the case of the NASA facility described earlier. In some cases, such as that one, it is moot whether it is the computer work or some other kind of work that is the dominant or leading function of the program. In the case of the NASA Scientific and Technical Information Facility a good argument could be made that printing, writing, indexing, and abstracting are closer to the main objective of the facility, in fact, and computer work is really incidental here—the means to accomplishment of the objective, rather than the end or objective itself. However, NASA, like a great many other organizations today, tends to equate "information" with the world of computer and data processing experts, and so far every contractor for that facility has been one prominent in the EDP field. Of course, it is the customer who decides what all the necessary qualifications are. (In one case, some years ago, the successful contestant for that particular project did some crash recruiting of technical writers and editors to assemble an instant publications department, something which had not existed in that organization before, to qualify as a bidder for the program.)

Like NASA with its Scientific and Technical Information Facility contract, EPA regarded its Pesticides Registration support contract as one that was essentially a computer contract or one calling for a computer/EDP contractor, at any rate, despite the fact that a large portion of the required staff were to be scientists from various other disciplines. And as in the NASA case and most other cases, it was the customer's perception that prevailed: The successful bidder had to show its main qualifications as those in the computer/EDP field.

Of course, the opposite situation may prevail, in which a contract calls for significant computer services, but is not a computer contract per se. An agency may call for a survey or study of some sort, for example, which requires extensive computer work, but requires extensive work of other specialists than those from the computer field. One example of this is the contract to poll the nation every 10 years, a contract let by the Bureau of the Census, in the Commerce Department. The Bureau is itself heavily computerized, and most of its work, including that contracted out, is usually heavily dependent on computer services. But the Bureau often looks to surveying/polling kinds of organizations for contracts related to gathering census data and derivatives therefrom, despite the fact that the work almost always requires extensive computer work also to complete the contract. We'll look a bit more closely at these situations later, when we discuss bidding strategies and proposal writing, but it is useful to bear this in mind in the meanwhile. Customers often tend to perceive their needs in terms of their own missions and functions, an understandable bias, of course, and one that the alert marketer must remain conscious of. But to do so, to understand and consider this, means also that the marketer must always understand and bear in mind the customer's mission, to understand the agencies and their objectives, that is.

Major Federal Agencies and Bureaus

If we were to count the many agencies, with their various and sundry bureaus, "administrations," "offices of," their various regional, district, and field offices, and their various bases, centers, and other physical facilities, we would arrive at a total of at least 30,000 targets, quite possibly many more than that. Most of these are occasional targets for marketing computer goods and services, but some are frequent or regular buyers of such goods and services. Following are brief listings of some of the major federal agencies and those of their subdivisions which appear to be the most likely targets for marketing computers and related services.

Agriculture Department (USDA)   USDA is a large and sprawling agency, with a great many offices and bureaus, including the following targets:

Farmers Home Administration   Forest Service
Agricultural Marketing Service   Soil Conservation Service
Commodity Credit Corporation   Food and Nutrition Service

Commerce Department   The Department of Commerce, already mentioned, includes many bureaus, in addition to the Census Bureau, some of which are generally heavy users of computers and EDP:

National Bureau of Standards   National Technical Information
                                       Service
National Oceanic and Atmos-   National Telecommunications
   pheric Administration   and Information Administration
United States Travel Service

Bureau of Economic Analysis
Bureau of Industrial Economics

Defense Department (DOD)   DOD has its own agencies, distinct from sub-divisions of the several military services. Here are some which are reasonably good marketing targets:

Defense Communications   Defense Logistics Agency
Agency
Defense Contract Administrative   Defense Advanced Research
Services   Projects Agency
Office of Economic Adjustment

Health and Human Services Department (HHS)   HHS is quite a large agency, even with the loss of its former Office of Education, now a separate Department. Its major subdivisions include these:

Public Health Service   Center for Disease Control
Alcohol, Drug Abuse, and Men-   Food and Drug Administration
tal Health Administration
   Health Administration   Health Resources Administration
Health Services Administration   National Institutes of Health

Housing and Urban Development Department (HUD)   HUD is an agency that spends money on a large scale, helping individuals acquire homes through mortgage and loan-guarantee programs and helping builders put up housing, including apartment projects, with loan guarantees and other services. A great many of HUD's many programs are carried out by these two HUD agencies:

New Community Development   Government National Mortgage
   Corp.   Association

Interior Department   Probably the most promising target in Interior is the Bureau of Geological Survey.

Justice Department   Justice has two well-known subdivisions of interest to potential contractors and some not so well known but also of interest:

Federal Bureau of Investigation   Drug Enforcement Administra-
                                     tion
Antitrust Division   Immigration and Naturalization
                                     Service
Office of Justice Assistance,   Tax Division
   Research & Statistics

Labor Department   The following agencies of Labor are suggested:

Employment and Training   Employment Standards Adminis-
   Administration   tration
Bureau of Labor Statistics   Office of Federal Contract Com-
                                     pliance Programs

Treasury Department   Not surprisingly, the Treasury Department is also highly computerized. Treasury does the bulk of government payouts—Postal

Service and a few others do their own check writing for payables, but most agencies have Treasury do it for them. The Treasury Department is, of course, made up of several subdivisions, including the well-known Internal Revenue Service, itself a major user of computers and related services, the Customs Service, the Secret Service, and the Bureau of Alcohol, Tobacco, and Firearms. But with such other special offices as these, also, you can well imagine the prominence computers must inevitably enjoy in Treasury Department operations:

Office of Financial Analysis	Office of Tax Analysis
Office of Special Studies	Office of Industrial Economics
Office of Revenue Sharing	Bureau of Government Financial Operations
Bureau of the Public Debt	Office of Computer Science
Office of Budget and Program Analysis	Office of Procurement
Office of Management and Organization	Office of Procurement
Office of Personnel	Office of Foreign Assets Control

Environmental Protection Agency (EPA)   Aside from the Pesticides Registration program, already referred to and discussed, EPA has other organizations of interest. That pesticides program and many other programs, offices, and bureaus are, in fact, within the overall structure of these six main divisions of EPA:

Planning and Management	Enforcement
Water and Waste Management	Air, Noise, and Radiation
Research and Development	Pesticides and Toxic Substances

General Services Administration (GSA)   Probably all of GSA's divisions are of some interest, but the principal ones are these:

Automated Data and Telecommunications Service	Federal Supply Service
Public Buildings Service	National Archives and Records Service

Postal Service   The U.S. Postal Service is another major user of computers and computer services. In its payroll alone, the Postal Service has a rather large operation, with nearly 700,000 regular employees and an annual payroll on the order of $17 billion, But there are also other billions of dollars accounted for in Postal Service purchasing: The main supply services of the Postal Service are in a facility at Topeka, Kansas, but even that is only a fraction of the procurement functions; there are also some 300 vehicle maintenance facilities throughout the United States (only the U.S. Army has more vehicles than the Postal Service does), and there is purchasing by major Postal Service centers and by the Postal Service Headquarters at its L'Enfant Plaza building in Washington, DC. The Postal Service therefore owns a number of mainframe computers, as well as microcomputers, which it manages to keep quite busy.

A major activity within the Postal Service is its real estate department, for the obvious reason that (1) the Postal Service owns and operates those thousands of post offices, large and small, and (2) must continually build new ones, to keep pace with the new residential areas constantly springing up. But there are other divisions, as well as these, of interest to marketers:

Payroll Systems	Finance Group
Research and Technology Group	Rates and Classification Service
Management Information Systems Dept.	
Real Estate and Buildings Dept.	Procurement and Supply Dept.

Veterans Administration (VA) It is likely that few understand the size, complexity, and scope of the VA. It is a highly complex agency, with many buildings—hospitals, domiciliaries, and regional centers—and its own highly complex agency, with many buildings—hospitals, domiciliaries, and regional centers—and its own centralized procurement and supply service to handle its huge procurement of foods, medical supplies, medical equipment, and various services connected directly and indirectly with veterans' benefit programs. These are among its many agencies and offices:

Office of Data Management and Telecommunications	Data Processing Center
Office of Loan Guaranty Service	Office of Planning and Program Evaluation
Records Processing Center	Procurement and Supply Division

Other Agencies

The foregoing have been only a relative handful of the thousands of government agencies and offices. They were selected as being among the most promising targets for government contracts on a more or less frequent or continuous basis. However, any government agency or office can be a source of lucrative business on occasion, if not with any regularity. Even agencies that do not often do any significant amount of contracting out, such as the SBA, have occasional need, as when the SBA let a fairly large contract to design and program its small- and minority-business register-directory.

Geographic Aspects

One other point ought to be made about doing business with the federal government: Where you are located and where the government agency with whom you wish to do business is located are usually of little importance, in terms of your right to pursue and win the contract. (Most certainly, it is not necessary to have a facility in or near Washington, DC, for even when the contract originates in a Washington, DC, headquarters office of an agency, the work is quite often to be done somewhere else. Moreover, it is often possible to pursue and win contracts without ever making other than mail and telephone contacts with the customer!) There are occasional exceptions, as in some cases where the agency believes it necessary for the contractor to be in proximity to the agency, if the work is to be done effectively and efficiently, and makes that a requirement of the contract. But even in those cases it is usually possible to meet such a demand by agreeing to establish a special field office near the agency for the purposes of handling the contract—a "project office," as it is often called.

On the other hand, you may not wish to do business far from your home base. But even then, be aware that the federal government is very much decentralized geographically, as well as administratively. Despite the heavy concentration of government buildings and government offices in and around Washington, DC, and the heavy proportion of contracting done in Washington, there are other concentrations of federal offices, and a great deal of contracting is done in other areas throughout the United States. The government divides the country up into 10 regions, for purposes of administration, and most major agencies maintain a regional office in each region. In addition to this, some cities and their environs are centers of major federal procurement activity because many major government suppliers are located there or because some major military or civilian federal facilities are there. (Often both situations prevail, one the result of the other, because contractors are attracted to areas of major government facilities, such as in San Diego, where the Navy maintains extensive facilities, or in Huntsville, Alabama, where the Army Redstone Arsenal and NASA's Marshall Space Flight Center are cheek by jowl, and contractors tend then to come in and establish factories and other manufacturing and supply establishments.)

The result is that there are a number of areas in the country that are concentrations of government activity, often with a wide variety of government offices and facilities, and where the government does a significant portion of its purchasing. Here are most of those kinds of areas in no particular order:

Washington, DC	Atlanta, GA
Boston, MA	Denver, CO
Chicago, IL	San Francisco, CA
Kansas City, MO	San Diego, CA
Dallas-Fort Worth, TX	Norfolk, VA
Los Angeles, CA	Louisville, KY
Seattle, WA	Huntsville, AL
Philadelphia, PA	Houston, TX
New York, NY	Honolulu, HI
St. Louis, MO	

Chapter 5

MAIN CUSTOMERS IN STATE AND LOCAL GOVERNMENTS

The state and local government markets are not exactly microcosms of the federal government, but there are many parallels and similarities, nevertheless.

Size is One Measure

The 50 states of the United States vary widely in size, of course, in terms of both acreage and population. The largest in acreage is Alaska, a quite enormous land mass, more than twice the size of the formerly largest state, Texas. Ironically enough, Alaska is also the smallest in population, having a smaller population than such large but sparsely populated states as Wyoming, Montana, New Mexico, and Nevada and even smaller than those of such tiny states as Rhode Island and Delaware. On the other hand, California is our most populous state, although New York State is not far behind California in population count.

Taking the state governments together, as a set of markets, some are better prospects than others simply because they are bigger markets—they buy more, in terms of both total procurement dollars and diversity of needs. One index to market size is size of the state in terms of population, because the tax base and procurement budgets bear a direct relationship to the tax base. Here are the 50 states, in descending order of approximate population:

State	Population (millions)	State	Population (millions)
California	20.0	Nebraska	1.5
New York	18.2	North Carolina	5.1
Pennsylvania	11.8	Missouri	4.7
Texas	11.2	Virginia	4.7
Illinois	11.1	Georgia	4.6
Ohio	10.7	Wisconsin	4.4
Michigan	8.9	Minnesota	3.8
New Jersey	7.2	Maryland	3.9
Montana	7.0	Tennessee	3.9
Florida	6.8	Louisiana	3.6
South Dakota	6.7	Alabama	3.4
Massachusetts	5.7	Washington	3.4
Indiana	5.2	Utah	1.1
Kentucky	3.2	New Mexico	1.0
Connecticut	3.1	Maine	1.0
Iowa	2.8	Rhode Island	1.0
South Carolina	2.6	Hawaii	0.8
Oklahoma	2.6	Idaho	0.7
Kansas	2.2	New Hampshire	0.7
Colorado	2.2	North Dakota	0.6
Mississippi	2.2	Delaware	0.5
Oregon	2.1	Nevada	0.5
Arkansas	1.9	Vermont	0.4
Arizona	1.8	Wyoming	0.3
West Virginia	1.7	Alaska	0.3

This is, of course, no guarantee that state-government markets will align in this precise order of activity and opportunity, for there are a number of other factors to be considered, such as preferences often accorded in-state firms over out-of-state firms, small-business preferences and set-asides, minority programs, and sundry other matters of state-government procurement programs, policies, and procedures. (These will be taken up and discussed in a later chapter.) But this is at least an approximate indicator of the size of each state-government market, at least in gross terms, and is therefore one of the several measures you may use to judge where your best opportunities lie.

Industrialization is a Factor

California and New York State are among our most highly industrialized states, in dollar volume and diversity of industry, as well as in numbers of industrial workers, and they are surely leaders among those with the largest tax bases and budgets. So it should be no great mystery that these two states and several others, even as individual governments, rival the federal government in the diversity and activity of procurement, if not in total dollar volumes of purchasing. In fact, if we compare the lists of goods and services normally purchased by each—the federal government and California, for example—we find a remarkable similarity. (Even the supply-classification numbers are similar.) On the official lists of items purchased regularly by the California purchasing and supply organization, for example, we find the following supply groups, using the same group number, 70, as the federal government uses for EDP equipment. (The federal classification, as published in the CBD, is "70 General Purpose ADP Equipment, Software, Supplies, and Support Equipment, incl Leasing." Compare that with California's wording of its supply group 70, reproduced here.) Detailed explanations and notations are supplied for some of the items in the official literature released by the California State government but have not been included here in the interest of brevity.

Group 70:   EDP Equipment, Software, Supplies, and Support Equipment

> 7010 EDP Configuration (computer systems)
> 7020 EDP Central Processing Unit, Analog
> 7021 EDP Central Processing Unit, Digital
> 7022 EDP Central Processing Unit, Hybrid
> 7025 EDP Input/Output and Storage Devices
> 7030 EDP Software
> 7035 EDP Accessorial Equipment
> 7040 Punched Card Equipment
> 7045 EDP Supplies and Support Equipment
> 7050 EDP Components

California's Office of Procurement (Department of General Services, Sacramento) buys no services but delegates to each state agency its own purchasing authority to buy engineering, programming, consulting, and other services, as necessary. Figures on California's total annual procurement are not readily ascertainable because of the decentralization of many classes of procurement, especially of procurement of services, but they are obviously in the multi-billion-dollar range.

New York State also reports a highly diversified list of goods and services purchased regularly, with the central Standards and Purchase Group (Office of General Services in Albany) alone accounting for nearly $1 billion. Like California and many other jurisdictions, New York State authorizes its many state agencies to negotiate separately for services they require. This again makes it difficult to determine with any accuracy the total state-government spending for all goods and services. However, listed on New York State's commodity lists are computers of various types and sizes and general computer supplies for all those types and sizes, which ensures that related services must also be required. And there is no doubt that procurement and purchasing by New York State rivals that of the purchasing divisions of other major state governments.

California, New York, and many others also rival the federal establishment in the diversity and number of state agencies, bureaus, and institutions scattered across their states. Each state government is articulated with many kinds of official support organizations, and many of these have a number of offices throughout their respective states. So the 50 states actually represent upward of 10,000 or more potential customers. For as in the case of the federal and commercial markets, computers and computer services respond to a "horizontal" market, rather than a "vertical" one: There is virtually no office or facility today, whether government, commercial, industrial, or other, that is not a customer or potential customer for computers and related supplies and services. So while there are some state government agencies that are more or less regular purchasers of EDP goods and services, and others that buy such goods and services only occasionally, they are all markets, at least potentially, for everyone selling computer equipment, supplies, and services of virtually any kind.

A Typical State Purchasing Organization

North Carolina, a state of some 5 million citizens, is partly agricultural and partly industrial, with a fair share of high-tech industries, and is reasonably representative of the typical state in its purchasing. Its Division of Purchase and Contract (Figure 5-1) is representative of other such organizations. It includes seven procurement teams, a purchasing consulting group, a data processing group, and a staff group, who report to a purchasing official in charge of the entire operation. Team 7 is charged with the procurement of data processing equipment and supplies, among other classes of supply, and Team 6, with three buyers, is charged with purchasing consulting and contractual services for the various state departments.

Some Typical State Agencies

Few of us are even dimly aware of the true complexity of government, the number and diversity of state agencies, bureaus, and institutions, for example, even at the federal level, much less at state and local levels. The Commonwealth of Massachusetts is a good example of this complexity. Relatively small in area, although with a substantial population approaching 6 million citizens, the state has a healthy economy and an active Purchasing Division in Boston, with a large number of buyers assigned to the various classes of supply. And, like other jurisdictions, the various agencies procure most of their standard commodities from the state's central procurement and supply organization, but are free to do at least some buying on their own, especially of custom professional services. Following is a list of Massachusetts state agencies. In each case the agency or institution listed has someone in charge of purchasing, often with the title of Purchasing Agent, in fact, although also with other titles, in some cases, such as Steward, Business Manager, Administrator, or other official designation which includes responsibility for purchasing functions.

Top-Level Agencies   The following agencies are entirely independent in their purchasing authority and can contract directly with suppliers:

Massachusetts Port Authority   Massachusetts Bay

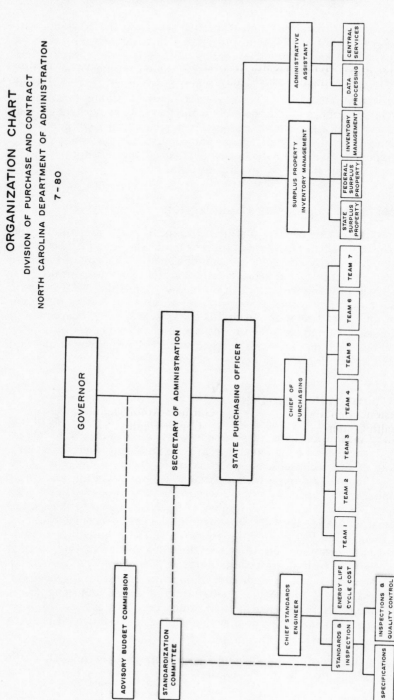

Figure 5-1 North Carolina state purchasing organization

Massachusetts Turnpike   Transportation Authority
    Authority

Department of Mental Health Institutions   The following are institutions of this department, which may do at least some of their buying independently:

Belchertown State School
Boston State Hospital

Cushing Hospital

Hogan Regional Center

Medfield State Hospital
Metropolitan State
    Hospital
John T. Berry
    Rehab Center
Monson Development Center

Paul A. Dever State School
Westboro State Hospital

Worcester State Hospital

Glavin Regional Center

Blackstone Mental
    Health Center
Brockton Multi-Service
    Center
Dr. Solomon Carter Fuller
    Mental Health Center
Northhampton Center for
    Children and Families
Tufts-Bay Cove
    Mental Health Center

Danvers State Hospital
Dr. John C. Corrigan
    Mental Health Center
Massachusetts Mental
    Health Center
Dr. Harry C. Solomon
    Mental Health Center
Northhampton State Hospital
Taunton State Hospital

Walter E. Fernald
    State School
Cambridge/Somerville
    Mental Health Center
Wrentham State School
Erich Lindemann
    Mental Health Center
Mystic Valley Community
    Mental Health Center
Pocasset Mental Health
    Center
Gardner-Athol Mental
    Center Health
Bridgewater Treatment
    Center

Department of Public Health Institutions

Lakeville Hospital
Massachusetts Hospital School
Pondville Hospital
Rutland Heights Hospital
Tewksbury Hospital

Lemuel Shattuck Hospital
Western Massachusetts Hospital
Soldiers' Home Chelsea
Soldiers' Home Holyoke

Department of Youth Services

Judge John J. Connelly
    Youth Center

University of Massachusetts
    Columbia Point

Worcester Detention Center

Westfield Detention Center
Stephen L. French
   Youth Forestry Camp
University of Massachusetts
   Amherst
Southeastern Massachusetts
   University

University of Massachusetts
   Medical School and Hospital
University of Lowell
University of Lowell
   Research Foundation

Board of Regional Community Colleges

Berkshire Community College
Bristol Community College
Bunker Hill Community
   College
Massachusetts Bay
   Community College
Massasoit Community College

Middlesex Community College

Mt. Wachusett Community
   College
Springfield Tech Community
   College

Cape Cod Community College
Greenfield Community College
Holyoke Community College

North Shore Community
   College
Northern Essex
   Community College
Quinsigamond Community
   College
Roxbury Community College

Massachusetts State College System

Boston State College
Bridgewater State College
Fitchburg State College
Framingham State College
Massachusetts College of Art

North Adams State College
Salem State College
Westfield State College
Worcester State College
Massachusetts Maritime Academy

Department of Corrections

Massachusetts Correctional
   Institute Bridgewater
Massachusetts Correctional
   Institute Concord
Massachusetts Correctional
   Institute Framingham
Massachusetts Correctional
   Institute Warwick
Massachusetts Correctional
   Institute Shirley Pre-Release
Medfield Prison Project
   Pre-Release
Norfolk Pre-Release
Lemuel Shattuck Hospital Unit

Massachusetts Correctional
   Institute Norfolk
Massachusetts Correctional
   Institute Walpole
Massachusetts Correctional
   Institute Plymouth
Park Drive Pre-Release

Boston Pre-Release

Lancaster Pre-Release

South Middlesex Pre-Release
Bay State Correctional Center

Shirley Training Academy	Reception Diagnostic Center
	Western Avenue Pre-Release
	Southeast Correctional Center

Colleges Affiliated with University of Massachusetts Amherst

Amherst College	Mt. Holyoke College
Hampshire College	Smith College

Worcester Consortium for Higher Education, Inc., Affiliated with University of Massachusetts Medical School

Anna Maria College	Central New England College
Assumption College	Clark University
Becker Junior College	Holy Cross College
Worcester Polytechnic Institute	The Worcester Foundation for Experimental Biology

Miscellaneous Massachusetts Agencies

Food and Agriculture Department	Transportation Department
Commerce and Development Department	Environmental Management Department
Labor and Industry Department	Consumer Protection Division
Insurance Department	Corporation and Taxation Department
Public Utilities Department	Arts and Humanities Council

Obviously, the nature of state agencies will vary somewhat from one state to another, if for no other reason than the geography of the state. Where Massachusetts and New York—and even Philadelphia, which is not on the seacoast, but has a major river leading to the sea—would have Port Authority agencies, one would not expect to see such an agency in Arizona or North Dakota. And the subordinate agencies within the major departments of each state government are even more directly affected. The Department of Agriculture in a desert state, such as Nevada, would have quite different concerns and therefore different bureaus and offices than such a department in a state having huge wilderness areas, such as Montana, one having a basically agricultural economy, such as Iowa, or one heavily industrialized, such as Michigan. And, of course, these differences can strongly affect the various agencies' needs for computers and related goods and services.

Major Cities

There are approximately 125 major metropolitan areas in the United States—that is, there are 125 of the country's approximately 18,000 incorporated communities (cities, towns, and townships), taken together with their suburban environs and including over 125 of the nation's 3,000-odd counties. Some of these coincide with the major centers of federal procurement activity alluded to earlier, but all the major cities and counties are important elements in terms of local government markets—in terms, that is, of their own purchasing power. All have their own government structures, which include a purchasing office and staff in the city hall or county executive building. In some cases, city boundaries and county boundaries coincide (in the case of Philadelphia, Pennsylvania, for example), and in some cases city/county purchasing is merged, at least in part.

Following are the 50 largest cities in the United States. (There is no significance to the order in which they are presented.)

Albuquerque, NM	Atlanta, GA	Austin, TX
Baltimore, MD	Boston, MA	Buffalo, NY
Charlotte, NC	Chicago, IL	Cincinnati, OH
Cleveland, OH	Columbus, OH	Dallas, TX
Denver, CO	Detroit, MI	El Paso, TX
Fort Worth, TX	Honolulu, HI	Houston, TX
Indianapolis, IN	Jacksonville, FL	Kansas City, MO
Las Vegas, NV	Los Angeles, CA	Louisville, KY
Memphis, TN	Miami, FL	Milwaukee, WI
Minneapolis, MN	Nashville, TN	New Orleans, LA
New York, NY	Norfolk, VA	Oakland, CA
Oklahoma City, OK	Omaha, NE	Philadelphia, PA
Phoenix, AZ	Pittsburgh, PA	Portland, OR
St. Louis, MO	St. Paul, MN	San Antonio, TX
San Diego, CA	San Francisco, CA	San Jose, CA
Seattle, WA	Tampa, FL	Toledo, OH
Tulsa, OK	Washington, DC	

Typical City Purchasing

To illustrate the scope and diversity of purchasing at the local government levels, consider the city of Dallas, Texas, as one example. In 1982, the most recent year for which figures were made available, Dallas spent approximately $40 million for goods and services in the public marketplace, excluding construction costs and certain other types of expenditures, according to the city's Director of Purchasing. Listed on the 'Commodity Index' furnished (a computer printout) were several items of interest to anyone selling computer equipment, supplies, and/or services:

Computer channel switch	Computer ribbon remanufacturing
Computer equipment lease	Computer supplies
Computer monitoring equipment repair	Computers
Computer output microfilm	Consulting, data processing
Computer parts	

The Central Purchasing Department of the City of San Diego reported about $45 million in 1982 purchasing (but excluding certain kinds of purchases and including, primarily, purchases of items for central stock in its own supply department) listing a staff of nine, including six buyers, with the purchase of computer equipment assigned to the senior buyer.

The City of Milwaukee operates a Central Board of Purchases, headed by a City Purchasing Agent, and lists word processing and business machines as regular items purchased.

The City of Memphis includes a purchasing agent in its Division of Finance and Administration, and says, "This department purchases all goods and services required by all City Divisions including the Park Commission." Exclusions are:

> The School System
> Memphis Light, Gas and Water Division
> City of Memphis Hospitals

All Shelby County Government agencies such as the Sheriff's Department, the City/County Health Department, and the Library System."

The City of Oakland Purchasing Department operates with a staff of several buyers, has a thoroughly structured set of procedures and policies, and specifically excludes about a dozen city/county agencies for which it does not buy, such as the school district, the local housing authority, and the local utility companies.

Some Major Counties

For purposes of illustration only—this is not a comprehensive list— here are a few of the larger counties in the United States (counties of 1 million or more population) along with their approximate population figures. (Again, there is no particular significance to the order in which the counties are listed, but not surprisingly the larger ones generally include a major city and even a major metropolitan area.)

County	Pop. (millions)	County	Pop. (millions)
Los Angeles, CA	7.032	Nassau, NY	1.429
Orange, CA	1.420	New York, NY	1.539
Alameda, CA	1.073	Queens, NY	1.987
Santa Clara, CA	1.065	Suffolk, NY	1.127
Dade, FL	1.268	Allegheny, PA	1.605
Cook, IL	5.492	Philadelphia, PA	1.949
Middlesex, MA	1.398	Dallas, TX	1.327
Wayne, MI	2.667	Harris, TX	1.742
Bronx, NY	1.472	King, WA	1.157
Erie, NY	1.114	Milwaukee, WI	1.054
Kings, NY	2.602		

In most cases the county has its own purchasing office, especially if it is a county of some size. (Despite the relatively small number of counties of over 1 million population, there are many counties of several hundred thousand population, as well as a few of only a scant thousand or two.)

Although on a smaller scale, most local governments follow procedures and employ procurement policies that are quite similar to those of the larger state and federal governments. Fairfax County, Virginia, for example, a county of nearly a half-million citizens, maintains a Purchasing and Supply Management Agency which is quite highly structured to handle the county's purchasing and supply needs (see Figure 5-2). Vendors are asked to register by completing a bidders application form; procurements of $5,000 or more must be solicited formally by bid invitation or proposal request and advertised in a local newspaper. Purchases under $5,000 may be made via informal bids, do not require formal advertising, but will be competed by getting at least three bids. The county's socioeconomic programs offer certain preferences to minority entrepreneurs and small business as well as to local business.

Organization

OFFICE OF GENERAL SERVICES
Purchasing and Supply Management Agency

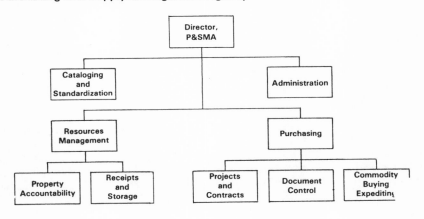

Figure 5-2 Procurement and supply organization of Fairfax County, Virginia

Chapter 6

BIDS AND PROPOSALS

This is the game of winners and losers, for it's basically competitive in every sense.

Market Research

In the commercial world the market targets are fairly obvious because they are out in plain sight: they advertise their goods and services, and they let the media know when they are seeking bids and proposals. In fact, there are various and sundry publications devoted to helping businesspeople learn promptly about all bid opportunities in their field (the F. W. Dodge reports in the construction industry, for example).

In doing business with governments the market targets are far less obvious, and many are overlooked completely by marketers who don't even suspect that the markets exist. In short, in many ways the biggest problem in selling to the government is "finding the doors," as some have put it; that is, learning where and how to uncover all the business opportunities. That is what market research means, essentially, when applied to government marketing.

Earlier in these pages a number of representative notices from the federal government publication, the *Commerce Business Daily* (CBD), were shown to illustrate one way to learn of government needs and opportunities to bid for contracts. The CBD carries several kinds of notices, in addition to synopses of solicitations available. There are also synopses of contracts awarded, which give the reader possible leads for subcontracts with winners of large contracts (winners of major prime contracts almost invariably award a number of subcontracts, since no one, no matter how big, does everything); notices of future procurements, often with invitations to readers to submit capability brochures to qualify as bidders later, when the solicitations are issued (they will be issued only to those who have qualified earlier by submitting acceptable capability brochures); and sundry other notices the U.S. Department of Commerce (publisher of the CBD) and other federal agencies wish to publicize. (Occasionally the Commerce Department will permit other than federal agencies to use the pages of the

CBD, when it appears to be in the interests of the government, as when they permit the winner of a large prime contract to use the CBD as an avenue for finding suitable subcontractors.)

The CBD probably lists about $20 billion of federal procurement, possibly a bit more (but certainly not a great deal more), which is only some 10 to 15 percent of all federal procurement. Even as a percentage of all competitive federal procurement it is only a relatively small fraction. A great deal of federal procurement is never announced in the CBD at all, despite the law that says that it must be so publicized.

This means that you must pursue sources of information other than the CBD if you expect to be made aware of more than a small fraction of federal government business opportunities. These other measures of conducting your market research include the following:

- Visit as many procurement offices as possible and make direct inquiries. All outstanding solicitations are available, either posted on a bulletin board or bound in a volume, but available for your scrutiny.
- File Bidders List applications with all the procurement offices you can discover. (Make a basic form out and then make a couple of hundred copies for distribution, because you must file a copy with each and every procurement office with which you hope to do business.)
- Get acquainted with as many people who request bids and proposals as you can and stay in touch with them by telephone and personal visits. Many of these will call you to let you know of a procurement that you might very well never learn of otherwise.
- Create opportunities by making sales calls. The law permits agencies to award up to $10,000 ($25,000 in DOD) by informal contracting procedures—purchase orders—and you can generate some of these by simple low-pressure salesmanship.

This does not mean that you should not use the CBD. Far from it, the CBD is an extremely valuable tool. It currently costs $81 per year for second-class mailing, $160 for first class, with no guarantee that the latter extra expense will truly speed delivery. Where once the paper arrived on its nominal date, when the postal service was at its former level of efficiency, it is rare to get an issue in the mail now that is not several days late, and issues do not even arrive in any order: you may very well get Thursday's edition before you get Monday's! (Instead of getting the paper daily, you generally get several issues at a time, once or twice a week, and first-class mail does not appear to help greatly; in fact, daily periodicals are "preferential" mail, by definition, and are supposed to get first-class treatment regardless of the postage fees paid, and perhaps they do, since all mail, including first-class mail, seems to get third-class treatment now.)

CBD Online

There is now a solution for this: The U.S. Department of Commerce has made arrangements with private-sector organizations to make the information available in a more timely manner by utilizing the newest technologies. You can now subscribe to "CBD Online," an electronic edition of the CBD, available as an online database which is accessible by computer and modem, and get the information even before it is printed. There are currently four organizations authorized by the Commerce Department to supply this service:

SOFTSHARE/MCR Technology, Inc.
55 Depot Road
Goleta, CA 93117
805/683-3841 (Collect)

United Communications Group
8701 Georgia Avenue
Silver Spring, MD 20910
301/589-8875

Data Resources, Inc. (DRI)
2400 Hartwell Avenue
Lexington, MA 02173
617/863-5100

Dialog Information Services, Inc.
3460 Hillview Avenue
Palo Alto, CA 94304
800/227-1927 (outside CA)
800/982-5838 (in CA)

As with most such services you pay for "connect time" online, but you do not have to subscribe for the entire edition. You can read and/or download just those portions of the CBD that interest you. This saves you time and money, as well as being far more efficient than reading the entire CBD. And overall, the time saved is well worth the investment, if you are serious about pursuing government contracts.

Using Your Own Computer for Market Research

One of the major advantages of using the CBD Online database is the currency of the information: Instead of waiting several days for your paper edition you get the information immediately, perhaps even before the paper edition goes into the mail. But, important although it is, that is not the only advantage. You can get marketing information that is simply not available to you by any other means, except at intolerable cost. You can, for example, do extensive searches of the database by entering keywords as search terms and get back data in minutes.

Each of the several services differs somewhat in details, although all offer the same basic capability. CBD Online, a division of United Communications Group of Silver Spring, MD, has been kind enough to give me not only permission to explain its system in some detail but also to reproduce portions of its user manual.

Basics of the System

As in all such subscriber systems, each subscriber is assigned a unique identification code, which the subscriber must use in logging on to the system. The system permits access and data transfer at either 300 or 1200 baud (rates of data transfer or transmission). Those in the local Washington metropolitan area can dial the system up directly, using a local telephone number. Those calling from anywhere else can access the system toll-free via either of two telecommunications networks, Telenet and Tymnet. (The manual furnishes many pages of Telenet and Tymnet telephone numbers for many cities in the United States.)

The manual promises the subscriber that "... you can quickly pinpoint government offerings, searching by keywords, categories, and through our amazing combination search."

Once signed on, the system responds thus:

> ITT Dialogue Computer Services 18.4A(50)
> On at (time and date)
> Last on at (time and date)
> LATEST CBD ISSUE ONLINE (day and date)
> >

Once you have logged on and been acknowledged, you are offered a Main Menu:

WELCOME TO CBD ONLINE

copyright 1982   UNITED COMMUNICATIONS GROUP
8701 GEORGIA AVE., SUITE 800
SILVER SPRING, MD 20910

HERE ARE YOUR CBD ONLINE OPTIONS:

1. U.S. GOVERNMENT PROCUREMENTS
2. CONTRACT AWARDS
3. RESEARCH AND DEVELOPMENT SOURCES
4. FOREIGN GOVERNMENT STANDARDS
5. BUSINESS NEWS
6. STATUS REPORT
7. ADD TO OR DELETE FROM AUTO KEYWORD LIST
8. SIGN OFF
50. HELP

If you respond by asking for any of the first five items, you are offered a menu listing the five most recent issues, including the current one, as the first five items on the menu, but you are also offered two other items: BACK CBD ISSUES and HELP. (HELP or an equivalent command, such as "main Menu" or "?," is usually an option on all menus of all systems, so that you can almost always ask for help if you get confused or "stuck" in some manner.)

Selecting a date causes the computer to fetch the appropriate file, and then ask you either to enter a keyword or select another option. If, for example, you are interested in training only, you can use *training* as your keyword, and the program will search for all synopses that have the keyword in them. But the options offered include these:

Auto Keyword Search
Category Search
Level-by-Level Keyword Search
The Amazing Combination Search

The auto keyword permits searching for more than one keyword at a time, and the computer saves the term so that you can order it up the next time you log on, if you want to search for the same keywords. But you can also change keywords, add new ones, or delete old ones, as you wish.

You can also do these same things with other categories than procurement. You can do keyword searches in the contract-awards sections, you can do searches of only certain categorical listings, and otherwise customize your search.

Doing Market Surveys

One special application of the system is for doing surveys of the government market as basic market research. In my work as a consultant in government marketing, I am occasionally called on to help a client make market estimates, which usually entails some preliminary market research. In the past, I had to do some laborious digging into my library of recent issues of the paper version of the CBD, a tedious and time-consuming job that, at best, produces only approximate estimates. Of course, I now utilize CBD Online for such work.

In one recent case I was approached by a client who was not doing any substantial amount of business directly with the federal government, but was interested to know whether the government bought enough shelters to make that an attractive market to pursue. The CBD Online capability was a "natural" for this, a way to get the information swiftly and economically.

I arranged to make a search of the awards section. A first search, using the keyword *steel*, was not very helpful; it produced little useful result. A second search, using the keyword *shelter*, however, produced rather dramatic results.

Figure 6-1 illustrates the point. It is an actual reproduction of a small portion of the printout resulting from that second search. I have condensed the printout to get as many examples as possible into the illustration.

You have a choice in such searches of doing merely a scan of headings (three lines, including customer name and address) or ordering the full text of the synopsis. (You can always go back to get the full text of any that interest you. And you can have the service order any solicitations you wish, as well.) The number or letter following the CBD Issue Date is the CBD category listing—for example, 54 = Prefabricated Structures and Scaffolding, H = Expert and Consultant services, K = Modification, Alteration, and Rebuilding of Equipment, Y = Construction, etc.

Since these are notices taken from the awards section, they include the useful information of dollar values and names of successful bidders, as well as names of customers, locations, and summary descriptions of the requirements.

R & D Opportunities and Capability Brochures

Frequently, the specific synopses will advise you that the procurement is to be made sometime in the future, but that the customer wants to gather expressions of interest now from suppliers, and asks those interested to supply a capability statement. This is a rather general document, which can be

RECORD # :   1
KEYWORD: SHELTER
CBD ISSUE DATE : 10/06/84
54 -- EXPANDABLE SHELTER/CONTAINER, ES/C, Model A, Empty, NSN 5410-00-009-9852
EJ-55 ea, ES/C, model A, nondestructive, NSN 5410-00-407-9579EJ-8 ea,
ES/C, model A, life support, NSN 5410-00-140-8963EJ-7 ea and 10 other
items with 1st, 2nd, 3rd program year option requirements. Contract
F09603-84-C-0015, 23 Mar 84, (Solic 2-53401), $18,588,825, Nordam, Tulsa, OK.<
Warner Robins ALC Directorate of Contracting and Manufacturing, Robins
AFB, GA 31098<

RECORD # :   2
KEYWORD: SHELTER
CBD ISSUE DATE : 10/06/84
54 -- S-280C/G SHELTER ELECT EQUIP, (No RFP), Contract DAAB07-84-C-B102,
Mod P00002, $1,983,400, 8 Jun 84, Gichner Mobile Systems, P.O Box B,
East Locust St, Dallastown, PA. (180)<
U.S. Army Electronics Command, Fort Monmouth, NJ 07703<

RECORD # :   3
KEYWORD: SHELTER
CBD ISSUE DATE : 10/11/84
H -- MODIFICATION OF MARINE EQUIPMENT SHELTER. Award of Contract No.
14-08-0001-20772, Modification No. 4, was made to Woods Hole Oceanographic
Institution, Water Street, Woods Hole, MA 02543, in the amount of $68,250.00
on June 8, 1984.<
U.S. Dept of Interior, Geological Survey, Eastern Region Management
Office, Procurement and Contracts Section, Room 2A233B, 12201 Sunrise
Valley Drive, Reston, VA 22092, 703/860-7817<

RECORD # :   4
KEYWORD: SHELTER
CBD ISSUE DATE : 10/11/84
K -- MODIFY GFP SHELTERS for the AN/TRQ-32 mobile, multi-station, ground-based
, direction finding and intercept system, Contract DAAK21-82-C-0072,
Modification P00016, dtd 22 Jun 84. $163,000, Magnavox Government and
Industrial Electronics Co., 1313 Production Rd, Fort Wayne, IN 46808.<
Harry Diamond Laboratories, Contracts Branch (Vint Hill), Attn: S.H.
Wake, DELHD-PR-CV, 703/347-6573, Vint Hill Farms Station, Warrenton, VA 22186<

RECORD # :   5
KEYWORD: SHELTER
CBD ISSUE DATE : 10/11/84
Y -- CONSTRUCTION OF HANDICAPPED ALTERATIONS, Heated Pump Shelters
& Improve Heating/Ventilating Systems at Holston AAP, Kingsport, TN,
DACA01-84-C-0088, Awarded 12 June 1984, DACA01-84-B-0038, National
Geothermal, Inc., Rt. 4, Box 32, Florence, MS 39073, Amount $198,336.00.<
Mobile District, Corps of Engineers, PO Box 2288, Mobile, AL 36628.<

Figure 6-1 Portion of CBD keyword-search printout (Courtesy CBD
Online, United Communications Group)

quite informal—typed, with a corner staple, for example—or it can be a printed brochure, as long as it contains all necessary information, demonstrating that your organization is qualified in terms of experience and resources—people, facilities, and know-how.

The purpose of asking for such a document is simply to compile a bidders list for future use, and in many cases you will be advised that only those who provide such a statement and demonstrate that they are qualified for the future project will be invited to propose later.

While these requests are sometimes made in regular procurement synopses, under any of the general category codes, there is a special section of the CBD that addresses this kind of need exclusively. It is headed Research and Development Sources Sought, and invariably invites readers to submit capability statements to be held in reserve for future use in some R&D procurement.

Marketing research efforts ought always to include the maintenance of up-to-date capability statements, while monitoring the CBD for opportunities to qualify for future procurement competitions. The capability statements, however, are most useful when they are in some kind of looseleaf form (and preferably in word processor files) so that they may be tailored (customized) for each need.

In general terms, all of this is as valid for researching state and local government markets as it is for marketing to federal agencies, although there is, so far, no counterpart for CBD Online at the state and local government level. However, all the purchasing offices of these other governments urge vendors to visit their offices and to file the forms, which are intended to serve as applications for inclusion on bidders lists, in most cases, but are used as registration forms in a few cases. And in a few cases a small fee is required to register, but most impose no fee for filing.

Like the federal agencies, the state and local governments do little to publicize their needs, other than to make the formal announcements in the local newspaper classified columns under "Bids and Proposals" headings, although on occasion a state or local government will utilize large display advertisements when it wishes to generate more intense competition. Therefore, like the price of liberty (per Thomas Jefferson), the price of success in finding opportunities to exploit in government markets is eternal vigilance, for basically the burden for learning of the bid and proposal opportunities is borne by you as the marketer, not by the government agencies.

Bids

Typically, in soliciting a bid from you, the federal government will employ one of two forms, a Standard Form 33, as noted earlier (Figure 2-2), which can be used for soliciting either a formally advertised bid (IFB) or a proposal (RFP), or a Standard Form 18, Request for Quotation (RFQ), a very much misunderstood and misused form. And state and local governments have parallel forms, generally.

Agencies often misuse the RFQ as an instrument to solicit bids and even proposals. Its proper use is as an instrument to determine what something is likely to cost, as a kind of price survey. The form states plainly, in fact, that the price quotations furnished by respondents are not binding on them, but are furnished entirely for purposes of providing information. However, many agencies use the RFQ as a preliminary to issuing a purchase order; that is, to get bids for supplies or services costing not more than $10,000 or whatever their limit is on small purchases. And where the RFQ is supposedly utilized only to determine prices, agencies often ask that respondents submit much other information that is tantamount to a formal proposal. Of course, respondents don't argue with this use, since it represents a sales opportunity.

The use of RFQs is fairly limited, and many who sell regularly to federal government agencies have never seen one. More commonly bids are solicited by use of the IFB or Standard Form 33, where the chief criterion—actually, for all practical purposes, the sole criterion—is price, with the low bidder winning the contract.

The rules surrounding the advertised procurement (the formal bid) are rather rigid, and there are few occasions on which any can be bent even slightly. For example, failure to sign the bid in the proper place disqualifies the bid automatically, as does failure to comply faithfully with all legitimate requirements of the solicitation, such as submitting it not later than the precise date and time of closing. Being as much as 30 seconds late disqualifies the bid.

Usually, when an agency sends you a formal bid solicitation, it attaches an alerting sheet advising you that you are signing a contract form, in signing your bid, and that all the government needs to do is sign the form also, and a contract will exist. You will be compelled under law to deliver what you have bid for the prices you have bid. Therefore, you are urged, check and double check everything before signing and submitting the bid; be sure that you are willing to be bound by what you have bid.

In practice, the government would gain nothing by compelling you to lose money, especially if the loss would put you out of business so that you could not complete the contract. Therefore, if the contracting officer believes that your bid is unrealistically low, and is low because it is based on error, oversight, or ignorance of the realities, you will usually be offered an opportunity to voluntarily withdraw your bid, which is ordinarily the only way it can be nullified after the opening. Theoretically, the government has the right to disqualify your bid on any of several possible grounds, but in practice it is almost impossible to disqualify you as a bidder if you have made out the forms properly, unless there is provable fraud or collusion of some sort, or you have been legally barred from bidding. (There are such cases occasionally, but they are quite rare, and even in some of these cases the bidder has gone to court over the matter and often prevailed there.) In practice, no matter how unrealistic your bid, if you happen to be the low bidder you can insist on having the contract and will almost always get it. (That is not always a blessing, as a few low bidders have discovered!)

Bidding Strategies

When we discuss proposal writing, we will spend time in discussing proposal strategies, one of which is cost or price strategy. In a bid situation, that is the only strategy that counts, for the obvious reason that price is the only factor on which the award decision is based. In fact, it is gilding the lily to refer to the action as a decision, for the price dictates the result. But that itself makes the idea of a cost strategy an apparent anomaly: A bid is, presumably, either the lowest or it is not the lowest. How, then, can we speak of strategy?

The answer to that question lies in the nature of many, if not most bid solicitations: They are by no means always simple, "for the job" or "for the lot" single-price quotations. Quite often the solicitation requires that an entire series of prices be furnished, and it is not at all simple to determine who is, in fact, the low bidder in many of these cases. In many cases, it is a question of who *appears* to be the low bidder. But let's look first at a hypothetical request for prices, as represented in Table 6-1.

Now there is no problem with determining who is the low bidder for this procurement, since everything is quantified. The grand totals for all the bids will be compared (after all extensions are verified correct), seeking the lowest grand total as the victor. (If extensions are incorrect, the unit prices will prevail, and the contracting officer will correct the extensions and the grand total.) But as it happens, this is quite often not the case, and instead a bid is called for in the format shown in Table 6-2.

Indefinite Quantity Bids

Table 6-2 illustrates the all too common indefinite-quantity bid, wherein the bidder is asked to furnish unit prices for a variety of items with little or no indication of the quantities of subsequent orders, or what the total size of the procurement is likely to be, either in numbers of items or in numbers of dollars. This is an indefinite-quantity bid, also known as a Basic Ordering Agreement (BOA) usually, in federal procurement, and as a term contract or term supply contract, usually, in state and local government procurement. It is used when the government has no dependable way of ascertaining just how much of something it will use over the next year but wants to pin down a source of supplies and agreed-upon prices for the year. (These contracts are usually for one year.)

There are several alternative versions of this basic situation. The customer might state that the contract is to be approximately of such and such a dollar volume or "not to exceed" some figure, which is a left-handed way of saying the same thing by implication, so as not to be bound by the figure stated. (Sometimes such contracts carry a guaranteed minimum of items or dollars, but these are usually virtually nominal and so not really significant.) Or the bid might specify the numbers of main items wanted—letter quality and dot matrix printers, in this case—but give no indication of how many replacement parts and supply items are likely to be ordered.

Table 6-1 Form for providing price quotations in formal bid

PRINTERS AND SPARE PARTS

Item	No. Req'd	Unit Price	Total
Letter quality printers, per specifications	10	$ _____	$ _____
Dot matrix printers, per specifications	20	_____	_____
Platens for letter quality printers	50	_____	_____
Replacement daisy wheels	60	_____	_____
Tractor mechanisms	12	_____	_____
Foreign-language PROMs for dot matrix printers	120	_____	_____
Sheet feeders	40	_____	_____
Replacement Print heads	40	_____	_____
Ribbons for letter quality printers	200	_____	_____
Ribbons for dot matrix printers	200	_____	_____
Additional copies of maintenance manuals	18	_____	_____
		GRAND TOTAL:	$

Table 6-2 An indefinite-quantity bid

PRINTERS AND SPARE PARTS

Item	Price Each
Letter quality printers, per specifications	$ _____
Dot matrix printers, per specifications	_____
Platens for letter quality printers	_____
Replacement daisy wheels	_____
Tractor mechanisms	_____
Foreign-language PROMs for dot matrix printers	_____
Sheet feeders	_____
Print heads	_____
Ribbons for letter quality printers	_____
Ribbons for dot matrix printers	_____
Additional copies of maintenance manuals	_____

This is a dilemma for the bidder, of course, even if the agency furnishes estimated (but not guaranteed) quantities, because the customer is not bound by these figures, so they are almost meaningless. Ordinarily, the profit markup on replacement parts and supporting supplies is much greater than it is on the main item, which must often be discounted. And if the spare parts and supplies order is great enough, many bidders will offer the main items at little or no profit, and sometimes even at a slight loss—as a loss leader—expecting to make up the difference in the other items. Obviously, this strategy goes out the window when the sales volume of these other items is unknown and in no way guaranteed.

But that is not necessarily fatal for the resourceful and determined marketer; there are some alternatives.

How to Become the Apparent Low Bidder

One thing you can and should do, when faced with such a situation as this, is to find out if there is currently a contract in force for these items (or services, for such contracts are also issued for services). If so, ask how many of each item was bought last year. (This is ordinarily public information, and you are entitled to ask for and get this information.) Caution: try to check back several years because last year might be an aberration or the first year, in which case it is unlikely to be dependably indicative of what you are likely to provide under the new contract. Seek to get figures for as many prior years as possible and study them, trying to find a pattern of some verifiable consistency.

There are two possibilities here for developing a price or cost strategy of some sort:

1. You may find that demand for high-profit items is high enough to furnish you a profit even if you go in very low on the main items, and you may opt to utilize that as your strategy.

2. You may find that the agency buys extremely little of one or two of the items, in which case quite another strategy is indicated. To explain this strategy, it is necessary to digress for a moment and look at the dilemma from the customer's viewpoint, for the customer has a problem too.

How to Determine Which Is the Low Bid

Bear in mind that it is the customer's problem to decide which is the low bid, and it is as difficult to decide that as it is to know how to bid when quantities to be furnished are totally indefinite. In fact, in the absence of specific quantification that dictates which is the low bid, the government is compelled to determine which is the *apparent* low bid by some arbitrary but nevertheless plausible and equitable evaluation scheme. (Otherwise, losing bidders are certain to protest and even sue in court.)

Consequently, the agency will generally employ a scheme to arrive at a weighted average, based on whatever it believes to be reasonable expectations. In practice, the agency will arbitrarily assume some hypothetical quantities of all the items, based on whatever it deems to be justifiable assumptions or best estimates of some quantity of each item listed, and use this as a measure to compare bids. That is, it will arrive at grand totals for each bid, based on those hypothetical quantities, and declare that bidder whose hypothetical grand total is the smallest to be the low bidder.

It is possible to finesse that tactic when you find, as you may very well, that the agency has rarely, if ever, bought one or more of the items for which you have been asked to furnish pricing. Bureaucracy being what it is, an item may get on the list one year because of a special, nonrecurring need, and it is likely to remain on that list forevermore, even if it is never needed again. Or it may be there simply because someone thought it wise to provide against the possibility of its need, however remote that possibility. That happens in a bureaucracy, too.

Once you find such items, you can risk low-balling them sharply, virtually giving them away. The risk is slight, since it is unlikely that you will ever be called on to furnish the item. But the salutary effect of such low-ball unit prices is reflected in the bottom line, immensely increasing your prospects to be the apparent, but not actual, low bidder.

A parallel situation exists with regard to such contracts for services and is often even more prevalent a situation when technical or professional services are being contracted for. That is, it is even more likely that the agency will not be able to predict with any great accuracy how many tasks it will have to contract out or how many hours of each category of labor it will buy during the year. The same methods of deciding who is the low bidder are used here, and the same strategies are available to bidders. In fact, when it comes to BOAs for service, you are sometimes offered an even better opportunity to finesse the competition through becoming the apparent low bidder, because in many situations you can decide which is the item the customer will use in zero or near-zero quantity! Here is why:

Many of these contracts for technical and professional services grow by accretion, just as the others do, acquiring labor classes not really needed, as a result of some unique, nonrecurring circumstance. For example, a contract may call for three or four classes (proficiency levels) of engineers, technical writers, analysts, programmers, and/or others. Unless the customer requires that the labor be provided as bodies to work on-site—on the government's own premises—you can usually decide for yourself which class or classes is/are excess and unneeded. Thus, you can offer these unneeded classes of labor at bargain rates, with that same beneficial effect on the bottom line. (But you will never actually use these classes of labor because to do so would mean losing money. So you get all the work done with the classes of labor remaining.)

Negotiated Procurement

The difference between the work on-site and the work off-site is this: When you provide services on the customer's premises, you generally provide bodies—people—and bill for each person in each labor category for hours worked. But when the services are performed on your own premises, you usually bill, not for people and hours worked, but for and by tasks performed. In the first case, you must provide the classes of labor called for; in the second case you must provide the end-results and/or end-products called for, giving you the opportunity to decide who will be assigned to each task. (You will never assign the classes of labor you have low-balled, of course.)

There is this difference, though, between the solicitation for goods and the solicitation for technical or professional services: Goods, particularly goods that can be specified with great precision or ordered by brand name or equivalent, are often bought by formally advertised procurement—sealed bids. But technical and professional services are far more often bought by negotiated procurement, which means after RFPs are issued and proposals are evaluated. And negotiated procurement and the proposal game are entirely different games than advertised procurement and sealed bids, despite a very few points of similarity. Here are the major differences:

1. Price is only as important as the customer wishes it to be. Low bid does not dictate the winner, although it may be a major factor and the cost strategies may be applied here also, for whatever influence they may have.
2. The competition is primarily a technical competition, rather than a price or cost competition, although it is a real enough competition, nevertheless.
3. Every proposal must be evaluated for its technical excellence (or lack of it), and the technical score so awarded is a major factor.
4. Preference may be given certain types and classes of proposers.
5. The rules that bind the customer and the proposer are not nearly so strict. The proposals must be submitted not later than the closing date and hour, but the customer can negotiate afterwards and accept changes to anything in the proposal, either in writing or verbally, across the negotiating table.
6. The contract normally goes to the best proposal writer, who may or may not be the best contractor.

That last point is the most important one made, and it is one that sometimes escapes notice. The goal of the proposal competition, from the customer's viewpoint, is to choose the best contractor. But the means for judging which is the best contractor is the proposal. (Even if the customer knows and is fond of the proposer, by law the proposer can get credit only for that which is in the proposal.) So inevitably the best proposal writers win the contracts.

Proposal writing is itself of such importance that it merits a chapter of its own, and the next chapter will be devoted to the subject.

Chapter 7

THE ART OF PROPOSAL WRITING

The purpose of a proposal, like the purpose of oratory, is persuasion, not truth.

A Few Preliminary Understandings

As in the case of most other important activities in our society, a mythology has sprung up around proposal writing. And like most myths these have some slender basis in fact, but they suffer from the syndrome of observing the exception and declaring it to be the rule.

Almost without exception the mythology consists of various declarations that only large and powerful organizations can win government contracts, that the system is less than honest, and that the "little guy" does not stand a chance of winning.

It is, of course, the cynics and those who have never mastered the art of bidding and proposing successfully to the government agencies that create and propagate the myths, at least partially as a rationale for their own failures in marketing. You will never hear these myths from those who manage to market successfully to government agencies, whether they are the large organizations or the small ones. The simple fact is that even the self-employed individual can do business with government agencies, and a great many do. In fact, many contracts are specifically set aside for small businesses, and large companies are not even permitted to bid for these. This is not to say that the system is perfect. It would be unreasonable to believe that with millions of purchases and contracts, representing the expenditure of hundreds of billions of dollars, occasional irregularities do not slip by the scrutiny of contracting officers, inspectors general, and others responsible for safeguards in the system. But these are the exceptions, and every day government contracts are awarded to both small and large organizations and even to self-employed individuals operating one-person enterprises.

It is important to understand this because your mental set is an important factor in all marketing, but especially in marketing to government agencies.

The markets are highly competitive, and the traditional verities of sincerity, dedication, and perseverance are necessities here. Moreover, positive and negative approaches somehow show through your writing and affect the customer's perceptions. And in marketing, the customer's perception is by far the most and in some cases the only important factor.

Proposal Premises

There are several basic premises upon which all ideas about successful proposal writing—and "successful" refers to proposals that win contracts, of course—must be founded. They are these:

- A proposal is a *sales* presentation.
- Proposals are the responsibility of the organization's marketing department, not the publications department.
- Proposal "writing" has far less to do with skills in writing than with skills in persuasion.
- Good proposal writers are good marketers at least as much as they are good writers and perhaps much more marketers than writers.
- Proposals do not win contracts by luck; they win as the result of determined and intelligent effort by their developers.
- The key to success in proposal competitions is strategy.

The Evolution of Strategy

Proposals are sales presentations, an element of marketing. And success in marketing is the result of successful marketing strategies. You may take it for granted that most of your competitors will deliver proposals which demonstrate that they can do the job and deliver the product about as well as you or anyone else can. But that is not enough to guarantee winning the contract. If every proposer manages only to prove equal ability to satisfy the customer's requirement, the competition becomes a lottery, where the customer might as well place all the proposals in a hat and have one withdrawn by someone who is blindfolded to ensure impartiality. But of course this is not the way it is done. Instead the customer evaluates the proposals, trying to determine who is best qualified, who has somehow demonstrated that he is both able and likely to do a far better job, deliver a far better product, or otherwise give the customer one or more compelling reasons for being selected as the winning proposer. That is what strategy is all about: reasons for selecting you as the winner and the methods you use to persuade the customer to agree with your arguments. Here are a few of the general categories into which those "compelling reasons" might fall:

- Cost
- Project design and/or features
- Product design and/or features
- Qualifications of proposed individual staff members
- Qualifications of organization
- Something special (ideally, unique) as inducements/considerations

Of course, that is not all there is to proposal writing or to the development of effective strategies. But those ideas contain some of the seeds of strategy and some of the categorical areas to consider when seeking a basis for strategies. And, as you will soon see, there are several kinds of strategy to consider:

- Technical or program-design strategy
- Presentation strategy
- Competitive strategy
- Cost strategy
- Capture strategy

All of these will be discussed individually, but first on to more fundamental discussions about the general basis for all strategy definition. For the identification of successful strategies cannot be arbitrary; it must be based on some rationale. That rationale is based on the same considerations on which all marketing and sales are based, so it is useful to first discuss those briefly.

The Basis for Strategy: Sales/Marketing Principles

The basis of all marketing and sales is buyer motivation, that which causes a prospect to become a customer, to agree to exchange dollars for what you offer. It has lots of names and related terms. Perhaps you have heard a few of these:

Persuasion
Sales arguments
Wants
Felt needs
Created needs
Inducements
Closing

Let us discuss a few of these terms to understand their relationships to each other and what they have to do with formulating successful strategies for marketing generally and for proposal writing especially.

Persuasion and Sales Arguments   Persuasion is not a complicated idea. It simply involves managing to convince someone that you are right or that he or she would be well advised or want to do as you suggest. The means for persuasion are the key to sales and marketing, the objective of sales arguments, of course, and we will discuss them shortly. But bear in mind that all persuasion has a common basis of self-interest. It is self-interest or the other party's *perception of self-interest* that is always the great persuader. Cynical although it may sound, we humans act out of self-interest, even when we do things that are commonly regarded as being selfless and altruistic or done out of love. We act "unselfishly" because it pleases us to do so, because it makes us feel better in some way. That is, "self-interest" is not necessarily venal or evil, but may underlie motivation for even the noblest acts. It is necessary to understand that when you are engaged in marketing.

What this amounts to, in marketing terms, is that to persuade someone to any course of action you must make the other party perceive his or her self-interest in believing what you say and/or doing what you suggest. It is necessary, also, to understand that every business is a service business, in this sense: People do not really buy *things*; they buy what things will *do* for them—or what they believe the things will do for them. Sometimes we buy clothes to keep warm, but we also buy them to make ourselves look good, to be in style, to keep up with the Joneses, and for lots of reasons other than the practical one of keeping warm and comfortable. (In fact, how often do we wear uncomfortable clothes because the other wants are more important to us than being comfortable?)

To persuade anyone, you must understand what the other person wants or thinks he or she needs. And the ablest marketers help the others perceive wants that coincide with what the marketer is selling. As the late Elmer Wheeler, lauded as "America's greatest salesman" said, if you want to sell people lemonade, you have to first make them thirsty. And it is rather well known that most people buy a great deal more when shopping in the super-market if they happen to be hungry when they are doing their shopping. (Writers on how to be thrifty almost always urge readers to shop only when they are definitely not hungry.)

Wants and Needs   We use that word *want* today as a synonym for *desire*, but it really means to be without something, as in the rhyme that has such lines as "For want of a nail." It is therefore a synonym of *need*, as well as of *desire*. And *need* is a key to much marketing wisdom, as in the often-quoted advice for success in business, "Find a need and fill it."

Marketers sometimes refer to felt needs, which are needs or wants the prospect has already recognized spontaneously, without external stimulus, and to creating needs, which means to cause the prospect to feel the need or want.

It is that latter idea that is most pertinent to proposal strategies. The customer has issued a request for bids or proposals because of a felt need, an idea that there is a requirement to be satisfied. The proposer must, however, study the request with a view to finding the basis for one or more alternative strategies.

- Agreement with the customer's definition of what is needed, and therefore seeking a means to outshine competitors in the methodology, services, results, and/or products to be delivered.
- Finding weaknesses in the solicitation, especially in the customer's idea of what is needed or wanted, and therefore changing the customer's mind as to the true need or want and offering a new and more accurate definition of the requirement as it should be stated.
- Find other wants, that perhaps the customer does not recognize yet (*create* wants) and make those the basis for offering what competitors cannot offer.

Store these thoughts away mentally for a moment, as we go on to a related subject, after which we'll bring the ideas together.

Worry Items

Experienced proposal writers often speak of the customer's "worry items," that is, his or her greatest concerns. If the customer dwells overly on the extremely tight schedule and the absolute need to meet that schedule without fail, you may safely assume that the schedule is an item of worry to the customer. But the customer may be worried about other things, such as cost, dependability, performance, or safety, for example. And successful strategies can often be built around those worry items for they are the keys to winning. The customer who imposes an "impossible" deadline to meet is going to be greatly influenced in favor of that proposer who can offer the best assurances of meeting that deadline without fail.

Sometimes the worry items are not apparent, and perhaps the customer really has no worry items and believes that there are no problems other than purely routine ones involved in satisfying the requirement. This presents something of a challenge. Assurances of meeting deadlines, of keeping the costs under control, of producing the desired results dependably, and of other such matters do little for the proposer strategically when the customer sees no problems with these. The experienced proposal writer knows that something must be done, and it is this: the customer must be *given* a worry item or two! It must be assumed that there are problems and hazards and that the customer is simply unaware of them. It is necessary first to create the proper worry items—and then reveal the solutions.

Promises and Proof

Marketers who write on the subject and train others often refer to the AIDA acronym to explain sales and advertising:

A	for	[get]	Attention	
I	for	[arouse]	Interest	(in your offer)
D	for	[generate]	Desire	(for what you are selling)
A	for	[ask for]	Action	(ask for the order)

I have always had trouble discriminating between I and D; they seem pretty much the same thing to me, but both are necessary, if the acronym is to be used. Asking for the order is legitimate enough, I believe; people do need to be instructed specifically in what to do; initiative, even in so minor a matter as saying, "I want one of those," is remarkably lacking in the populace at large.

In proposals and bids we do not face the problem. The customer will place the order. Our problem is solely one of persuading the customer to place the order with us. In fact, in my opinion we do not need an acronym to remember the basics of sales and advertising, for it requires only one letter, repeated: P and P. And they stand for Promise and Proof:

PROMISE: What this product/service will *do* for you.

PROOF: The evidence that it will do so.

Let us put this theory to the test by considering some successful applications:

Beer commercials on TV: No one even attempts to sell beer as a product, and any reference to the quality of one's beer is an afterthought and a minor theme. Brewers sell the good times—fun at the corner tavern and on the beach—that allegedly result from drinking their beer. A few sell the diet benefits of their light (lower calorie) beer, and occasionally a brewer sells the macho image of booted men on camping, hunting, and fishing trips, but the latter are very much in the minority.

The "ring around the collar" commercial: This is an oldie, which has worked well for many years. The benefit is avoidance of embarrassment— never sell the fear motivation short; it's a powerful one, as the next example shows also.

"Do you make these embarrassing mistakes in English?" was the head- line of a magazine advertisement for the Cody correspondence school in English. It ran successfully without change for over 40 years, offering that same benefit of avoiding embarrassment.

Insurance is sold through fear motivation for the most part, appealing to the desire to protect one's family. But it also appeals to the fear of feeling guilty if you do not have enough insurance. Watch the insurance advertise- ments closely for this connotation of guilt, as well as appeals to a sense of greater security.

Successful proposals, like successful advertisements and commercials, make such appeals and focus primarily on promises of benefits, even of negative benefits, such as the avoidance of disasters. And of course the major promise should be keyed to the major worry item. That's the point of deciding on what the worry items are or, failing that, generating at least one important one by explaining potential problems and hazards to the custo- mer.

The promise, like the worry item, must not be something trivial, if it is to be effective. It must be something important to the customer. And there may be more than one promise, but it is possible to dilute and weaken the effect, so there should always be one major worry item and one major promise, with others clearly subordinate, and not too many others, in any case, so that the major impact is focused. That is an important factor in the strategy.

The Search for Worry Items and Strategies

Searching for worry items and evolving strategies upon which to base a pro- posal is primarily a job of analyzing the RFP, with its work statement and other factors, each of which merits some discussion here, for they contain the clues to the development of winning proposals.

The Solicitation Package   The original solicitation package (RFP, in this case, since we are discussing proposal preparation in this chapter) issued by the government agency ordinarily includes at least three kinds of material:

1. General instructions and explanations of what is required as a response—what must be in your proposal, when it is due, where or to whom to address questions, notice of a preproposal conference, if one is to be held, how proposals are to be evaluated, and other such data.
2. A statement of work, which is the detailed description and specifications of what is to be done, what product(s) must be delivered as a result, and other data pertaining to the specific project.
3. Forms, copies of controlling and pertinent regulations, and sundry other such "boilerplate" material.

Often there are appendices or attachments, listing formal government standards and/or specifications, and other more detailed information regarding the procurement. Usually these are technically part of one of the three categories of information mentioned here.

The Statement of Work   The work statement is in most respects the most important part of the package. Unfortunately, it does not always carry out its mission well. The general instructions are often considerably less than crystal clear, but the statement of work is often even more so, and fails to include true specifications; that is, what is supposed to be the specifications is anything but specific.

There are many reasons for this, most of which are not of any value that makes them worth exploring here. The reason for providing a statement of work, philosophically, is to explain generally what the requirement is, while encouraging the respondent to offer ideas, so that the government may choose what appears to be the best approach to satisfying the requirement. Therefore, the statement of work (SOW), should be specific enough to explain the government's want, but open enough to permit and even encourage innovative thinking. But few SOWs manage to achieve that ideal middle ground; most tend to one extreme or the other.

The extremes are overly vague, almost-impossible-to-decipher work statements, on the one hand, and work statements so detailed in dictating exactly what the contractor is to do as to prevent any exercise of imagination or independent, innovative ideas on the part of the respondent. However, the specificity or lack of it can obtain in more than one area of the work statement, and these will be of critical importance, as you seek worry items and strategies. Those can include any or all of the following:

1. The problem the customer is facing or needs to solve.
2. The results the customer wishes to achieve.
3. The end item or product the customer wishes delivered.
4. The time schedules to be imposed and met.
5. What the government will provide or do.
6. Procedures or methodology the contractor must pursue.
7. Quantification of whatever requires quantification.
8. How proposals are to be evaluated. (This is probably not part of the work statement itself, but is worth mentioning here, since any serious discussion of proposal writing must consider it.)

Pros and Cons of Responding to the Vague RFP   In the actual case, work statements are more likely to be vague and noninformative, rather than overly detailed. Many prospective proposers are discouraged by this apparent difficulty, and choose not to respond to the RFP as a result. Others see this as a advantage because there is reduced competition resulting from the discouragement of many who might otherwise respond, and further because the very vagueness of the work statement opens the door wide to imagination and innovation. It is significant that in questioning attendees at many seminars on proposal writing I have found that the experienced and successful proposal writers prefer the vague statement of work to the overly detailed one. There are at least two major considerations involved in this rationale:

1. The very omission of clarifying detail suggests, in fact reveals, the customer's lack of information and/or ideas about the matter, and should be considered a pointed clue to areas in which the customer most needs your help.
2. The lack of detail certainly suggests that the customer will be highly receptive to your ideas, for the same reason. In fact, that lack of detail, especially when it occurs in the most critical areas, is probably a loud cry for help.

These are direct aids to identifying worry items or advising the customer about what ought to be worry items, and to devising a suitable strategy for the proposal. Instead of representing a problem and bringing discouragement, the very vagueness of the RFP generally and the work statement especially should be regarded as a great opportunity, offering excellent prospects to the imaginative and hard-working proposal writers. In fact, the deficiencies are especially revealing and diagnostic when some portions of the RFP and SOW are highly specific and detailed with crystal clarity, while others are equally vague and nonspecific. This contrast highlights both those areas that the customer has clear knowledge and ideas about, and those in which he or she does not. And this is an arrow-straight pointer to worry items and strategies, and is one of the specific things to look for in studying and analyzing RFPs and their work statements.

The Requirements Analysis

(The methods recommended here are based on the assumption that a team of several people is involved in proposal preparation. However, in most respects—and the exceptions will be self-apparent—the methods are readily adaptable to use by individuals writing proposals alone. I have, in fact, been able to write many successful proposals alone on the basis of methods and techniques described here.)

The first mistake made by those new to proposal writing is writing too soon, before they have a clear understanding of what the requirement is, what the worry items are or ought to be, and what strategy is to be employed. The analysis should precede any writing, other than that of notes and planning material, and serious writing of proposal draft should not begin until the analysis has progressed to at least the point of main-strategy definition.

Probably you should spend as much time in analysis as in the writing itself. You will save yourself much wasted effort and resulting rewriting by doing so. You can write a better proposal in one week when you know in advance exactly where you are going than you can in three weeks of "playing it by ear" as you go. Here are the steps you should follow:

Initial RFP Study and List   Read and study the solicitation with a writing pad and prepare four lists of items derived from your reading:

1. Those proposal items required—what information, statements, or declarations the RFP says clearly must be furnished in your proposal.
2. Those specific items that must be included in your proposed project, program, product, or whatever is to be done, as described in the statement of work.
3. Those criteria by which your proposal will be evaluated.
4. Anomalies—items that contradict each other, potential or probable problems to be anticipated, "impossible" demands, non sequiturs, and other such special items. (What you are to look for here and why is probably already apparent, but if not will shortly become so.)

In compiling these lists, make notations of where each item was found—section, page, and where paragraphs are numbered, page numbers. These are important references, as you will see.

You will almost surely not develop a complete list in your first reading of the RFP. It usually requires successive readings. And you may very well find yourself adding items missed earlier throughout the proposal-development process. But another aid and an excellent idea is to have others read copies of the RFP and make their own lists, which all of you can compare. This makes it far more likely that you will not miss anything important. (One such omission can cost you the award, even if your proposal is superb in all other respects. Conversely, one such item can deliver the winning strategy into your hands, even if your proposal is not outstanding in other respects.)

As you develop the lists, or after you have completed them, compile redundant items—many RFPs have redundancies as well as anomalies—making a single entry of the item, followed by all the section, page, and/or paragraph numbers that identify each occurrence of the item.

This set of lists has several important uses, so it is a good idea to type up the composite set and make a number of copies for the follow-up uses, one of which is to supply each member of the proposal team with a copy.

Graphic Analysis   The next step is to put the list and work statement to work as the definitive inputs to a functional flowchart of the project defined and called for by the RFP—to translate and convert the statement of work to a graphic representation, not quite the way a computer program is flowcharted, and yet not remarkably different either. The basic idea is to make the flowchart as simple and as uncomplicated as possible, concomitant with completeness and accuracy. Figure 7-1 is one example of such a chart. Note that each box contains a statement in simple language. In fact, this flowchart lists the major functions in proposal development, and illustrates where and how some of the functions belong in the general flow.

The resulting flowchart may represent the project as described by the work statement, where the work statement is suitably definitive and descriptive. And where that is the case, the flowchart may be prepared in advance by the same individual who prepares the lists, and should ordinarily be the first step in planning the project. The flowchart serves nicely as a planning tool, a basis and guide for discussion where several people are involved in the proposal preparation, and ultimately finds its way into the proposal itself as an important element.

In this case, to avoid the awkwardness of a foldout drawing—one that cannot be contained in a single page and so must be printed on an oversize sheet and folded to fit in the final document—this drawing is arranged on three tiers, with lines defining the direction of flow. Unlike computer program flowcharts, which are usually constructed in a vertical orientation, these charts are usually oriented in the same way as we read: horizontally, progressing from left to right because this makes it easier for those unfamiliar with flowcharts to understand them. However, there are no hard-and-fast rules, and you can orient your own flowcharts as you wish, but do make the direction of flow clear to the reader.

The very act of translating a work statement into a flowchart is in itself a functional analysis, as you devise the logical flow of phases and functions of work to reach the desired goal. The chart you thus develop must be considered to be only a beginning, a rough draft that is subject to and almost certainly in need of refinement. You may find, as you prepare that first rough-draft chart or when you review what you have drafted, that the job simply cannot be done that way, even if you have translated the words of the work statement faithfully in converting them into a graphic presentation. That, in fact, is one of the reasons for making up this chart immediately: many anomalies, problems, and other important factors become clear insights only when you have a graphic representation.

One reason for this is that when you study text without illustrations you are compelled to juggle concepts mentally, and it is thus quite difficult to perceive sequences and relationships among the functions. But when you represent them as a logical flow, you sometimes discover that "you can't get there from here"—that the work statement has flaws. Or you perceive that there are more efficient ways to do the job than the text suggested or than you deduced from reading the text. The RFP, the lists, and the flowchart then become the beginning materials on which to base your first planning meeting with the proposal staff.

The chart of Figure 7-1 shows the logical flow in proposal development, beginning with the bid/no-bid analysis by management in reviewing the solicitation and deciding whether to write a proposal—to make a try for the award, that is. The chart goes on then to assume that a decision is made to bid and a proposal leader and proposal staff are assigned. The next step is the drafting of the proposal checklists. (Probably a preliminary briefing meeting has been held with the proposal team already, or at least a memo and copy of the RFP has gone to each member.) And then the drafting of

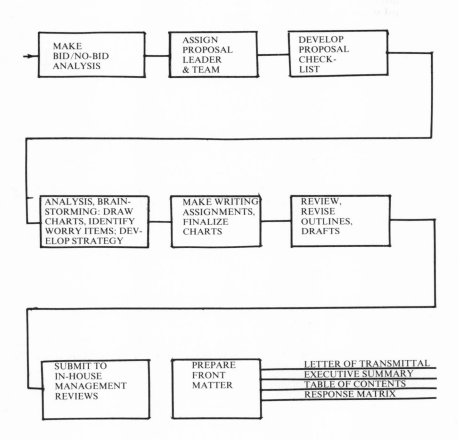

Figure 7-1   Simple functional flowchart

the functional flowchart (or charts, in the case of some complex projects) is carried out.

Who Drafts the Flowchart?

Unfortunately, not every RFP/SOW lends itself to direct translation into a flowchart. The vague RFP and its work statement may defy such immediate translation, and you may have to construct a flowchart from a few scraps or clues in the RFP and a great deal of your own imagination and initiative. Or the requirement may be a highly technical one that requires inputs from technical specialists to construct a plan. In such case, a brainstorming meeting should be convened to undertake the drafting of the flowchart. A leader conducts the meeting, of course, but as a first step the discussion should center on the lists, to reach agreement on them. (Group averaging of estimates and consensus in making judgments proves to be more accurate than any individual estimate or opinion surprisingly often and is well worth employing in the analysis of an RFP and proposal planning.) Then the leader leads a group discussion, before a large blackboard, and through discussion and agreement among the team members a flowchart is constructed that reflects, finally, the consensus of the entire team.

The Benefits of the Group Method

There are many advantages in working this way, not the least of which is the unanimity and cohesion of the proposal team thus achieved. In most cases a proposal team is an ad hoc group assembled at least partially on the basis of who is most readily available, rather than on the basis of who is best qualified for the task. The members have usually not worked together as a team before, and the group is not really a team, no matter how able the individuals are as individuals; it is just a bunch of people. But working together in the early brainstorming sessions and arguing out their differences of opinions and estimates to reach agreement does a great deal to make a team of this bunch of people and to persuade them to adopt a proprietary interest in the proposal effort, a highly desirable effect.

Aside from that, there is the enormous benefit of agreement itself, with the members of the team now endowed with the same understanding of what they are trying to achieve and how they are to achieve it. When this mutual understanding has been achieved, communication among the team members is improved, and there are fewer false starts and less rewriting, as a rule.

Identifying the Main Strategy

At this point, assuming that the group has identified and come to agreement on what either appear to be the customer's chief worry items or on what can and should be made the chief worry items in the proposal, it is time to address the question of general strategy. It will be based, usually, on those worry items, of course, but the question arises as to where and how the worry items will be responded to directly. For example, if it is decided that cost is the customer's chief concern, the response would logically be in the cost proposal, a separate document that is to be kept secret during the proposal-evaluators' deliberations. But they will be deliberating on only the technical proposal, with no knowledge of costs, which appears to invalidate the idea of cost strategies. However, that is not true, either, for it is permissible to discuss costs in a general and philosophical sense, especially in conjunction with an explanation of your approach and program designs, as long as you do not reveal any of your cost figures in the technical proposal. Moreover, as you will see, there are places in the technical proposal where you can at least provide the basis for comparing your proposal with others for relative efficiency and economy. Also, how you handle this depends on how costs are to be evaluated. Since costs are evaluated differently in different proposal competitions, your cost strategy must be dictated at least partly by this factor. (For example, some RFPs assign actual point values to costs, while others make only general statements about the impact of costs on the evaluation by remarking that the government will select that proposal which appears to be in the best interests of the government, "costs and other factors" considered.)

At the same time, if cost strategy is your main capture strategy (i.e., cost control or cost reduction is your main promise), it is necessary that you draw attention to it and dramatize it as much as possible to get the necessary impact. Therefore you must be at pains to explain why and how you can offer such cost advantages (present your proofs). If they derive from program design strategies, make your case and explain how your design strategy reduces costs (or controls costs, if cost control, rather than cost reduction, is your strategy). If they derive, in part or in whole, from administrative and management strategies you propose to employ, the explanations need to be dramatized also in the other appropriate sections of your proposal.

In short, every proposal is necessarily based on many strategies: the strategies of program design, of management and administration, of general cost control, of overhead cost control, and of every other specific area of concern in satisfying the requirement. However, one or more of these will coincide with whatever you plan to employ and pursue as your main capture strategy, that strategy upon which you plan to persuade the customer to opt for your offer as the most attractive one. (Do remember that your proposal is not a plea and never adopt a begging tone; it is a dignified, businesslike *offer*, and both you and the customer must understand that clearly.) It is that strategy, then, which must be dramatized and made the cornerstone of your proposal—your main argument for your plan—with all those other strategies clear enough, but subordinated so as not to draw attention away from your chief argument.

Typical Required Proposal Elements

Typically, the government wants your technical proposal to address certain matters, many of which are evaluated on their own merits, in an absolute sense, but are also made the specific elements to be considered in evaluating your proposal in comparison with others. Not unreasonably, the customer wants some assurance that you are addressing yourself to the right problem and will so address your proposed project, that you have all the capabilities for solving the problem or satisfying the requirement, and that you are a dependable contractor. That is the sum and essence of all the many specific requirements and criteria listed by government agencies in RFPs and their work statements. There are many typical points often specified as items to be covered in your proposal and listed as criteria to be evaluated in weighing your proposal against others submitted. (Despite the implication that your proposal will be evaluated independently in an absolute sense by assigning point values for each of the criteria cited, inevitably, much if not most of the evaluation necessarily is on a comparative basis.)

Here are some typical criterion items, found in many RFPs:

- Your understanding of the requirement.
- Your approach—its practicality and prospects for success, as the customer appraises it.
- Conformance of your proposal with all points of the RFP ("responsiveness").
- Qualifications of your organization *as an organization*.
- Qualifications of key staff proposed as individuals (résumés).
- Demonstrated ability to foresee problems and plans to handle them.
- Your management plan and quality of management plans and measures proposed.

In some cases the criteria and specifics called for are peculiar to the requirement, and are therefore special applications or extensions of one or more of the above general classes of items, as when some highly technical criteria are involved. In one case, for example, the requirement was for the design and manufacturing of a specific piece of digital communications equipment, and the technical specifications were quite rigid, especially with regard to the capability of the equipment to survive the electromagnetic pulse (EMP), a massive concentration of electrical/electronic energy that accompanies a nuclear explosion and blacks out all local communications for a period. In fact, that is a special application of the concern for responsiveness—for strict conformance with the design specifications and standards. Some discussion of these items is in order here, although more information will be offered on each of these again, in presenting a recommended outline and format for proposals and for many of the elements within the proposal.

Obviously, each of these should be addressed in your proposal and in fact must be addressed when they are listed as specific evaluation criteria. However, even when some of these are not specifically listed as information to be furnished and/or evaluation criteria, it is wise to address them nevertheless, for they are all important to proposal success.

Understanding of the Requirement   A shockingly large percentage of all proposals submitted (estimated to be about one-third) reflects a complete lack of understanding of the requirement. Part of the problem appears to be careless and indifferent reading of the RFP. Part appears to stem from responses made by unqualified proposers who hope to somehow stumble through the process and win a contract; part is probably due to poorly written RFPs, and part is undoubtedly due to the practice of writing "cheap and dirty" proposals, proposals written in haste and under the philosophy that if one writes enough proposals, no matter how badly they are written, the law of averages will produce an occasional contract—it doesn't.

The problem is so common that many proposal evaluators will not spend time reading the entire proposal if he or she becomes convinced that the writer of the proposal did not understand what the customer wanted or needed, but will set it aside with a sigh and go on to the next one. The mere fact that understanding of the requirement is a specific item to be evaluated, and prospective proposers are so advised, is itself an indication of the seriousness of the problem.

Your entire proposal reflects your understanding or lack of it, of course, but it is a good idea to include an introductory special section or subsection devoted to the subject specifically. In doing this do not simply echo the customer's own words drawn from the RFP or SOW, because that will not demonstrate understanding. Restate the *essence* of the requirement in your own words. Avoid restating the trivial or extraneous aspects in this subsection. In fact, your ability to identify the essential core of the requirement and discriminate between it and details of less importance is itself good evidence of your understanding. Time enough to deal with the trivia later. Remember that this a first hurdle, and if you don't surmount this one you may not even get to the second hurdle.

Responsiveness   About two-thirds of all proposals, on a broad average, are rejected on the basis of their being *nonresponsive* or allegedly so. That latter term refers to a great many faults, including the failure to demonstrate an understanding of the requirement, failure to furnish all information called for, taking exceptions or deviations (offering something substantially different from that which the RFP called for), and/or in any other way failing to conform completely with the stated requirements listed in the RFP.

Unfortunately, sometimes a proposal is mistakenly condemned as being nonresponsive because evaluators simply miss certain items in the proposal. This is due to the difficulty in rating each of a large number of proposals when each proposal has its own format. Sometimes an agency tries to overcome this problem and facilitate equitable evaluation by mandating a standardized format, but this is far more the exception than the rule and is less than a perfect solution even when it is employed. But there is a way to cope successfully with the problem, and the recommended checklists are a key to this method, which will be explained later in this chapter.

Approach   Your proposed approach to satisfying the requirement is often an item to be evaluated for its practicality and probability of success in satisfying the customer's requirement. Many RFPs specifically ask you to define your approach, if not your overall design, in those cases where there is a specific problem to be solved or where a large universe of approaches is possible. In discussing the format and specifics of writing proposals later in this chapter this will be shown to be a specific objective and, in fact, a transition between proposal chapters. As such, it is a natural milestone you would and should address, in any case.

Ability to Foresee Problems   Proposal requestors are usually well aware that most projects, and especially custom projects, are likely to encounter many problems. Therefore, a number of RFPs ask proposers to discuss the problems they foresee and describe the measures by which they expect to handle such problems and solve them. Of course, this is an invitation to create the worry items the inventive proposal writer would seek in any case. But the customer expects this information to reflect several things about the proposer, including understanding of the requirement, technical/professional competence, planning ability, and honesty, at least. It would be a mistake and might well be taken as evidence of dishonesty and/or lack of understanding and technical competence to insist that there are no problems to be foreseen. (It would also be poor strategy in general, of course, to deliberately ignore the invitation to explain the worry items.)

Management   Management is often a major concern of the customer, but this must be broken down into several parts: There is the management of your organization, for one, but there is also the management of the project or effort being proposed, and the specific management plans and procedures described in the proposal. (The RFP may call for detailed explanations of all project plans and procedures.)

There is also general management versus technical management, which can be an especially important distinction when the project is a large one and requires a large staff, with sundry other needs, such as a contract administrator, recruitment of extra personnel, use of consultants, and many other matters of sufficient scope to require that the project manager be supported by others. In such case, the project manager ought to be primarily a technical manager and not be directly responsible for all the support functions. The customer will want to know how all the support will be provided by the organization: who will administer the contract, recruit the personnel, find and retain the consultants, handle the printing, etc.

In fact, in many large requirements of this nature, and especially in those which involve a cost-plus or any other type of cost-reimbursement contract, you may be required to furnish copies of your personnel policy manual, purchasing procedures manual, and other such documentary backup. (If you don't have such things formally documented you will have to either describe them in detail in your proposal or create the required documents and enclose copies.)

Qualifications of Staff   In brief, this is a collection of résumés of the key staff members proposed for the project, reflecting each individual's pertinent education, experience, and achievements. These résumés are critically important in most cases, especially where the program is a labor-intensive service. In that case the qualifications of the staff represent the quality of the service, naturally, and the customer will equate your proposal with the apparent quality of those qualifications. It is of utmost importance that you do not use "boilerplate" résumés here, but write, edit, rewrite, and polish all included résumés to a high luster. Make them as strong as you can by concentrating on those individual qualifications and achievements that are most directly related to the requirement. Relevance *is* part of quality here, for the best experience and greatest achievements make no contributions if they are not relevant to the requirement.

Qualifications of Organization   This requirement is distinct from the qualifications of the individual staff members, and is a kind of company résumé in which you describe the company's facilities, resources, relevant past projects, and anything else bearing on the subject of the organizations's experience and related qualifications.

OTHER ELEMENTS

The elements listed here are those most often included in descriptions of the criteria by which proposals will be evaluated but they are by no means all the elements that should be included in your proposals. There are many others, some of which are requested occasionally although not specific proposal-evaluation items. These will be covered, one by one, in considering and discussing proposal organization and format. Here we will bring it all together—the marketing principles, the worry items, the strategies, and the implementation of it all to create a final product: the winning proposal.

PROPOSAL FORMAT

In some cases, relatively few, the agency mandates a format for your proposal, even to the extent of furnishing a rather detailed outline to be followed and often with the injunction that failure to follow the format faithfully will result in your proposal being rejected as nonresponsive. Much more often the RFP lists the kinds of information required, sometimes in great detail and sometimes in rather vague terms (as noted earlier), but without dictating any specific format or proposal outline to be followed. Of course, where the customer has enjoined you to follow a dictated format, by all means do so. However, since this is markedly the exception, rather than the rule, you do need some standard format of your own. A basic format is suggested here, one that is usually readily adaptable to all needs, even to the mandated format. (This is so because the recommended format is a logical one that proceeds along rather natural grounds.)

In general, this is a four- or five-chapter approach, including an introductory chapter, a chapter of discussion and argument, a chapter of specific proposed measures, and a final chapter of qualifications. Where the requirement makes it appear advisable, the third chapter may be split into two chapters, one devoted exclusively to management. The outline is presented in somewhat more detail in Table 7-1. However, that merits additional explanations and information. The remainder of this chapter will be devoted to those discussions, and they will be presented in this manner: Each chapter title listed in Table 7-1 will be listed as a sidehead, with the listed subjects under each chapter title discussed individually in the text. However, the front matter, important although it is, will be discussed last, for reasons that will be apparent then. The titles suggested for the proposal chapters and subsections are generic ones, and it is by no means suggested here that these are titles and sideheads you must use. In fact, in some cases other titles and sideheads will be suggested during the discussions, but not because they will be right for you necessarily or even better than the generic ones used here, but to start you thinking independently.

Table 7-1   Recommended general outline/format

	FRONT MATTER a. Title page b. Executive Summary c. Response matrix d. Table of contents
CHAPTER 1:	INTRODUCTION a. About the Offeror b. About the Requirement
CHAPTER 2:	DISCUSSION a. Analysis of the requirement b. Alternatives and rationales (technical and sales arguments) c. Conclusions d. Approach selected
CHAPTER 3:	PROPOSED PROGRAM a. Management and organization of project (with chart) b. Key staff and résumés c. Labor-loading estimates (with chart) d. Deliverable items (qualitative and quantitative data) e. Schedules (tabular and/or with chart)
CHAPTER 4:	QUALIFICATIONS & EXPERIENCE a. General description of organization b. Facilities and resources c. Most pertinent current and past projects d. Testimonials and references

APPENDICES

Bear in mind, in thinking of titles, that they need not focus on the same idea that my suggested titles do. For example, the first sidehead need not be of the same genre as "About the Offeror," but might be about some new or startling idea introduced in the first paragraph or two. (See some of the suggested other titles for illustrations of this.)

There are other reasons for doing a lot of thinking about your sideheads and titles, including the following:

- Every sidehead/title should be considered for its sales impact. Does it suggest a benefit (promise) or some evidence? Every sidehead should make a contribution to your sales effort, should furnish reasons to the reader for buying what you are selling. Make your sideheads work for you.

- Make your sideheads demand attention. Use some imagination. Make the reader notice and remember your proposal by novel and interesting, but not bizarre, phrases.
- Make your sideheads tell the story, even if the reader does not read the body text with full consciousness. At the least, make the sideheads telegraph what is in the text that follows. That helps the reader to grasp your main points easily.
- Use a new sidehead for each major point you are making, even if you have several sideheads on each page. If the point is important, it is worth a sidehead.

PROPOSAL CHAPTER 1: INTRODUCTION

The introductory chapter is a brief one, usually, and includes only the two items shown, each of which merits a brief discussion of its own. "Introduction" is most definitely generic and is not suggested as the best title for the opening chapter. Try to use something more imaginative and more descriptive, such as that used by one proposer who was bidding to displace an incumbent contractor and wanted to dramatize how hard he would work to do a better job than the incumbent was doing. He suggested tactfully in his proposal that perhaps the incumbent had been on the job too long and had grown complacent, and in introducing this idea titled his opening chapter "A New Broom."

About the Offeror   This subsection should introduce the proposing organization to the customer, *even if you are already well known* whether well-known generally (e.g., a division of IBM or General Motors) or well-known to the customer (e.g., contracted with the customer previously). The reason is simple: Under the normal regulations you cannot be given credit for what is not in your proposal. Your qualifications are based on what you state (subject to verification, if the customer entertains any doubts) and you cannot get credit unless your qualifications are explained. Of course, this is not the section where you are presenting those qualifications, but the principle is the same: act as if you were an unknown organization, whether that is true or not.

On the other hand, make this section brief, since you will provide details later (you can, in fact, so state that here). Say only enough here to make your general credentials and legitimate interest in the contract apparent. Especially try to get attention and arouse interest here by introducing something that is likely to command attention and arouse interest. Normally, one writes an introduction last, after the rest of the proposal is written. You then have the entire proposal from which to select what you believe to be the most attention-getting, interest-arousing item to use in your opening. It may be a worry item, some novel feature of your plan, some cost-cutting eye-opener, the use of some unusually well-qualified and perhaps well-known consultant, or even a collection of several items. In fact, it is sometimes proved to be a successful technique to set up the worry item in the introductory chapter and then promise the customer that the solution to the problem will be found in the pages to follow.

Other possible titles: About _____ Corporation, An Energetic Contractor, An Innovative Approach to Cost Control, How to Have Your Cake and Eat it, Too.

About the Requirement   This is your direct address to the question of how well you understand the requirement. Keep this brief because its main purpose is to demonstrate conclusively that you not only understand just what the customer wants but understand it clearly enough to grasp the very essence of the requirement, even when it is masked by extraneous and trivial details, or excess verbiage, as is so often the case. State the problem or requirement, as you see it, explore it only briefly here (enough to prove your understanding and clear insights), and then promise thorough examination and discourse to follow immediately.

If you think the customer is mistaken in what is needed or is confusing the problem with its symptoms so that you will have to justify your approach, don't say it too bluntly here but do lay the groundwork for what is to come.

Other general sideheads you might use for this subsection are these: Appraisal of the Requirement; Understanding of the Requirement, and Understanding of the Problem; Another View of the Requirement; Symptoms Versus Problems; or Another Approach; but you might also use a sidehead related more directly to the specific requirement.

PROPOSAL CHAPTER 2: DISCUSSION

This chapter follows the second subsection of the first chapter thematically, as well as physically, as an extended discussion of the requirement.

Some other possible titles: Technical Discussion, Analysis of Alternatives and Approach, Logic of the Approach Selected. But the title may also be geared to the specifics of the requirement and, even better, to the main worry item, if it is an appropriate fit.

Analysis of the Requirement   This is a discussion that takes the reader through your own analysis of the requirement, step by step. Often this is a problem-definition stage, in which it is the problem that is explored, and discriminations made between problems and symptoms, and is quite closely related to the subsection that precedes it. (It is often an expansion of that preceding discussion.)

Alternatives and Rationales   This is really part of the analysis, but focuses more on alternative attacks on the problem or requirement—on ways to solve the problem or satisfy the requirement. There are usually alternatives, and this discussion presents and examines them, showing the pros and cons of each.

Conclusions   This section identifies the logical results of the analyses and points to the approach.

Approach   The approach is identified and defined clearly here, in direct preparation for the next proposal chapter.

The subsection titles here are entirely generic, intended only to show the general philosophy of this chapter—what it is and what it should accomplish. Sideheads should be selected for their relevance to the requirement and the project proposed.

PROPOSAL CHAPTER 3: PROPOSED PROGRAM

This chapter is the specific proposal, and it should stem directly and thematically from the final subsection of the previous chapter, which identified the approach proposed. This chapter explains how that approach is to be implemented. The first two chapters have been prologue, preparation for this chapter, designed largely to argue your case and prove the superiority of your proposal. Now you are about to tell the reader precisely what you offer to do. There is no special virtue in the order in which subsections are presented here, and the order of presentation may be changed to suit your own ideas, but all the elements do belong here, with the possible exception of the résumés, which may be in an appendix, if you prefer that, as some do. Subsection titles may be chosen for their relevance to the requirement, but the ones shown are generally satisfactory in most applications.

Other possible chapter titles include A Plan for Action, Methods and Procedures, _____ Corporation's Specific Offer, and others chosen for more direct relevance.

Management and Organization   This subsection should describe the project team or group that will satisfy the customer's requirement, explaining how it is organized. Discuss management principles, both general management and technical management, explain your standard procedures and/or special procedures to be developed and adopted for the project. Cover all special matters, such as recruitment of additional staff specialists, retention of special consultants, field work, and anything else that requires special measures.

Key Staff and Résumés   Identify all of your key staff, with brief words of individual qualifications and the notation that résumés will be found wherever you have decided to place them. (My own preference is for placing them at the end of this chapter.) A simple organization chart, showing the main functions and functionaries, the reporting order, and the linkage of the team with the main organization, should be presented here. (See Figure 7-2.)

HOWARD JEREMEE
PROJECT DIRECTOR

FRED GREENE   RHONDA SMITH   HARRY JONES
SR. ANALYST   PROGRAMMER   PROGRAMMER

Figure 7-2   Simple organization chart

Some RFPs mandate a résumé format, and in such case you've no choice but to follow the mandated format. However, where there is no such dictated format, by far the more common situation, you need to devise your own, and you should design it carefully, to accomplish at least these objectives:

- Make the format simple and uncomplicated (easy to follow).
- Make the individual's regular position and proposed special project responsibility clear.
- Use a uniform format so as not to require the reader to familiarize himself or herself with more than one format.
- Use a design that maximizes the immediate impact of the most relevant information.
- Use a design that lends itself to easy customizing for each proposal.

This should be interpreted to mean that, for one thing, you should not use the individual's unique personal résumé from your personnel files. Most individuals write poor résumés, and even the best of résumés written in pursuit of a job are rarely suitable for proposal purposes. It also means that you must *rewrite* each résumé and *tailor* it to the requirements of the proposal. Rarely will any given résumé presentation be suitable for all proposals.

The format offered here is one that meets these criteria reasonably well, and is the one recommended. The opening paragraph should be carefully tailored to maximize the individual's credentials for the proposed project or contract responsibility, but in many cases it is only that and the proposed position that need revision. In any case, this format is relatively easy to tailor individually to each proposal, especially if you are using a word processor and have the originals on file, readily available for copying and modifying.

NAME

REGULAR POSITION OR TITLE

PROPOSED POSITION OR TITLE

for proposed project

INTRODUCTORY PARAGRAPH: general description of individual's most relevant and important experience and other qualifications.

FOLLOW-UP PARAGRAPHS: both general and specific background experience and qualifications of individual, as they relate to the proposed position.

ROUND-UP INFORMATION: less-relevant details, such as general educational background (any major achievement, such as doctorates, patents, or awards, would have been mentioned earlier, but details of such are covered here) as is information about prior employment and positions, and other such data.

Labor-Loading Estimates.   Some RFPs ask for your identification of all major functions, phases, and/or tasks and estimates of how key staff will be assigned vis-à-vis these tasks, including estimates of time required for each task. But whether the RFP calls for it or not, it is an excellent idea to provide this information for at least these reasons:

It demonstrates your understanding of the requirement.

It proves your technical and managerial competence.

It supports your cost estimates (although they are in a separate document).

It enables the customer to evaluate what you are offering, as compared with your competitors' offerings, in a way that *quantifies* the offer well beyond the mere comparison of bottom lines (total dollars).

It is necessary for your own sake if you are to present your cost estimates with any confidence in your own figures.

The labor-loading chart can be organized in a variety of ways, of course, according to your own ideas, but an example of one way to do it is shown in Table 7-2. This is the hypothetical beginning phase of a small project, with only three key people on the staff, but the principle is the same, no matter how large or small the project. Of course, the actual chart may very well be many pages long or may be on one or more large foldout pages, but the methodology and philosophy is the same: it is immensely valuable to you as a planning tool and verification of your cost estimates (it ought, in fact, to be a major foundation for your cost estimates). In fact, even if I did not include this set of figures in my proposals I would prepare them before I prepared my cost proposal. I would find it difficult to place trust in any cost estimate without having prepared this labor-hour estimate first.

Table 7-2   Portion of labor-loading chart

Tasks/subtasks	Proj. Dir.	Sr. Analyst	Programmer	Totals
Labor-Loading Chart				
Labor Hours				
PHASE I				
Postaward meeting	8	8	—	16
Preliminary analysis	24	60	—	84
Revised project plan	8	16	—	24
TOTALS	40	84	—	124

As you can easily see from even a brief scan of this chart it provides you and the customer with four different estimates or appraisals of the proposed program:

- The full complement of phases, functions, tasks, and/or subtasks that constitute the program overall, representing an appreciation of the project.
- The degree of participation by and assignment of roles and responsibilities to each key staff person for each phase or task.
- Total estimated time commitment of each key staff member for entire program.
- Total estimated time commitment for each listed phase or task.

This makes the chart more than a valuable planning aid, although it is certainly that also. It becomes a powerful selling tool, too, for a reason that is itself a lesson to be learned about credibility: This chart provides the *details*, and they are always powerful selling influences because while anyone can philosophize or generalize about almost anything under the sun, it takes real knowledge to present the "how to" in implementable detail. So, although generalization means nothing, specifics tend to convince and persuade. They lend the extremely important characteristic of *credibility* to the sales argument.

Incidentally, with respect to titling this chart, perhaps the term used here, *labor-loading chart*, is not the best in the world, but it avoids the sexist and less accurate term *man loading*.

Deliverable Item   It is necessary to be highly specific about precisely what you propose to deliver, sometimes even more specific than the customer has been in describing the requirement. And you must be both qualitative and quantitative in your specification of whatever is to be delivered.

It is a rare contract that does not have a tangible deliverable of some sort, even if the contract is entirely for services. At the least, the client normally wants reports, manuals, or some other sort of paper end item. However, whatever the items, they should be carefully defined, and in detail. If it is to be a report or other paper, for example, your proposal should offer the most detailed estimates you can provide of the content (with a detailed outline), number of pages, illustrations, and anything else that is pertinent, such as binding, type, number of copies, etc. (Of course, your labor-loading chart furnishes at least some detailed quantitative descriptions of the main labor hours of services pledged.) Bear in mind that it is this section of your proposal that is chiefly referred to and included in any resulting contract. (Government contracts based on proposals generally include the proposal "by reference" as specifications of what is contractually agreed to and pledged by the contractor.) It is as much in your interest as it is in that of the customer that everything to be agreed to in the contract be carefully defined in quantity as well as in kind. It will serve you well to spend some time on this and review carefully what you have promised.

One caution: Do not assume that what the customer has described or specified is precisely what you should promise. Remember that a proposal request is at least nominally (and in many cases actually) a call for help. The requestor concedes that you are the expert and wants you to study the stated need and *propose* what you believe to be in the best interests of the customer in satisfying the requirement described. You may very well believe that the customer's descriptions or specifications require modification or, at least, enhancement and greater detail. If so, your proposal is the place to provide that ancillary coverage.

Schedules   Most RFPs include schedules. They are sometimes suggested schedules, sometimes mandated schedules. Sometimes the customer insists that this is a schedule that must be met, and that acceptance of the schedule and agreement to meet it is a required condition of any contract resulting. In other cases, the schedule is suggested, and the customer invites other suggestions, or even states that a better schedule is desirable and the promise of earlier delivery will be to the proposer's advantage in proposal evaluation.

Unfortunately, quite often the schedule offered by the customer is as vague as some RFPs and SOWs are generally. For example, a schedule may be expressed along the following lines:

Item	Due (days after award)
Preliminary design	10
Government review complete	20
Final changes	30
First-module tryout	60
Debugging complete	90
Final delivery of first module	120

Many proposers fall into the trap (not deliberately planned by the customer, but a trap nevertheless) of simply echoing this schedule and pledging themselves to it in their proposals. And the results can be disastrous.

There are two things wrong with this suggested schedule. The first is that the customer failed to specify whether those "days after award" are calendar days or working days. There is quite a difference. If they are working days, the 120 days represent 24 weeks, or nearly 6 months. But if they are calendar days, they represent only four months, which is quite a different thing and may make quite a difference in costs as well as in the staffing plan and labor-loading chart; that is, they may be all wrong.

The other problem is in the promise to review the preliminary design in 10 days. It may or may not happen; experience reveals how often that 10 days can stretch into several weeks and even months. In the meanwhile, your schedule has committed you to now impossible deliveries.

Of course, the government is not so unreasonable that you cannot later adjust this if the government's action leads to such a problem, but why plant the seeds of a future problem? Why not change that "days after award" definition to days following government approval?

You can use this same tabular approach to presenting your schedule, changing the heads appropriately to working days but skirting that other problem, possibly along the following lines:

Item	Due (working days)
Preliminary design	10 days after award
Government review complete	20 days after award
Final changes	10 days after government review
First-module tryout	40 days after final changes
Debugging complete	30 days after tryout
Final delivery of first module	30 days after debugging complete

Another way to present the schedule, in place of or in addition to the tabular presentation, is via a graphic method such as a milestone chart (see Figure 7-3). The advantage of such a chart is that it shows the schedule graphically, along with a revelation of those tasks and functions that are consecutive and those that are concurrent, for at least some portion of their duration. It is thus far more definitive than a tabular presentation, as many graphics are more definitive and have greater impact than do textual passages.

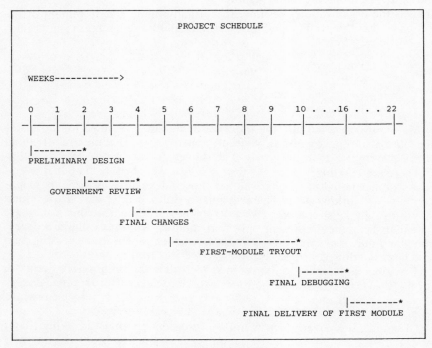

Figure 15. Milestone chart

Figure 7-3   Milestone chart

PROPOSAL CHAPTER 4: QUALIFICATIONS AND EXPERIENCE

This is the organization's résumé. It is usually made a requirement of the proposal that the proposer offer the organization's credentials as an organization, in addition to the individual credentials of the proposed key staff members. And while the specification of what is required here is usually rather general, it is rather common for RFPs to request a list of the organization's relevant projects, current and recent, with clear identification of contract numbers, customers, and names to call for verification. But there are many other things you should present as evidence of not only your technical/professional abilities but also as evidence of your dependability as a contractor. That latter concern is important, too, and contracting officers do consider that in entering their own opinions as to the acceptability of a contractor.

General Description of the Organization   This chapter ordinarily opens with a general description of your organization—full corporate name, where incorporated, where headquartered, other addresses, subsidiaries, if any, and similar data. There should be identification of your primary business, names of officers and other key people, and a top-level organization chart. It is a good idea to include on that chart an indication of where the proposed project fits in and how it interfaces with the main corporate entity.

Figure 7-3   Milestone chart

Facilities and Resources   The chief resources of an organization are physical—buildings and equipment; human— personnel; and financial— liquid assets and lines of credit. In all cases the presentation of an abundance of resources is reassuring to customers, helping make the proposer appear to be solidly stable and dependable. It therefore is a positive step to list all resources, even those that have no bearing on the project pursued. The "when in doubt leave it out" philosophy does not apply here. You will never be penalized for furnishing too much information and too many details, but the reverse is not true: As a great many chagrined proposers have learned in the past, you may very well lose a contract award because you failed to furnish enough detail.

Pertinent Contracts   This is another of those items that the customer may or may not ask for, but that you should supply in any case. Typically, the customer wants to learn not only what kind of experience you have had but for whom you have done work and how well you performed. The request for this information is therefore likely to include a request for information regarding the quality of your performance. To that end such requests often ask for the following information on each current and/or recent project that is relevant to the contract being sought:

- Name, address, and telephone number of customer
- Name, telephone number of customer's purchasing agent or contracting officer and/or project manager

- Contract/project name and number
- Description of contract/project
- Type contract (fixed price, cost plus, etc.) and amount
- Outcome (overruns, underruns, on schedule, ahead of schedule, behind schedule, etc.)
- Special achievements, anything else deemed noteworthy

There are several ways to handle this requirement. One is to maintain a separate write-up of each current and past project, and simply make copies, putting them in the order of most relevant and best performances first. Another is to construct a matrix or table listing all this information. This is slightly less flexible, in terms of its amenability to tailoring it to each proposal, although it makes a more efficient and possibly more impressive presentation if you have a large number of contracts to cite.

Testimonials and References   It has come to me as something of a shock to learn during my seminars that few proposers include testimonial letters and references in their proposals. (Of course, the list of current and recent projects includes a list of references, but that is not quite the same as furnishing a simple, lengthy list of names and telephone numbers as references.) I discovered that most individuals are reluctant to *ask* for such letters and permission to list former customers for reference. (You should always have the individual's permission to list him or her.) It is perfectly acceptable to ask for such letters and permission of customers you have done a good job for. Some will be unwilling to go along with your request, but many will be happy to accommodate you.

Such letters are a great help, especially with customers who do not know of your company and would like to talk to some people who do know your company as customers.

APPENDICES

Although appendices are not always employed judiciously, they can be most valuable, especially for proposal applications. But first, some background information is desirable.

You may recall the admonition earlier about the inclusion of clarifying detail to add credibility to the proposal and to the proposer's claims and promises. It is true enough that the lack of detail can easily be a fatal error in making any kind of sales presentation. The details of *how* you propose to make good on your promises and claims of superiority have two aspects bearing on credibility: one is the general effect; that is the impact of a wealth of detail on even those who are not technical experts and thus cannot make direct use of the detail; and the other is the effect on the customer's technical experts who will study those details carefully to judge how sound your plans and promises are.

But there is a problem that arises with this, too: at least some of those who must read and evaluate your proposal do not want to fight their way through many pages of tedious detail or be obliged to skim through many pages, seeking the lay language again. In fact, these individuals are often interested in only certain areas, such as your management plans or the résumés of your proposed key staff people. (In large procurements, proposals can be quite large, and the evaluators are split up into teams, each assigned a different area of the proposals to study and judge, so that few of the readers are required to read the entire proposal.) They tend to complain about proposals that are difficult (for them) to read.

It is for the solution of precisely this kind of paradoxical problem that the appendix is most useful. The appendix is a place to have your cake and eat it too, to present or make available information that is of interest to some of your readers but not to all. If you have cited a paper presented at a conference, for example, and want to include the entire paper, refer the reader to a suitable appendix, where the paper will be available in its entirety, rather than reproducing it in the body of the proposal. Many kinds of material are suitable to be included in one or more appendices. (Use different appendices for different kinds of material.) Here are a few illustrative examples:

Reprints of published papers and articles
Technical drawings
Standards and specifications
Detailed charts
Commercial brochures
Samples of your work, such as documentation and training programs
Photographs
Floppy disks
Slides (in flat holders)

FRONT MATTER

As you were advised earlier, front matter is being presented last in this chapter, which is fitting, since front matter is usually prepared last. That is necessary because it is introductory and summation material, and you can hardly introduce your proposal before you know precisely what it says or will say, nor can you summarize anything before it is written, of course. But that is not to minimize the importance of some of that front matter; it is often of critical importance. Let's consider it in the order listed in Figure 7-1, which is the order in which it generally appears. But there is one special notation first: the figure does not list the Letter of Transmittal, which is a separate item, but one that many proposal writers include in the front matter of the proposal; that is, they bind a copy of the transmittal letter inside the cover of the technical proposal. That letter will be discussed separately, since it is technically not part of the proposal itself.

Title Page   Most organizations use the same copy on the title page as they do on the cover of the proposal except for the inclusion of the date and a proprietary notice. In general, here is what should be presented on that title page:

- Title of your proposal, which is probably the title furnished by the customer in the RFP or something based directly on that.

- The number of the RFP and the indication that the proposal is in response to that RFP.
- The addressee's (customer's) name and address.
- The proposer's name and address. (Some have a standard printed form to use for covers and/or title pages, while many use a copy of their letterhead or formal stationery.)
- A proprietary statement (optional), as suggested in most RFPs, advising the reader of any proprietary or confidential information that you claim protection for (immunity from dissemination to others under the Freedom of Information Act [FOIA]). You have the right to do this, as long as the information you are claiming as proprietary is not clearly nonproprietary. You cannot make the entire proposal proprietary, however. That would be the easy way, but it is not acceptable, since obviously much of the information there is not confidential or proprietary.

Executive Summary   Most organizations do offer an executive summary in the front matter., This is a summation of the key points of the proposal, ostensibly for the convenience of the top-level managers who do not wish to read the entire proposal but want only a kind of abstract from which to draw the salient facts. However, everyone reads the executive summary, usually before they read anything else, and it is a common practice to use it to present the most important and most impressive selling points of the proposal. Avoid being overly technical here so as to make all the points clearly and with equal communicability to all readers. But do not make the executive summary overly long, or you defeat your own purpose. Make it short, sharp, clear, and hard hitting. Seed the reader's interest in reading the rest of the proposal by telegraphing the most attractive features yet to come.

Response Matrix   The checklists that you made up at the beginning of your proposal effort have a final and most important use now, as the basic input for a useful species of front matter I refer to as a "response matrix." Put as simply as possible, this is a table or matrix which directs the customer's attention to each requirement called for in the RFP and your specific proposal response to each requirement. Table 7-3 illustrates the idea in principle by presenting a fragment of a hypothetical response matrix.

In the hypothetical example it is assumed that both the RFP and the proposal have numbered paragraphs. This will not always be the case, of course, and frequently the reference will be to section/chapter number and page number alone, or even to page number alone. For that reason—because in such cases the reference is rather general—the summary description of the item is provided so that there is no doubt as to just what part of the page is referred to by the item in the matrix and the proposal reference. The right-hand column in the figure has been left blank intentionally. It is provided for the convenience of the evaluator, so that he or she may easily check off your compliance with each requirement.

Table 7-3   Portion of response matrix

RFP Ref. Sec/Pg/Par	Item	Prop.Ref. CH/PG/PAR	Notes
I/11/3.2, II/4/5.4	Validation testing	1/4/2.3, 3/3/3.7	
I/23/1.4	Safety programs	3/3/3.8	
II/45/2.5, II/46/2.11, III/65/3.4	Compliance with technical standards and military specifications	3/3/4.10, 3/5/5.1, 3/34/9.8	
II/40/2.3	Provisioning requirements	3/38/10.1	
II/28/1.15	Program installation	3/39/10.3	
IV/14/4.5	Staff buildup	3/41/10.5-7	
IV/17/4.6	Provide contact office	3/42/10.8-10	
IV/18/4.9, 4.11-12	Plans for phaseover of of program to government staff	3/44/10.12; 3/46/11.14, 16, 18	

Of course, there is nothing sacred about the matrix design used in the figure to illustrate the principle. It may be modified to suit your own ideas and the needs of the proposal. It is an important asset to have such a matrix, however, for it accomplishes more than one purpose:

- It helps you to prevent important items from "slipping between the cracks," something that often happens, rendering proposals vulnerable to charges of being nonresponsive.
- It helps ensure that the reader (evaluator) will not miss items and thus fail to credit you with responses. (Such slipups are fairly common, even government employees being only human.)
- It demonstrates your own thoroughness and adds to the general impact of your proposal in the same manner that the provision of detail adds to your credibility generally as a contractor.

Experience has demonstrated that this device tends to maximize technical scores awarded to proposals, for the reasons given. In any case, it is very little extra work, if you have developed your checklists carefully, and especially if you are using word processing assistance in all these efforts.

Table of Contents   You should provide a table of contents, of course, and my own inclination is to make that as definitive as possible. Scanning the table of contents ought to provide some insight into what the proposal will present and should, in fact, be a virtual outline of the proposal.

LETTER OF TRANSMITTAL

If you ask experienced marketers to government how important a letter of transmittal is, you will get a wide range of opinions, ranging from the view that it is a completely unimportant pro forma act of courtesy, to the view that it is even more important than the proposal itself. Not surprisingly, all these opinions are right and all are wrong, at the same time. There are individual cases where the transmittal letter has been a decisive factor, and there are cases where it has been totally unimportant. Usually, that was the result of individual circumstances or the act of the proposer writing the letter of transmittal who made the letter important or unimportant.

In most cases the truth lies somewhere between those extremes. Certainly, the letter can be made to provide some benefits, although it is rarely as decisive as some would have it. But it is addressed to the contracting officer, and may be the only thing, other than the cost proposal, that the contracting official will read. So it is not a bad idea to incorporate in it some of the information a contracting officer is interested in learning.

One objective of the letter is to validate the proposal as a bona fide offer. The signer of the transmittal letter should make it clear that he or she is authorized to make the offer in behalf of the organization, and to state for what period of time the offer is firm.

Another item considered obligatory for such letters is a pledge of best efforts and assurances that the proposed contract and program is an important one to the proposer and will get the direct attention of top management in the organization.

Contracting officers tend to be interested in fiduciary matters, and especially in contractors' consciousness of cost control and related measures. I have personally found it useful to point out to customers that cost consciousness is not only cost reduction but includes cost avoidance (as distinct from cost reduction) and cost control in general. (And, of course, your program should reflect your commitment to that philosophy, if you wish to embrace it.)

I have touched only fleetingly and sometimes only indirectly on the subject of writing itself, in this chapter. That is not because I underrate its importance, but because I wanted to lay primary stress here on marketing strategies and methodology. But it is time now to discuss writing per se—*persuasive* writing, that is.

Chapter 8

WRITING TO PERSUADE

To accomplish anything, writing must persuade as well as communicate. And there is more to the accomplishment of both of those qualities than is ordinarily appreciated.

Can "Persuasiveness" be Measured?

In writing almost everything but a laundry list the writer wishes to persuade the reader to belief and even to action, whether or not this objective is readily apparent. Of course, in the case of advertising and sales presentations there is no doubt that the writer wishes to persuade the reader to a specific action, a buying action. The writer is quite open about it. And if writing can be graded by the degree of persuasiveness that the writer attempts to embody in the written product, proposals must necessarily be rated rather high on that scale. In this case the major, even sole, objective is persuasion, and techniques for maximizing the persuasiveness content of the proposal is or ought to be a primary concern of the writer.

Of course, we have no precise measures of persuasiveness, and achieving that quality is at least as much a matter of art as it is of science. But we can at least judge the persuasiveness of the writing on the yes-no scale of whether the reader was or was not persuaded to do what the writer urged. And that is especially easy to observe in the case of proposal writing.

The Ingredients of Persuasive Writing

Two ingredients, promises and proofs, necessary to and the key for achieving persuasiveness in writing (and in marketing and sales generally, for that matter) have already been cited several times, with the clear implication that these are the sum and substance of persuasiveness. However, these have been given as *the* secret of persuasiveness on the premise of clear communication. Obviously you cannot persuade a reader to whatever you wish to persuade the reader if the reader does not understand what you are saying—if you fail to send your message "in the clear," as military security people might say. It seems so obvious as to be almost banal to point out that clear and accurate communication is a first requirement of persuasive-ness. And yet we find that many who write, especially in the business world, give rather little time or thought to their effectiveness as communicators via the written word.

About Communication

The word *communication* and such phrases as "the failure to communicate" and "a problem in communication" have been used and overused so much that the very word is almost a cliché and the phrases almost platitudes, equating disagreement or failure to persuade with failure to communicate. That is highly significant because while the phrases are often used merely as excuses for the failure to be convincing they often do describe accurately at least one major reason for the failure to persuade. Indeed, we do fail to communicate, far more often and far more commonly than many of us are willing to concede.

A great deal of energy has been expended by a great many writers, teach-ers, and lecturers in efforts to describe, identify, explain, and teach the art of what we call communication. To boil down its definition to the simplest explanation without losing accuracy, it can be fairly said that *accurate and reliable* communication takes place when and only when the message received is the same message as the one that was sent.

That definition is somewhat different from many other definitions of communication that are offered because it focuses attention on the receiver as well as on the sender. And that appears to imply that there is some question as to whose has the responsibility for clear communication. Is it the reader's own fault if the message recorder in his or her brain is a different one from that which was in the writer's brain? Or did the writer fall down on the job and fail to make the message plain enough? So we must face a rather important philosophical question which we do not always face directly when we discuss means and methods for achieving improvement in our writing.

Most admonitions and courses of instruction about writing clearly appear to offer sets of rules and measures ("fog index" and word lists for different grade levels of readability, for example). The evident implication of this is therefore that communication must inevitably result if these rules and guidelines are followed faithfully. But this invokes the inescapable corollary that if communication fails to take place despite careful observation by the writer of all these "rules," the fault must then lie with the reader.

Unfortunately, even if this appears to be a justified conclusion, it is an unsatisfactory one. For one thing, while it apparently relieves the writer of any responsibility for inadequate communication, it also meekly surrenders control of communication to chance. It surrenders control to the chance that the reader also understands those "rules" of communication and that they work for him or her, as they do for the writer.

Obviously, this won't do. A parallel may be drawn between writing and education in our modern world. In recent years educational technologists (as many behaviorists who work in developing training and educational materials and systems characterize themselves) have pursued a new standard which says that students do not fail in their studies, but teachers and materials fail. The responsibility for communication in training and education is thus clearly fixed on the sender of the messages.

In precisely this same philosophy the writer must be in control of communication to whatever extent that is possible and must at least accept responsibility for the communication. The writer must somehow gain a reasonably accurate idea of the reader to whom the writing is to be addressed and then see to it that the writing is as unambiguous and as clear as writing skills can make it.

What *Is* the Message?

A serious study of writing that fails badly to do its job, writing that has been categorized by such terms as *bureaucratese, gobbledygook* (a term coined by Congressman Maury Maverick), and *purple prose*, suggests one inescapable conclusion that surprises many, namely that the writer did not have a clearly formulated message to send; small wonder, then, that he or she failed to send it. A reader can hardly be expected to get the same message as that sent when the sender is unsure of what the message is. Not surprisingly, the reader's understanding or, more exactly, misunderstanding, is a reflection of the writer's own confusion.

This idea of what is often responsible for what we call "bad" or "poor" writing is confirmed by many editors who have found this to be a common cause of the problem. It is certainly logical enough to assume that what the writer has recorded on paper is what is in the writer's own brain. (What else could the writer write?) Fuzzy thinking or inadequate knowledge of the subject simply finds its reflection in what the writer has written.

It is really not difficult to confirm this simply by reading a few samples of such writing and interpreting or translating their central ideas or messages into simple, lay language. Translated, we usually find that the original messages were either so insignificant that they were hardly worth the paper on which they were written, or they were something utterly meaningless. Here, to demonstrate that, are a couple of examples of such writing and their interpretations:

From a training manual on the subject of solar energy: "This amount of potentially useful energy is staggering, but logical. Since all forms of energy originate from the sun, the basic source is, by necessity, a reservoir of almost unimaginable size."

Aside from the fact that this entire passage is a non sequitur (this is not a logical argument, as expressed here), the point of the passage (the message, that is) is unclear. Literally, it states that the sun is a reservoir (of energy?) of almost unimaginable size. But that has no significance to the text in which this passage appears. What the writer apparently wanted to get across to readers was that all energy on earth comes from the sun, has done so for the several billion years of the earth's existence, and will continue to do so for many millennia more, hence the enormous reservoir of energy the sun represents.

That's a mild case. Here is another, from the same source: "A heat pump is correctly identified as a refrigerant machine that can extract usable heat from a source that is at a temperature too low for *direct* comfort applications."

Laboriously, the text winds on discussing the nature of heat pumps until we finally discover what the writer apparently had in mind, which was this: A heat pump is a device to convert large volumes of cold air to smaller volumes of warm air. Having made that main point, the writer should then go on to explain in more detail how a heat pump does this, and perhaps then mention that it is in principle quite similar to a refrigerator. It took some study on my part, plus the application of whatever technical knowledge I myself possess to reason out the intended message, which the writer never really did make very clear. And saying that the writer intended to say this is giving the writer the benefit of the doubt, for perhaps the writer never really reasoned the matter out at all and did not really understand how a heat pump works.

As evidence for that latter notion I can cite a particularly illustrative example from my own experience while functioning as an editor on a technical writing project. We were preparing manuals and other texts for the use of U.S. Air Force personnel operating the Ballistic Missile Early Warning System (BMEWS) at Thule, Greenland. One of the manuals a writer in my own group was writing included an explanation of the telephone system at the site, and especially of how the telephone priority system worked.

When I read the manuscript I had some trouble following the explanations, which included references to engineering drawings of the circuits that were to be included in the manual. However, by studying the drawings and analyzing the circuits for myself, I was able finally to understand the system.

I called the writer to account and explained that only by employing my own technical knowledge and analyzing the drawings was I able to understand the manuscript, and we could hardly expect the reader to do that. I suggested that perhaps the writer did not himself understand the system.

Of course, he insisted that he understood the system well. But I was rather sure of what I was saying because he was obviously a bright enough young man, certainly had fluency in English, and certainly had had proper technical training. I therefore asked him to indulge me by spending the rest of the day studying the drawings, and then trying an entirely new and fresh approach to writing the section on telephone priority.

The result confirmed my suspicions. The second manuscript was everything I could have wished for, and the writer sheepishly admitted that he now recognized that he really did not know what he was talking about when he wrote the first manuscript. It's quite easy to deceive yourself in this manner and to believe what you would prefer to believe.

Here is another, somewhat different example (this one more of the nature best described as "purple prose") from a brochure published by the U.S. Department of Labor: "The following objectives provide qualitative and quantitative milestones toward which the program can strive."

Translation: Here are the objectives for the program.

The U.S. Department of Energy enriched our literature with this prose gem: "The ratio (or amplification factor) of private sector activity to federal activity can be characterized by the ratio of the number of privately financed to federally financed solar heating and cooling systems installed annually."

Translation: You can measure the ratio of private-sector solar-energy activity to federal solar-energy activity by the ratio of spending in each sector. Which says that the ratio equals the ratio!

You Must First Understand Your Own Message

A first rule for writing clearly, for communicating well, must be that you first understand yourself *precisely*, not generally, what you want to say: what your *exact* message is. And that is also the second and third rules, and is more important than any other rules you can think of, and even more important than the sum total of all those other rules.

The simple fact is that few of us who have a reasonable fluency in our language have that much difficulty in expressing ourselves in writing *when we know what we are trying to say*. (And bear in mind at all times that grammar, punctuation, and spelling are not the skills of writing; they are only the tools of using the language, mechanical disciplines, whereas writing is at least in large part an art.)

This kind of problem arises when you don't know your subject well enough and fail to do adequate research. It arises when you fail to invest the time and effort to think matters out and identify the precise points to be made and the precise information necessary to make the points. It arises when you try to write without advance planning of any kind, such as developing outlines and some kind of organization plan. It arises when you begin writing too soon—before planning and thinking the material out thoroughly. It arises when you fail to do adequate self-editing of your rough drafts—when you are unable to be sufficiently objective in self-editing to recognize your lapse into vague generalizations and self-deceit about them.

Admittedly, it is extremely difficult to be objective in reviewing and editing your own rough drafts, but with practice it does become possible. You learn to recognize those abrupt changes in your manuscript from the clear detail of the subjects you know well to the rambling generalizations of those you do not know well. And that is by far the most important thing to search out and detect in editing your own material.

A Plan of Action

Writing is part art, part science, or at least part definable method. There are some rules that will help you overcome the worst problems, which are not your shortcomings in spelling and punctuation. You can engage the services of a competent editor to handle those matters. What the editor cannot do is rewrite bad material—that is, supply missing information and accomplish total reorganization of a manuscript. Both of those needs stem from the same basic problem that we have been discussing here. But there are steps and procedures you can follow (an organized plan) that will help you overcome these problems.

Step 1: Identify Your Goal

At least part of the art of writing lies in knowing when you are ready to write, when you know where you are going with your writing. You would hardly start out on a long journey without knowing your destination and having at least some idea of how you are going to get there, even if you do not have a completely detailed itinerary. In writing, as in other things, if you don't know where you are going before you start, you are likely to end up in some other place than you should.

Overall, you should by now (by the time you are ready to begin writing seriously) have set your main strategy and therefore know what main points you want to prove in your proposal. However, you must plan a little more closely than that. You have at least four chapters, and each of those has to have some strategic goal and specific objectives. Here, in fact, are the general goal-objective requirements for each chapter:

Chapter 1: Introduction   The overall goal here ought to be to command attention and arouse serious interest immediately, with at least these three general objectives:

1. Introduce yourself as impressively as you can, although briefly, demonstrating that you are well qualified to bid for the contract.
2. Find some eye-opener to get attention early in the proposal and generate some interest in reading the rest of your proposal.
3. Demonstrate an unusually perceptive insight into the customer's needs or problems, vis-à-vis the RFP, with a hint of unusually able planning to satisfy the requirement.

Chapter 2: Discussion   Generally speaking, the goal for this chapter is to define, justify, and sell your approach. These are two specific objectives:

1. Prove, through rational discussion and analyses, that your insight into the customer's problems or needs is undoubtedly the right one.
2. Prove, as a result of the arguments and discussions, that your approach is undoubtedly the right one.

Chapter 3: Proposed Program   Show here an effective implementation of the approach you identified, with at least these objectives:

1. Sell your proposed implementation of the approach through your plans for organizing and managing the project.
2. Be crystal clear about what you will deliver, how much of each item you will deliver, and when you will deliver.
3. Provide staff of unquestionable qualifications.

Chapter 4: Qualifications and Experience   Prove your organization's qualifications, making at least these points:

1. Your organization has all the necessary qualifications of experience, facilities, and resources.
2. Your organization is dependable, as proved by your track record of successful accomplishment.

These are general statements. Before you begin serious writing, you must translate these into the specific statements that apply to the proposal you are about to write. Just what will you say to demonstrate your qualifications clearly and briefly? How will you demonstrate unusually clear or perceptive insight into the requirement? What are the arguments (the main points) you will use in your discussion?

Admittedly, most proposals are written under severe time pressures; rarely is there "enough" time to do a proper job. But everyone labors under that burden, and one characteristic of those who win is that they cope successfully with it. The common mistake is, of course, to begin to write frantically without preparation. The proper thing to do is to take the time to prepare, to plan. There will not be time to do it over, so you must get it right the first time. (Failure to do this, resulting in the clear need, but no time to do it over, has caused more than one organization to abort a proposal project after spending a great deal of money on the effort.) And the first step in planning, after having decided on main strategies and devised the checklists and flowcharts, is to develop a reasonably detailed outline. That is the guide you need.

Outlining

There is a planning document many people refer to as a *topical outline*. The term is as vague as the outline many produce as their idea of what that term defines. Here is that kind of outline for the first chapter:

A: INTRODUCTION
  1. Who we are
     a. Our formal name
     b. What we do
     c. Who we have done business with
  2. Why we are proposing
     a. Our interest in the project
     b. Our special qualifications
     c. Something special about us/our offer
  3. Our understanding of the requirement
     a. The essence of what it is, in our own words
     b. Our special insight into it
     c. A hint of what this will mean

This is much too vague to be useful. It describes what the proposal should talk *about*, but not what it is to *say*. It would do fine as a general outline of the "blanks" to be filled in, before actual writing begins, along the following lines:

A: INTRODUCTION
   1. Who we are
      a. Our formal name: _____
      b. What we do: _____
      (Describe activities in terms most closely related to requirement.)
      c. Who we have done business with: _____
      (Choose names of customers most similar to requestor's organization.)
   2. Why we are proposing
      a. Our interest in the project: _____
      (How it relates especially to some interest of ours.)
      b. Our special qualifications: _____
      (Some experience or facilities closely related to the requirement.)
      c. Something special about us/our offer: _____
      (Some attention-getter we can produce.)
   3. Our understanding of the requirement
      a. The essence of what it is: _____
      (Summarize, in our own words, and in the most attention-getting phraseology possible.)
      b. Our special insight into it: _____
      (Some special, insightful commentary.)
      c. A hint of what this will mean: _____
      (Suggestion of how this will affect our choice of approach and implementation.)

Getting and Keeping Control of the Proposal

Most of those blanks ought to be filled in before writing begins, especially when an ad hoc team is writing the proposal. These can be preliminary objectives, which can be revised later, if further effort suggests that they should be revised; they do not have to be "graven in stone," but there must be something specific, at least tentative objectives clearly specified. Otherwise, you have no control: you and everyone else working on the proposal are each writing what you happen to think is relevant and appropriate at the moment to the general "topic" specified, based on spur-of-the-moment thinking.

Successful proposals are not written that way. They are written after some specifics are formulated and set as objectives, based on thoughtful reading and analysis. As a small sample, let's take a current small requirement from the U.S. Army. The summary description of the work is as follows:

Contractor is to provide all labor and equipment necessary to perform Computer Communications Analyst Services at the U.S. Military Academy West Point, NY in accordance with the attached statement of work for the period 1 December 1984 through 30 September 1985.

The detailed statement of work that follows explains that the project will require from 160 to 200 hours per month on-site, that the contractor may be required to furnish verbal and/or written information to satisfy requirements, and may have to do some actual programming. It requires five typed pages to complete the descriptions of the various tasks, all of which concern such technical matters as network design, configuration control, cost/benefit estimates, technical specifications, and numerous other matters related to the subject of computers, communications, and networks. A number of specific makes and models of equipment are also listed.

Although the statement of work never uses the term, this appears to me to be obviously a consulting project, as evidenced by the recurring mention of the necessity for advice, reports, recommendations, and other such typical requirements of consulting projects. Moreover, I am impressed by the vast scope of knowledge and skills required of the contractor, which includes specific familiarity with a number of different makes and models of equipment, operating systems, and software.

Were I to analyze this project with a view to writing a proposal, I would think hard about two things that strike me about this requirement:

1. The customer appears to expect a single individual to be supplied for the project, although the statement never specifically says so, but instead merely lists a number of hours per month.
2. The requirement is quite varied in the skills and knowledge required, so broad, in fact, as to be probably beyond the range of many experts in the field.

This would compel me to consider the advisability of offering to supply the services of more than one individual, pointing out the unlikelihood of finding a single individual willing to and capable of handling all the varied tasks with equal ability. (For example, would a consultant who can advise on such advanced matters as networking—who would necessarily be a rather advanced individual of unusual professional qualifications—be willing to spend time on the laborious and lower-level work of actual programming?)

In short, it is necessary to make such decisions before writing and to set these decisions as specific objectives to be cited in the outline. This then directs and guides you or whoever is the writer and also serves the editor/reviewer later in judging how well the proposal text achieves the objective. But unless the writer understands clearly, in advance, what point is to be made, it is not likely to be made.

The Necessity for a Theme

Every proposal ought to have a central theme, and you should know in advance what that theme is to be. It is necessarily closely related to the main strategy, of course, and is a reminder to the reader of that strategy. For example, in writing the successful proposal to the U.S. Navy for a standard teleprinter, the main strategy was to point out that the proposed teleprinter was a new, state-of-the-art design, prepared especially for the proposed project, and to contrast that with the makeshift adaptations of existing commercial models that others would offer. To follow up that point thematically the proposal established the theme of "monolithic" design, albeit with a detachable keyboard, versus the more typical "separates" or "components" design used in commercial models.

The effect was all that could be desired. The very term *monolithic* became something of a buzzword among those concerned with evaluating the proposals, and the subliminal impression gradually evolved there that any design that was not monolithic was substandard.

Theme reminds the reader of the main strategic thrust, and helps materially to maximize the effectiveness of the strategy. If the strategy is well chosen, the effective use of a theme can help make it a winner.

Theme is a unifying influence, helping lend focus to the proposal, and a constant reminder to you as the writer, as well as to the reader, of where you are wending and what your central orientation is. Without a theme a proposal tends to become a rambling discourse, meandering aimlessly, and thus almost certainly doomed to failure. You would have trouble getting a customer to read it all the way through, let alone select it as the winning proposal.

Note that almost all the discussions and methods advocated in this chapter have had a common characteristic: they are elements related directly to clarity, unity, and specificity. And when they are consciously and deliberately employed, they help you keep your own feet on the path of specificity.

Editing

Every writer should learn to do some self-editing, even when a professional editor is employed to support the proposal writers. A brief study of what the editing functions are will show why this is true:

The word *editor* has more than one meaning, and is often modified with adjectives to discriminate between various kinds and levels of editorial responsibility. Hence you may come across such terms as *line editor, copy editor, editor-in-chief,* and *technical editor,* among others. However, without discriminating among the many different levels of responsibility assigned editors, here are the principal editorial functions:

- Reviewing and/or correcting grammar, punctuation, spelling, and other mechanics of usage.
- Clarifying unclear passages.
- Uncovering non sequiturs, such as illogical transitions, confused (and confusing) organization, missing information (such gaps are often apparent to any astute reader), and other weaknesses.
- Covering a few legal matters, such as proper use of trademarks and proper attribution of other people's material, especially copyright material for which use you have been given permission.

Some of this the editor can do spontaneously, but much of it can be handled only by querying the author and getting the author to straighten things out.

In this way an editor is or should be the writer's alter ego, providing the objectivity that most people find difficult to achieve in reviewing their own work critically. Unfortunately, one major question arises inevitably: at what point does the work of shoring up weaknesses in the writing cease to be "heavy" editing and become rewriting and/or revision? For it is neither fair nor practicable to make an editor responsible for rewriting poor copy. The editor's function is to identify weaknesses in the copy and bring them to the writer's attention; the writer then, presumably, revises the material according to the criticism and suggestions, if any. Editors are not generally responsible for directing the rewrite, but a good editor will often be specific enough in pointing out the weaknesses to guide the writer in making the proper revisions. However, when the copy is technical and rather specialized, even the best of editors are hard put to do this, because editors are not necessarily technical experts in the subject matter.

That last point is one compelling reason for you to do at least some editing of your own copy. And just as vagueness, rambling ideas, and purple prose may indicate to readers that you have not properly thought out and planned your proposal, they should suggest the same problem to you as the writer. Therefore you should develop the ability to spot that kind of fault in your own writing. And when you detect that kind of symptom you should question your own knowledge and preparation—your own *understanding* of your subject. It is likely that you have unconsciously gone on ahead and "written around" the subject, concealing your lack of preparation even from yourself. (It is quite easy to deceive yourself about this unless you guard against it. I do it myself occasionally, even though I have schooled myself to catch it most of the time, and I am quite embarrassed when I fail to catch it and an editor must do it for me.) In self-editing, then, strive to become objective about your own writing. It is possible to do so.

A Definition of Understanding

One of the problems we encounter in trying to examine writing and what makes some writing good and some bad is the problem of trying to determine what the word *understanding* means. Behaviorists have come up with their own definition, stipulating that it can be defined only in terms of what one *does* that demonstrates understanding. But that is a rather ponderous mechanism, and totally unsuited to our use as writers. For myself, as a simple but helpful definition, I maintain that one can demonstrate his or her own understanding only by the ability to explain the matter to an absolute layperson who is totally ignorant of the subject beforehand. It is that very ability to explain something adequately in lay language that is the proof of understanding. On the other hand, the lament sometimes heard that, "I understand it, but I don't know how to explain it," is pure hogwash, in my opinion. I believe that it is, instead, a confession of the lack of understanding, although phrased as a denial of that deficiency. If you truly understand something, you ought to be able to explain it.

Therefore, I myself interpret any difficulties I have in explaining something as evidence that I do not myself have a true and full understanding. I am immediately convinced, from that, that I am unprepared to write about it until I have perfected my knowledge and therefore my understanding, and I then set about doing more research, more thinking, and more planning before I attempt to rewrite. To test this, when you suspect that you are writing from less than adequate knowledge and planning, try to explain the matter in the simplest possible language. (A few scientists, including the late George Gamow and the late Bertrand Russell, managed to explain even Einstein's theories of relativity—there were actually two such theories—in simple language for the lay reader.)

A Helpful Tip or Two

Here are some tactics and techniques you can use to help prompt and prod yourself into thinking your material out, doing adequate research, and planning your presentations properly before you run into trouble.

Using Exact Numbers   Use the same tactic you should employ to make your writing more credible: Be specific not only in the details you provide but also in quantifying, as well as qualifying all information that can be quantified, and in quantifying it as accurately as possible. For example, refrain from the temptation to round off numbers. A reader finds "99,575" far more credible than "100,000" or even "nearly 100,000." Even when you are estimating, don't grandly round off your "ballpark" figures. If you used a formula to arrive at an estimate, use the exact number your formula produced, not the rounded-off next-higher integer. Round numbers are all too easy to guess at and to use. *Compel* yourself to find the exact numbers, and you'll be steering away from the potential problem.

Forget About Modifiers   Minimize your use of adjectives and adverbs. Stick to the nouns and verbs, and you will not only do wonders for your style—purple prose and government-style gobbledygook are much harder to create without adjectives and adverbs—but you will be driven in the direction of far greater accuracy and far greater specificity.

The reason for this is simple enough. It is not the clean and trim noun or verb, but the rotund and little-known modifier we drag out of the unabridged dictionary (`a la one-time Vice President Spiro Agnew) behind which we so often manage to conceal even from ourselves our lack of something substantial to say. Try to write badly using only nouns and verbs, and you'll soon see that cutting modifiers from your writing regimen does as much for your writing as cutting sweets from your diet does for your figure.

Analyze and Synthesize   Break things down when discussing them, especially when explaining them. Show your readers the constituent parts of your reasoning, in both analysis of the requirement and synthesis of the solution. Analysis *forces* you to think things out until you have yourself achieved understanding. Try "thinking on paper" as a boon to improving your writing.

Outlining   Outlining, done properly, *is* analysis. (Since we have been over this subject, we'll be brief here.) But it's easy to fall into the trap of listing what you will write *about*, rather than what you will *say* when you write. Learn to outline in specific detail as an effective preventive to writing about something before you understand it.

The Burden Is on You   A final test of your understanding, then, is whether another does actually grasp your own explanations. This is one excellent argument for having editors who are not technical experts. If the nontechnical editor understands your technical explanations, you have done well. (Of course, you are not necessarily writing for laypeople, so it is not always appropriate that your writing be intelligible to the layperson, but you can often use editors to help you judge your success in getting your points across.)

Chapter 9

THE FEDERAL MAZE AND RELEVANT COMPUTER APPLICATIONS

All the federal government's thousands of agencies and offices are prospects, but they are as varied in their locations and needs as are the prospects in the market generally. You need some kind of road map to find your way through the maze.

The Federal Small-Computer Market

As a market for computers, computer services, and all related accessories and supplies, the federal government is a microcosm of the national market: There is probably not one item sold in the market generally that is not also sold somewhere in the federal-government marketplace. And the posture of the federal government vis-à-vis such purchases has changed to reflect the changes that have taken place in the computer field. In the era of mainframe computers the General Services Administration (GSA) established the Automated Data and Telecommunications Service (ADTS), making it "responsible for a comprehensive government-wide program for the management, procurement, and utilization of automatic data and telecommunications equipment services." While this official language suggests that the ADTS is the government's sole purchaser of and standards setter for computer hardware, software, and services, it is not literally the only computer customer among the agencies, nor does it actually control all computer procurement by the government, although it does serve other agencies as a consultant and as an advisor, and it operates the Federal Telecommunications System (FTS), and handles sundry related services for the federal government generally. Even in the field of the costly mainframe computers and minicomputers many agencies have done and do their own purchasing, but this is especially the case with respect to standalone desktop or personal computers.

The intrusion of the personal computer into the market affected federal computer purchasing deeply, as it has affected computer procurement generally in the economy, and as some of the earlier pages (especially reproductions of solicitation announcements) have demonstrated. The purchasing of personal or desktop computers for federal offices has burgeoned mightily, and GSA has responded to this development by assigning to its own Office of Information Resources Management (OIRM) responsibility for appropriate action. OIRM published a report, *Managing End User Computing in the Federal Government*, the product of an interagency task force that was commissioned to develop a buyer's guide and procedures for buying what they referred to as end-user's computers. (The term *EUC* is being used to refer to end user computing.)

A Federal Buyer's Guide to Small Computers

The buyer's guide has since been published (August 1984), titled, *End User's Guide to Buying Small Computers*. (GSA will furnish single copies on request. Address requests to General Services Administration, Office of Information Resources Management, Washington, DC 20405.) It is a slender volume of 32 pages, although a great deal of highly varied information is packed into its pages, and most of that information is of great value to anyone who wishes to sell "EUC equipment" to the government, as it is referred to in the Guide.

The volume is divided into two major parts. The first part, Chapters I through VI, covers all the areas of identifying needs, procurement procedures (including alternatives), and justifying procurement. The second part is a series of appendices, presented as Chapters VII, Appendix A through Chapter XIII, Appendix G, offering a variety of useful references—intended to be useful to the federal managers and procurement specialists, that is, but equally useful to vendors who take the trouble to study this little manual.

For example, the Guide points out that under the new Federal Acquisition regulations (FAR) and current law, small-purchase procedures may be used if the procurement is for not more than $25,000. On the other hand, formal solicitation procedures may be used also, but the Guide does not recommend this and suggests other alternatives available.

Requestors must usually manage to justify their purchase requests if they want to spend beyond the limits of petty cash, and Chapter VII presents an example of such a justification, offering first a detailed problem statement concerning travel-fund reports, which are at present not timely, not available on a cumulative basis, and not capable of comparisons of plan versus obligations. It then makes what is represented as an exemplary effective argument for the requested purchase of hardware and software.

The next chapter offers a second example, in which the problem is one of the agency's felt needs for a faster system for tracking contracts, calculating payments due, and authorizing progress payments to contractors meeting the milestone objectives in their contracts.

Other appendices discuss advantages and disadvantages of standardization, local area networks in government office complexes, relevant regulations, records management, and some miscellaneous matters.

The Growing Diversity of the Federal Computer Market

This is by no means the death knell of the federal market for mainframe and minicomputers, along with all related purchasing. Like the business and industrial worlds generally, the federal establishment will continue to have needs for all three levels of computer sizes and capabilities and will undoubtedly become a prime customer for the inevitable "supercomputers" of the future. Federal agencies face all the same computer problems that business and industry do, such as those concerning micro-to-mainframe communications and other networking problems, and communication among computers with different operating systems and using programs speaking different languages.

Aside from these general considerations, different agencies have different kinds of needs. Military agencies, for example, have a great many contracts to manage, as do a few other agencies, such as the Postal Service and the National Aeronautics and Space Administration (NASA). Some agencies, including the Departments of Housing and Urban Development (HUD) and Health and Human Services (HHS), among others, have many grant programs and grant awards to monitor and manage. Financial matters on a macroscopic scale are among the chief concerns of the Treasury Department and the Social Security Administration (SSA). The National Bureau of Standards, NASA, and other agencies are largely concerned with the use of computers for scientific and engineering work. But even those agencies that do not do a great deal of contracting, awarding of grants, tracking major financial matters, or carrying out challenging scientific and technical assignments have use for at least a few mainframe computers and/or minicomputers to help manage their day-to-day affairs. (Most agencies have at least several large computers.)

Government Organization

Every government entity of size, whether a department, an administration, an "office of," or some other such designation, is made up of subordinate units, many of which are themselves quite large. The Department of Defense (DOD), for example, includes the three military departments (Army, Navy, and Air Force), with the Marine Corps a unit within the Navy. The Coast Guard, although an element of the Armed Forces and assigned to the Navy in wartime, is otherwise a unit of the Transportation Department, as are many other organizations.

The logic of some of these assignments may escape you because there is no apparent logic in many of them. Sometimes the motivation for the assignment was political, sometimes pure expediency, sometimes pure chance. Many of these organizations have been kicked around from one assignment to another. The Bureau of Indian Affairs, for example, was once part of the then War Department; later it was assigned to the Interior Department when the latter was formed.

On the other hand, some of the organizations appear to be highly redundant, duplicating other government organizations and their functions. It may puzzle some of us that the Interior Department's National Park Service, its Bureau of Land Management, and the Department of Agriculture's Forest Service appear to replicate similar functions. And we may wonder why the Navy can't carry out the duties and functions currently assigned to the Coast Guard, or why we need both a Marine Corps and an Army in these days of air transport of troops. However, many today believe that this kind of redundancy and replication of function is to be expected in any large bureaucracy.

The following is a list of the major federal government agencies and the most relevant of their subordinate units or programs. (However, many of these subordinate units are themselves quite large and are in turn made up of numerous bureaus and offices. In the case of DOD, its three major components, Army, Navy, and Air Force, are treated as though they were independent departments.)

U.S. Department of Agriculture (USDA)

Farmers Home Administration (FmHA)
Agricultural Stabilization and
  Conservation Service (ASCS)

Agricultural Marketing Service (AMS)
Soil Conservation Service (CS)
Forest Service (FS)

U.S. Department of Commerce (DOC)

Maritime Administration
National Bureau of Standards (NBS)
National Oceanic and Atmospheric
  Administration (NOAA)
Bureau of the Census
United States Travel Service

Minority Business Development
  Agency (MBDA)
National Technical Information
  Service (NTIS)
Office of Telecommunications

U.S. Department of Defense (DOD)

Defense Advanced Research
  Projects Agency (DARPA)
Defense Logistics Agency (DLA)
National Security Agency (NSA)

Defense Communications Agency (DCA)
Defense Intelligence Agency (DIA)
Defense Contract Administrative
  Services (DCASR)

U.S. Department of the Air Force (USAF)

Air Force Logistics Command (AFLC)
Air Training Command (ATC)
Military Airlift Command (MAC)
Tactical Air Command (TAC)

Air Force Systems Command (AFSC)
Air University
Strategic Air Command (SAC)
Air Force Communications Service

U.S. Department of the Army (USA)

U.S. Army Forces Command
U.S. Army Material and Readiness
  Command
U.S. Army Tank-Automotive Material
  Readiness Command
U.S. Army Tank-Automotive Research
  and Development Command

U.S. Army Training and Doctrine
  Command
U.S. Army Communications Command
U.S. Army Military Academy
  (West Point)
U.S. Army Troop Support and Aviation
  Material Readiness Command

U.S. Army Aviation Research and Development Command

U.S. Army Material Readiness Command

U.S. Department of the Navy (USN)

Naval Air Systems Command
Naval Facilities Engineering Command
Naval Supply Systems Command
Naval Oceanographic Office
U.S. Naval Academy (Annapolis)

Naval Electronic Systems Command
Naval Sea Systems Command
Bureau of Naval Personnel (BuPers)
Naval Telecommunications Command

U.S. Department of Education (D/E)

Office of Bilingual Education and Minority Language Affairs
Howard University
Rochester Institute of Technology

American Printing House for the Blind
Gallaudet College
National Technical Institute for the Deaf

U.S. Department of Energy (DOE)

Office of Energy Research

Office of Energy Technology

U.S. Department of Health and Human Services (HHS)

Office of Human Development Services
Alcohol, Drug Abuse, and Mental Health Administration
Health Resources Administration (HRA)
National Institutes of Health (NIH)

Public Health Service (PHS)
Center for Disease Control (CDC)
Food and Drug Administration (FDA)
Health Services Administration (HSA)
Social Security Administration (SSA)

U.S. Department of Housing and Urban Development (HUD)

New Community Development Corporation
Policy Development and Research

Government National Mortgage Association
Community Planning and Development

U.S. Department of the Interior (DOI)

U.S. Fish & Wildlife Service
Bureau of Mines
Bureau of Indian Affairs (BIA)
Bureau of Reclamation

National Park Service
Bureau of Geological Survey
Bureau of Land Management (BLM)

U.S. Department of Justice (DOJ)

Federal Bureau of Investigation (FBI)
Bureau of Prisons
Antitrust Division
Immigration and Naturalization

Drug Enforcement Administration (DEA)
U.S. Marshals Service
Civil Rights Division
Community Relations Service

U.S. Department of Labor (DOL)

Employment and Training Administration
Occupational Safety and Health Administration (OSHA)

Office of Comprehensive Employment Development Programs

U.S. Department of Transportation (DOT)

U.S. Coast Guard (USCG)
Federal Highway Administration
National Highway Traffic Safety Administration (NHTSA)

Federal Aviation Administration (FAA)
Federal Railroad Administration (FRA)
Urban Mass Transportation Administration (UMTA)

U.S. Department of the Treasury

Internal Revenue Service (IRS)

U.S. Customs Service
Comptroller of the Currency
Bureau of Government Financial
  Operations

Bureau of Alcohol, Tobacco and
  Firearms
Bureau of Engraving and Printing
Bureau of the Mint
Bureau of the Public Debt
U.S. Secret Service

U.S. Environmental Protection Agency (EPA)

Planning and Management
Water and Waste Management
Research and Development

Enforcement
Air, Noise, and Radiation
Pesticides and Toxic Substances

General Services Administration (GSA)

Automated Data and Telecommunications
  Service (ADTS)
National Archives and Records
  Service (NARS)

Federal Property Resources Service
Federal Supply Service (FSS)
Public Buildings Service (PBS)
Transportation and Public Utilities
  Service

U.S. National Aeronautics and Space Administration (NASA)

Ames Research Center
George C. Marshall Space Flight
  Center
Jet Propulsion Laboratory
Langley Research Center
Lyndon B. Johnson Space Center
National Space Technology
  Laboratories NASA Headquarters

Hugh L. Dryden Flight Research
  Center
Goddard Space Flight Center
John F. Kennedy Space Center
Lewis Research Center
Wallops Flight Center

U.S. Veterans Administration (VA)

Department of Veterans Benefits
Department of Memorial Affairs

Department of Medicine and
  Surgery

Even this gives only an extremely broad picture, since there are some 60 "autonomous" or "independent" agencies, in addition to literally thousands of lower-level units too numerous to include here. (The official *United States Government Manual*, issued annually to describe the federal government and list all the organizations and key personnel, itself runs to approximately 1,000 pages of small print.) But the complexity does not stop with the several hundred agencies of the government, or even with all the subordinate units of the many organizations, for there is the further *geographic* proliferation of federal agencies and offices. Most federal agencies have regional offices (in most cases one in each of the 10 federal regions), and the regional offices usually have a full complement of subordinate units.

And it does not stop even there, for certain federal agencies have far more than 10 offices scattered across the considerable geography of the United States: Many have district offices. The Small Business Administration (SBA), for example, has nearly 100 offices throughout the United States, as does the Department of Commerce, and others, many of whom have an even greater number of field or district offices.

Some of these offices buy centrally through their regional or even their national (Washington) headquarters offices, but much buying is also done locally and independently by these offices, especially when the purchase qualifies legally as a small purchase or there is such urgency as to preclude the fairly lengthy delays inherent in centralized procurement. So the end result is the existence of many thousands of federal purchasing offices (at least 15,000) employing some 130,000 procurement specialists. (It requires a great many people to spend $170 billion annually.)

Needs and Applications

All agencies have need for computers for general applications, such as maintaining personnel records, recording and managing inventory, and monitoring budgets and expenditures. But some agencies have special needs, as well. For example, many agencies have use for what is often referred to by irreverent young computer professionals as "number crunching," or use of computers for quantitative work—mathematical calculations of some kind. But even here the applications vary enormously, according to the missions and responsibilities of the agency, for there are many kinds of number crunching. The National Bureau of Standards (NBS), NASA, the Environmental Protection Agency (EPA), the Department of Energy (DOE), many of the military organizations, and numerous other federal agencies have needs for technical applications, such as engineering and scientific calculations. The Treasury Department deals primarily in financial matters, of course, and therefore does most of its number crunching with reference to dollars and cents—budgets, deficits, international exchange, tax revenues, and related matters. Military agencies must keep track of a wide variety of resources maintained in many places—personnel, vehicles, weapons of many kinds, and sundry other assets, representing a kind of inventory reporting and control. The Commerce Department's Census Bureau is concerned with counting the population and gathering many kinds of statistics in its many kinds of demographic bases. (Census-related work goes on steadily throughout the 10 years between official nose-countings.) But the Commerce Department's National Oceanic and Atmospheric Administration does some technical number crunching, too. The Labor Department's Bureau of Labor Statistics counts labor classes and the unemployed, and Labor also uses computers to perform calculations for such requirements as determining which counties of the United States are "labor surplus areas," that is, areas of exceptionally high unemployment rates. The Department of Housing and Urban Development keeps track of millions of government-backed mortgages, government-backed loans to builders, rental-subsidy programs, grant programs, and sundry other programs related to residential housing, while the Interior Department must keep track of oil leases, Indian reservation lands, and other matters concerning government-owned land. (Approximately one-third of all U.S. land, concentrated largely in the West and Northwest, is owned by the federal government.)

Of course, number crunching is only one broad area of computer applications. NASA must also utilize computers for computer-assisted design (CAD), word processing, and many other applications. The Department of Education maintains computer cataloging and monitoring of documents related to education. The Department of Health and Human Services operates the National Library of Medicine, with its vast computer-resident stores of medical information. The National Archives and Records Service does something similar for general information and documents of national interest. And the National Technical Information Service (Department of Commerce) has a vast library system of documents to catalog and monitor.

Meanwhile, the military organizations use computers to play war games, modeling a variety of hypothetical situations to appraise the readiness and adequacy of U.S. forces in today's world, but also appraising similar appraisals of foreign forces.

There is virtually no possible application of computers and related technology that the government does not have a need for somewhere in the federal bureaucracy. And selling to the government requires that you understand the operations and needs of the many agencies, at least in principle. However, selling to the government is at least as much of a problem in "where to" as it is in "how to." Dealing with the bureaucracy is as frustrating with respect to the sheer numbers and dispersion of agencies and offices as it is in other respects. Often the winning of government business is no more complicated than finding the right door to knock on.

The Need for "Where To" Information

Personal experience has demonstrated clearly that many awards are made spontaneously, via purchase orders rather than via formal contracts, on the basis of expediency: A suitable vendor happens to call on the agency at the right time. That may very well be a time when the busy executive is aware that a problem exists, but he or she has not had the time to discuss it with others or even to think about it seriously and has no thoughts about it other than a vague feeling of discontent and concern. Or it may also be at a time when the customer is giving thought to seeking a vendor to satisfy some felt need but has not yet decided to take the time to carry out the series of preliminary steps necessary to make a procurement. In fact, the customer, a person often hard-pressed for time to get even routine things done, may very well never get around to taking those steps if the need is not especially urgent, but will put it off indefinitely, waiting for a "slow" time that never comes. And a few words to expand briefly on the various procurement alternatives open to government customers will explain why such procrastination is often the case and why, consequently, it is important to do as much marketing by personal and direct calls as possible.

The Procurement Cycle

Federal Acquisition Regulations (FAR) authorize both "advertised" and "negotiated" procurement, as explained earlier. But each method has its own pros and cons.

Advertised procurement is usually far more expeditious than negotiated procurement and can usually be consummated in far less time. Advertised procurement generally requires far less paperwork of the requestor, too, and far less labor in selecting an awardee. Moreover, it also requires far less paperwork of the bidder, and so encourages a greater number of bids, usually. Advertised procurement, however, imposes on the customer a practical obligation to accept the lowest bid (despite regulations which nominally authorize alternatives), even when that bidder appears to be an unsuitable and even unqualified supplier. That limits the choices rather severely, allowing no real discretion to the customer. And more than one federal government requestor has discovered that being compelled to select a contractor on the basis of price alone has resulted in procurement disasters, so they are rather bearish about this form of procurement if anything other than commodities or the most workaday routine services are required. Moreover, there are numerous cases where advertised procurement is simply not a suitable method for procurement of the goods or services required.

Negotiated procurement overcomes some of these drawbacks: The customer has a wide degree of discretion in choosing a supplier from among those submitting proposals, and is not obligated to select the lowest bidder as the winner. However, it involves much time and paperwork from both customer and proposer, and often this tends to limit the number of proposers, thus offering the customer relatively few options. But worst of all is the time required. The typical negotiated procurement can take many months to consummate as it proceeds through many steps and stages:

- Preparing the solicitation package, which includes writing the statement of work, specifications, proposal requirements, and other information and instructions. The writing of the work statement and specifications can itself be a difficult and time-consuming task and is rarely undertaken with any great degree of joy. (Frequently the customer has only a set of symptoms, and must spend the time to try to translate these into a problem definition and at least the suggestion of an approach to solution.)
- Announcement of the solicitation in the CBD and via mailing solicitations to suitable prospective suppliers on the bidders' lists.
- Proposal writing by prospective suppliers.
- Evaluation of proposals.
- "Best and final" requests and other negotiations.
- Final selection.

All of this takes months, often as long as a year or more for major procurements, but easily 3–6 months for even small procurements made through the formal contracting process.

Small purchase procurement overcomes both of these problems, to a large extent, despite the limitations of purchase size, and is a relatively informal and rapid process involving these steps:

Submittal of a purchase request by the customer to his or her contracting office. The purchase request is little more than a form with a brief statement of work or specification of services to be performed, along with a dollar figure and specified vendor or supplier.

This results in issuing a purchase order to the specified vendor, which order includes the work statement, the price, and any other relevant details, such as a delivery date.

This whole process can be consummated usually in two or three weeks.

As a practical matter, frequently the process works this way: The vendor has approached the customer in very much the same manner a vendor would approach any prospect anywhere, and has persuaded the customer to become interested. The customer invites the vendor to submit an informal "letter proposal," which is in fact a letter of a page or two describing the offer briefly. The customer abstracts the work-deliverable description of the letter proposal as the statement of work and requests the issuance of the purchase order. It's that simple, in practice, although the customer may be required, under the law (and depending on the dollar size of the purchase) to get two other bids by informal means.

This does not mean necessarily that the customer has been feeling a need of some kind. You may have to "create" the need by probing to find out what the customer's problems and concerns are, and then suggesting some appropriate products or services. And in an environment where $10,000 and even $25,000 is considered to be a small purchase you may win a substantial order awarded you rather casually to find out what you can offer, if you succeed in arousing the customer's interest enough.

Obviously, from the viewpoint of the customer this is a much-to-be desired method for making purchases, when the size of the purchase is small enough. And a great many of these small purchases are the result of conventional selling through personal calls to government offices. Hence the desirability of understanding the various agencies' missions and special interests with regard to computers.

From the vendor's viewpoint there are two advantages: One is the obvious one of expeditious procurement of business, even in small segments. But of much greater importance to a great many suppliers is the foot-in-the-door benefit of winning a first small contract. This gives the vendor an opportunity to become familiar with the agency's needs and personnel, and to become highly "visible" to the executives of the agency, both assets for future marketing and pursuit of larger contracts.

The next chapter will offer a directory of major federal government customers, as a kind of starter list.

Chapter 10

DIRECTORY OF FEDERAL GOVERNMENT PROSPECTS

A starter list of government offices throughout the United States, all of which do at least some independent procurement, and many of which buy a wide variety of goods and services, frequently and in substantial quantities.

Major Government Offices and Facilities

The following lists are by no means a complete directory of all U.S. Government offices and facilities, nor is there much purpose in listing all of them. The U.S. Forest Service, for example, has dozens of forestry stations and forest supervisors' offices, but these are generally rather small installations and not especially significant from the viewpoint of independent procurement. There are listed here, however, the Forest Service Regional offices and the Forest Service special test stations and research facilities. Nor are all units of the Department of Agriculture (USDA) itself covered here, except as listed for USDA's central headquarters in Washington, DC; there would be little to be gained by listing some of the units as prospects for computer-related business. Moreover, most of the offices not listed here do their purchasing via offices that are listed here. (Note the many centralized purchasing and procurement offices listed.) This general philosophy will be followed throughout the listings offered here.

The U.S. military services are a special problem insofar as providing coherent and complete listings is concerned because of the special problems of DOD being a department, within which there are the three military organizations also called "departments," and because of the complex structure of military organizations. Bear in mind, however, that every military base does at least some independent purchasing and therefore has its own procurement office and sometimes more than one such office, especially where the base serves as a headquarters for some major function within the military department.

U.S. Department of Agriculture

Central Offices
Independence Avenue & 12th-14th Streets, SW
Washington, DC 20250,
(202) 655-4000

Agricultural Marketing Service, Administrative Services Division, Property and Procurement Branch

Contracting Officer, Cotton Division, Marketing Programs Branch, Agricultural Marketing Service

Agricultural Stabilization and Conservation Service, Management Services Division, Procurement and Contracting Branch

Economics, Statistics and Cooperatives Service, Administrative Services Division, Procurement and Property Management Branch

FmHA Business Services Division, Procurement and Property Branch
Procurement and Property Branch

FCIC, Administrative Management Division, Administrative Services Branch

Food Safety and Quality Service, Administrative Services Division, Procurement and Property Branch

Contracting Officer, Poultry Market Program Branch, Poultry Dairy Quality Service, Food Safety and Quality Service

Contracting Officer, Meat Quality Division, Food Safety and Quality Service

Contracting Officer, Fruit Branch, Fruit and Vegetable Quality Division, Food Safety and Quality Service

Contracting Officer, Vegetable Branch, Fruit and Vegetable Quality Division, Food Safety and Quality Service

Contracting Officer, Specialty Crops Branch, Fruit and Vegetable Quality Division, Food Safety and Quality Service

Contracting Officer, Dairy Market Branch, Poultry Dairy Quality Division, Food Safety and Quality Service

Foreign Agricultural Service, Management Services Division

Office of Operations and Finance, Procurement Division (Operations Unit), Rural Electrification Administration, Management Services Division, Management Analysis and Services Branch, Supply and Space Management Section

Soil Conservation Service, Administrative Services Division, Procurement Management Branch

Forest Service, Director of Administrative Services

Forest Service

1765 Highland Avenue, Montgomery, AL 36101
Federal Office Bldg, POB 1628, Juneau, AK 99802
1960 Addison Street, Berkeley, CA 94701
630 Sansome Street, San Francisco, CA 94111
11177 West 8th Avenue, Lakewood, CO 80225
240 West Prospect Avenue, Fort Collins, CO 80521

POB 2417, Washington, DC 20013
1720 Peachtree Street, NW, Atlanta, GA 30309
701 Loyola Avenue, USPS Bldg, New Orleans, LA 70113
1992 Folwell Avenue, St. Paul, MN 55101
Federal Building, Missoula, MT 59807
POB 2570, Post Office Building, Asheville, NC 28802
517 Gold Avenue, Albuquerque, NM 87102
809 NE 6th Avenue, POB 3141, Portland, OR 97232
319 SW Pine Street, Portland, OR 97208
327 Reed Road, Broomall, PA 19008
POB AQ, Rio Pedras, PR 00928
507 25th Street, Ogden, UT 84401
633 West Wisconsin Avenue, Milwaukee, WI 53203
5130 N. Walnut Street, Madison, WI 53711

Science and Education Administration

2850 Telegraph Avenue, Berkeley, CA 94701
2000 W. Pioneer Parkway, Peoria, IL 61614
POB 53326, New Orleans, LA 70153
Rm 329, Building 003, BARC-W, Beltsville, MD 20705
Federal Building # 1, 6505 Belcrest Road, Hyattsville, MD 20782

Food and Nutrition Service

550 Kearny Street, San Francisco, CA 94108
2490 W. 26th Avenue, Diamond Hill Complex, Bldg D, Denver, CO 80211
1100 Spring Street, NW, Atlanta, GA 30309
536 S. Clark Street, Chicago, IL 60605
34 3rd Avenue, Burlington, MA 01803
1100 Commerce Street, Dallas, TX 75202

U.S. Department of Commerce

Central Office
14th Street and Constitution Avenue, NW,
Washington, DC 20230,
(202) 377-2000

Maritime Administration
Minority Business Development Agency
Bureau of the Census
International Trade Administration
National Oceanic and Atmospheric Administration
Bureau of Economic Analysis
Bureau of Industrial Economics
National Telecommunications and Information Administration
United States Travel Service

Maritime Administration

26 Federal Plaza, New York, NY 10007 (Eastern Region)
International Trade Mart, 2 Canal Street, New Orleans, LA 70130
(Central Region)
Room 576, 666 Euclid Avenue, Cleveland, OH 44114 (Great Lakes
Region)
450 Golden Gate Avenue, San Francisco, CA 94102 (Western Region)
Suite 430, 400 Oceangate, Long Beach, CA 90802 (Area Office)
Room 1894, 915 2nd Avenue, Seattle, WA 98174 (Area Office)
Kings Point, LI, NY 11024 (U.S. Merchant Marine Academy)

National Bureau of Standards

Route 70 and Quince Orchard Road, Gaithersburg, MD 20852
(Headquarters and Laboratory)
National Bureau of Standards, Boulder, CO 80303 (Director,
NBS/Boulder Laboratories)
JILA, University of Colorado, CO 80302 (Quantum Physics Division)
2000 E. County Road 58. Fort Collins, CO 80524 (Standard Frequency
Stations WWV and WWVB)
POB 417, Kekaha, Kauai, HI 96752 (Standard Frequency Station
WWVH)
5800 W. 69th Street, Chicago, IL 60638 (Master Railway Tracks
Scale Depot)

National Oceanic and Atmospheric Administration

585 Stewart Avenue, Garden City, NY 11530
601 E. 12th Street, Kansas City, MO 64106
819 Taylor Street, Fort Worth, TX 76102
125 S. State Street, Salt Lake City, UT 84111
POB 23, 701 C Street, Anchorage, AK 99513
Prince Kuhio Federal Bldg, Rm 4110, 300 Ala Moana Blvd, Honolulu,
HI 96850
5200 Auth Rd, Camp Springs, MD 20233
Gable One Tower, 1320 S. Dixie Hwy, Coral Gables, FL 33146
439 W. York Street, Norfolk, VA 23510
1801 Fairview Avenue E., Seattle, WA 98102
POB 1188, Gloucester, MA 01930
9450 Koger Boulevard, St. Petersburg, FL 33702
2725 Montlake Boulevard E., Seattle, WA 98112
POB 271, La Jolla, CA 92036
POB 1668, Juneau, AK 99802
Federal Building, Asheville, NC 28801
2001 Wisconsin Avenue, NW, Washington, DC 20235
3100 Marine Avenue, Boulder, CO 80302

National Technical Information Service

5285 Port Royal Road, Springfield, VA 22161

Patent and Trademark Office

2021 Jefferson Davis Hwy, Arlington, VA 22209

Bureau of the Census

1365 Peachtree Street, NE, Atlanta, GA 30309
441 Stuart Street, Boston, MA 02116
230 S. Tryon Street, Charlotte, NC 28202
55 E. Jackson Boulevard, Chicago, IL 60604
1100 Commerce Street, Dallas, TX 75242
575 Union Blvd, Denver, CO 80225
231 W. Lafayette, Detroit, MI 48226
4th & State Streets, Kansas City, KS 66101
11777 San Vicente Blvd, Los Angeles, CA 90049
26 Federal Plaza, New York, NY 10007
600 Arch Street, Philadelphia, PA 19106
1700 Westlake Avenue, Seattle, WA 98109
1201 E. 10th Street, Building 48, Jeffersonville, IN 47132
Walnut & Pine Streets, Pittsburg, KS 66762

U.S. Department of Defense

Defense Logistics Agency, Cameron Station, Alexandria, VA 22314
Defense Supply Service, The Pentagon, Washington, DC 20310
Headquarters, Defense Personnel Support Center, Defense Logistics
Agency, 2800 S. 20th Street, Philadelphia, PA 19101
Defense Electronics Supply Center, 1507 Wilmington Pike, Dayton,
OH 45444
Defense Atomic Support Agency, Sandia Base, Albuquerque, NM
87115

U.S. Air Force

Headquarters, Audiovisual Service, Norton AFB, CA 92409
Electronic Systems Division, L.G. Hanscom Field, Bedford, MA 01731
Air Force Communications Service, Scott AFB, Belleville, IL 62225

Army and Air Force Exchange Service

Fort Sam Houston, TX 78234 (Alamo Exchange Region)
Building 6, Cameron Station, VA 22314 (Capitol Exchange Region)
POB 3553, San Francisco, CA 94119 (Golden Gate Region)
Building 2501, Indiana Army Ammunition Plant, Charlestown, IN
47111 (Ohio Valley Exchange Region)
1280 Kershaw Street, Building T-5, Montgomery, AL 36108 (Southeast
Exchange Region)

U.S. Air Force Bases

Elmendorf AFB, Anchorage, AK 99506
Eileson AFB, Fairbanks, AK 99702
Williams AFB, Chandler, AZ 85224

Luke AFB, Glendale, AZ 85309
Davis-Monthan AFB, Tucson, AZ 85707
Blytheville AFB, Blytheville, AR 72315
Little Rock AFB, Little Rock, AR 72076
McClellan AFB, Sacramento, CA 95652
Mather AFB, Sacramento, CA 95655
Edwards AFB, CA 93523
Travis AFB, Fairfield, CA 94535
Vandenberg AFB, Lompoc, CA 93437
Beale AFB, Marysville, CA 95903
Castle AFB, Merced, CA 95340
March AFB, Riverside, CA 92508
Norton AFB, San Bernardino, CA 92409
George AFB, Victorville, CA 92392
USAF Academy, Colorado Springs, CO 80840
Ent AFB, Colorado Springs, CO 80912
Peterson AFB, Colorado Springs, CO 80914
Lowry AFB, Denver, CO 80240
Dover AFB, Dover, DE 19901
Andrews AFB, Washington, DC 20331
Bolling AFB, Washington, DC 20332
Patrick AFB, Cocoa Beach, FL 32925
Homestead AFB, Homestead, FL 33033
Tyndall AFB, Panama City, FL 32401
MacDill AFB, Tampa, FL 33608
Eglin AFB, Valparaiso, FL 32542
Dobbins AFB, Marietta, GA 30060
Moody AFB, Valdosta, GA 31601
Robins AFB, Warner Robins, GA 31908
Anderson AFB, Guam, APO San Francisco 96334
Hickam AFB, Honolulu, HI 96853
Mountain Home AFB, Mountain Home, ID 83648
Scott AFB, Belleville, IL 61820
Chanute AFB, Rantoul, IL 61868
Grissom AFB, Peru, IN 46796
McConnell AFB, Wichita, KS 67221
England AFB, Alexandria, LA 71304
Barksdale AFB, Shreveport, LA 71110
Loring AFB, Limestone, ME 04750
L.G. Hanscom Field, Bedford, MA 01731
Westover AFB, Chicopee Falls, MA 01022
K.I. Sawyer AFB, Marquette, MI 40843
Wurtsmith AFB, Oscoda, MI 48753
Keesler AFB, Biloxi, MS 39534
Columbus AFB, Columbus, MS 39701
Whiteman AFB, Knob Noster, MO 65301
Malmstrom AFB, Great Falls, MT 59402
Offutt AFB, Omaha, NE 68113

Nellis AFB, Las Vegas, NV 89181
Pease AFB, Portsmouth, NH 03801
McGuire AFB, Wrightstown, NJ 08641
Holloman AFB, Alamogordo, NM 88330
Kirtland AFB, Albuquerque, NM 87117
Cannon AFB, Clovis, NM 88101
Plattsburgh AFB, Plattsburgh, NY 12903
Griffis AFB, Rome, NY 13441
Pope AFB, Fayetteville, NC 28390
Seymour-Johnson AFB, Goldsboro, NC 27530
Grand Forks AFB, Grand Forks, ND 58201
Minot AFB, Grand Forks, ND 58701
Rickenbacker AFB, Columbus, OH 43217
Wright-Patterson AFB, Dayton, OH 45433
Altus AFB, Altus, OK 73521
Vance AFB, Enid OK 73701
Tinker AFB, Oklahoma City, OK 73145
Kingsley Field, Klamath Falls, OR 97601
Charleston AFB, Charleston, SC 29404
Myrtle Beach AFB, Myrtle Beach, SC 29577
Shaw AFB, Sumter, SC 29577
Ellsworth AFB, Rapid City, SD 57706
Arnold AF Station, Tullahoma, TN 37389
Dyess AFB, Abilene, TX 79607
Bergstrom AFB, Austin, TX 78743
Carswell AFB, Fort Worth, TX 76127
Goodfellow AFB, San Angelo, TX 76901
Randolph AFB, San Antonio, TX 78148
Kelly AFB, San Antonio, TX 78241
Sheppard AFB, Wichita Falls, TX 73611
Hill AFB, Ogden, UT 84056
Langley AFB, Hampton, VA 23665
Fairchild AFB, Spokane, WA 99011
McChord AFB, Tacoma, WA 98436
Francis E. Warren AFB, Cheyenne, WY 82001

U.S. Army

Computer Systems Selection and Acquisitions Agency, The Pentagon, Washington, DC 20310
Development and Readiness Command, 5001 Eisenhower Avenue, Alexandria, VA 22333
Corps of Engineers, Department of the Army, Washington, DC 20314
Office of the Surgeon General, The Pentagon, Washington, DC 20310
Medical Material Agency, Frederick, MD 21701
Medical Research and Development Command, Fort Detrick, MD 21701
Walter Reed Army Institute of Research, Washington, DC 20012
Health Services Command, Fort Sam Houston, TX 78234
Communications Command, Fort Huachuca, AZ 85613

Ballistic Missile Defense Systems Command, POB 1500, Huntsville, AL 35807

Military Traffic Management Command, 5611 Columbia Pike, Falls Church, VA 22041

Publications Directorate, Forrestal Bldg, Washington, DC 20314

Defense Mapping Agency, 6500 Brooks Lane, NW, Washington, DC 20315

Fort Lesley J. McNair, Washington, DC 20319

U.S. ARMY BASES

Fort McClellan, Anniston, AL 36201

Redstone Arsenal, 106 Wynn Drive, Huntsville, AL 35807

Fort Rucker, Ozark, AL 36362

Fort Richardson, Anchorage, AK 99505

Proving Grounds, Yuma, AZ 85364

Pine Bluff Arsenal, Pine Bluff, AR

Sharpe Army Depot, Lathrop, CA 95330

Fort Ord, Monterey, CA 93941

Oakland Army Base, Oakland, CA 94626

Riverbank Army Ammunition Plant, CA 95367

Sacramento Army Depot, Sacramento, CA 95801

Presidio of San Francisco, San Francisco, CA 94129

Fort MacArthur, San Pedro, CA 90731

Rocky Mountain Arsenal, Denver, CO 80240

Fitzsimons General Hospital, Denver, CO 80240

Fort Carson, CO 80913

Fort McPherson, Atlanta, GA 30330

Fort Gordon, Augusta, GA 30905

Fort Benning, Columbus, GA 30905

Fort Stewart, GA 31214

Construction Engineering Research Lab, Belleville, IL 61820

Fort Sheridan, Chicago, IL 60037

St. Louis Support Center, Granite City, IL 62040

Joliet Army Ammunition Plant, Joliet, IL 60436

Rock Island Arsenal, Rock Island, IL 61201

Indiana Army Ammunition Plant, Charlestown, IN 47111

Fort Benjamin Harrison, Indianapolis, IN 46218

Army Ammunition Plant, Newport, IN 47966

Jefferson Proving Ground, Madison, IN 47250

Iowa Army Ammunition Plant, Burlington, IN 56201

Fort Leavenworth, KS 66027

Fort Riley, KS 66442

Sunflower Army Ammunition Plant, Lawrence, KS 66044

Kansas Army Ammunition Plant, Parsons, KS 67357

Armor Center, Fort Knox, KY 40121

Fort Campbell, Hopkinsville, KY 42223

Fort Polk, LA 71459

Louisiana Army Ammunition Plant, Shreveport, LA 71102

Aberdeen Proving Ground, Aberdeen, MD 21005

Harry Diamond Laboratories and Electronics R&D Command, 2800 Powder Mill Road, Adelphi, MD 20783

Fort Ritchie, MD 21719

Fort George G. Meade, MD 20755

Fort Devens, MA 01433

Natick R&D Development Command, Natick, MA 01760

Materials and Mechanics Research Center, Watertown, MA 02172

Tank-Automotive Readiness Command, Warren, MI 48090

Fort Leonard Wood, MO 65473

Lake City Army Ammunition Plant, Independence, MO 64056

Gateway Army Ammunition Plant, St. Louis, MO 63143

Army Aviation R&D Command, 12th & Spruce Streets, St. Louis, MO 63166

Cornhusker Army Ammunition Plant, Grand Island, NE 68801

Army Cold Regions R&D Lab, Hanover, NH 03755

Army Armament R&D Command, Dover, NJ 07801

Fort Dix, NJ 08640

Fort Monmouth, NJ 07703

White Sands Missile Range, White Sands, NM 88002

Fort Drum, Watertown, NY 13603

Watervliet Arsenal, Watervliet, NY 12189

U.S. Military Academy, West Point, NY 10996

Fort Bragg, Fayetteville, NC 28307

Army Research Office, Research Triangle Park, NC 27709

Ravenna Army Ammunition Plant, Ravenna, OH 44266

Fort Sill, OK 73503

Fort Indiantown Gap, Annville, PA 17003

Carlisle Barracks, Carlisle, PA 17013

Letterkenny Army Depot, Chambersburg, PA 17201

New Cumberland Army Depot, New Cumberland, PA 17070

Scranton Army Ammunition Plant, 156 Cedar Avenue, Scranton, PA 18501

Tobyhanna Army Depot, Tobyhanna, PA 18466

Fort Jackson, Columbia, SC 29207

Volunteer Army Ammunition Plant, POB 1748, Chattanooga, TN 37401

Holston Army Ammunition Plant, Kingsport, TN 37662

Milan Army Ammunition Plant, Milan, TN 38358

Corpus Christi Army Depot, Corpus Christi, TX 78419

Fort Bliss, El Paso, TX 79916

William Beaumont Army Medical Center, El Paso, TX 79920

Fort Hood, TX 76544

Longhorn Army Ammunition Plant, Marshall, TX 75670

Brooke Army Medical Center, San Antonio, TX 78241

Lone Star Army Ammunition Plant, Texarkana, TX 75501

Dugway Proving Grounds, 1750 S. Redwood Road, Dugway, UT 84022

Fort Douglas, Salt Lake City, UT 84113

Tooele Army Depot, Tooele, UT 84075

Fort Belvoir, VA 22060
Fort Eustis, VA 23604
Fort Lee, VA 23801
Fort Monroe, VA 23651
Radford Army Ammunition Plant, Radford, VA 24141
Army Electronics Material Readiness Command, Vint Hill Farm
Station, Warrenton, VA 22186
Madigan Army Medical Center, Tacoma, WA 98431
Fort Lewis, Tacoma, WA 98433
Badger Army Ammunition Plant, Baraboo, WI 25721
Fort McCoy, WI 54656

U.S. Navy

Navy ADP Selection Office, Crystal Mall # 4, Washington, DC 20376
Navy Regional Contracting Office, Washington Navy Yard,
Washington, DC 20374
Naval Regional Contracting Office, Terminal Island, Long Beach, CA
90822
Navy Resale System Office, 29th Street & 3rd Avenue, Brooklyn, NY
11232
Naval Air Systems Command, Washington, DC 20361
Naval Facilities Engineering Command, 200 Stovall Street, Alexandria, VA 22332
Naval Sea Systems Command, Washington, DC 20376
Naval Material Command, Crystal Place # 5, Washington, DC 20360
Naval Electronic Systems Command, National Center, Washington,
DC 20361
Naval Research Laboratory, Washington, DC 20375

U.S. NAVAL BASES

Marine Corps Air Station, Yuma, AZ 85634
Naval Air Station, Alameda, CA 94501
USMC Logistics Support Base, Pacific, Bldg 236, Barstow, CA 94501
Marine Corps Base, Camp Pendleton, CA 92055
Naval Weapons Center, China Lake, CA 93555
Naval Weapons Station, Concord, CA 94521
Naval Weapons Station Annex, Corona, CA 91720
Naval Air Station, Lemoore, CA 93245
Naval Regional Contracting, Long Beach, CA 90822
Long Beach Naval Shipyard, Long Beach, CA 90822
Naval Supply Center, Oakland, CA 94625
Naval Air Station, Point Mugu, CA 93042
Naval Construction Battalion Center, Port Hueneme, CA 93043
Naval Facilities Engineering Command, POB 727, San Bruno, CA
94066
Naval Supply Center, 271 Catalina Blvd, San Diego, CA 92131
Naval Regional Medical Center, San Diego, CA 92134
Naval Air Station North Island, San Diego, CA 92135

SUPSHIP, Conversion and Repair, POB 119, Naval Station, San Diego, CA 92136
Navy Public Works Center, San Diego, CA 92137
Navy Public Works Center, San Diego, CA 92138
Marine Corps Recruit Depot, San Diego, CA 92140
Naval Air Station, Miramar, San Diego, CA 92145
SUPSHIP, Conversion and Repair, San Francisco, CA 94135
Marine Air Station Toro, Santa Ana, CA 92709
Naval Weapons Station. Seal Beach, CA 90740
Marine Corps Base, Twentynine Palms, CA 92278
Mare Island Naval Shipyard, Vallejo, CA 94592
SUPSHIP, Conversion and Repair, Groton, CT 06340
Naval Submarine Base, New London, CT 06340
Guantanamo Bay, Cuba, FPO, Box 25, New York, NY 09593
U.S. Naval Observatory, Washington, DC 20305
Military Sealift Command, 4228 Wisconsin Avenue, Washington, DC 20390
Washington Navy Yard, Washington, DC 20374
Naval Air Station, POB 21-A, Jacksonville, FL 32212
Mayport Naval Station, Jacksonville, FL 32228
Naval Air Station, Key West, FL 33040
Naval Training Equipment Center, Orlando, FL 32813
Naval Coastal Systems Center, Panama City, FL 32407
Naval Air Station, Pensacola, FL 32508
Naval Aerospace and Regional Medical Center, Pensacola, FL 32512
Marine Corps Logistics Supply Base, POB 18, Albany, GA 31704
Marine Corps Air Station, Kaneohe Bay, HI 96863
Naval Facilities Engineering Command, Supply Center, and SUP-SHIP,
Conversion and Repair, Pearl Harbor, HI 96860
Naval Training Center, Great Lakes, IL 60088
Naval Weapons Support Center, Crane, IN 47522
Naval Avionics Center, Indianapolis, IN 46218
SUPSHIP, Conversion and Repair, and Naval Support Activity, New Orleans, LA 71046
SUPSHIP, Conversion and Repair, 574 Washington Street, Bath, ME 05430
Naval Air Station, Brunswick, ME 04011
Naval Supply Depot and Purchase Division, Guam, FPO San Francisco, CA 96630
U.S. Naval Academy, Annapolis, MD 21402
National Naval Medical Center, Bethesda, MD 20014
David W. Taylor Naval Ship R&D Center, Bethesda, MD 20084
Naval Surface Weapons Center, White Oak Laboratory, Silver Spring, MD 20910
Naval Ordnance Station, Indian Head, MD 20640
Naval Air Station, Patuxent River, MD 20670
SUPSHIP, Conversion and Repair, 666 Summer Street, Boston, MA 02210

Naval Oceanographic Office, Bay St. Louis, MS 39522
Naval Construction Battalion Center, Gulfport, MS 39501
SUPSHIP, Conversion and Repair, Pascagoula, MS 39567
Naval Air Station, Van Voorhis Field, Fallon, NV 89406
Portsmouth Naval Shipyard, Portsmouth, NH 03755
Military Sealift Command, Military Ocean Terminal, Bayonne, NJ 07002
Naval Weapons Station Earle, Colts Neck, NJ 07722
SUPSHIP, Conversion and Repair, Flushing & Washington Avenues, Brooklyn, NY 11251
Navy Aviation Supply Office, 700 Robbins Avenue, Philadelphia, PA 19111
Naval Facilities Engineering Command, Philadelphia, PA 19112
Naval Regional Contracting Office, Philadelphia, PA 19112
Navy Ship Parts Control Center, Mechanicsburg, PA 17055
Naval Air Development Center, Willow Grove, PA 19090
Naval Construction Battalion Center, Davisville, RI 02854
Naval Underwater Systems Center and Naval Regional Contracting Office, Newport, RI 02840
Marine Corps Air Station, Beaufort, SC 29902
SUPSHIP, Conversion and Repair, Naval Weapons Station, and Naval Supply Center, Charleston, SC 29408
Naval Facilities Engineering Command, 2144 Melbourne Street, Charleston, SC 29411
Marine Corps Base, Parris Island, SC 20905
Naval Air Station, Corpus Christi, TX 78419
Office Of Naval Research, 800 N. Quincy Street, Arlington, VA 22217
Naval Surface Weapons Center, Dahlgren Laboratory, Dahlgren, VA 22448
SUPSHIP, Conversion and Repair, Newport News, VA 23607
Naval Facilities Engineering Command, Naval Base, Norfolk, VA 23511
Navy Public Works Center, Norfolk, VA 23512
Naval Supply Center, Norfolk, VA 23513
Naval Amphibious Base, Little Creek, Norfolk, VA 23521
Norfolk Naval Shipyard, Portsmouth, VA 23709
Marine Corps, Quantico, VA 22134
Naval Air Station, Virginia Beach, VA 23460
SUPSHIP, Conversion and Repair, POB 215, Portsmouth, VA 23705
Naval Regional Medical Center, Portsmouth, VA 23708
Naval Weapons Station, Yorktown, VA 23691
Naval Facilities Engineering Command, 5610 Kitsap Way, POB UU, Wycoff Station, Bremerton, WA 98310
Naval Supply Center, Puget Sound, Bremerton, WA 98314
Naval Torpedo Station, Keyport, WA 98345
Naval Air Station, Whidbey Island, Oak Harbor, WA 98274
SUPSHIP, Conversion and Repair, Sturgeon Bay, WI 54235

U.S. Department of Education

Central Office
400 Maryland Avenue, SW
Washington, DC 20202

Office of Contracts, 7th and D Streets, SW, GSA Administration
Building, 5th Floor, Washington, DC 20407
National Institute of Education, 1200 19th Street, NW, Washington,
DC 20208

U.S. Department of Energy

Central Office
Forrestal Building, 1000 Independence Avenue, SW
Washington, DC 20585

Regional Offices and Special Facilities

111 Pine Street, San Francisco, CA 94111
POB 26247, Belmar Branch, Lakewood, CO 80226
1655 Peachtree Street, NE, Atlanta, GA 30309
Argonne National Laboratory, 9800 S. Cass Avenue, Argonne, IL
60439
175 West Jackson Blvd, Chicago, IL 60604
150 Causeway Street, Rm 700, Analex Bldg, Boston, MA 02114
112 E. 12th Street, Kansas City, MO 64142
26 Federal Plaza, New York, NY 10007
1421 Cherry Street, Philadelphia, PA 19102
POB E, Oak Ridge National Laboratory, Oak Ridge, TN 37830
2626 W. Mockingbird Lane, Dallas, TX 75235
915 2nd Avenue, Federal Building, Seattle, WA 98174

U.S. Department of Health and Human Services

Central Office
200 Independence Avenue, SW,
Washington, DC 20201

Public Health Service, 200 Independence Avenue, SW, Washington,
DC 20201
Alcohol, Drug Abuse, and Mental Health Administration, 5600
Fishers Lane, Rockville, MD 20857
Center for Disease Control, 1600 Clifton Road, NE, Atlanta, GA
30333
Food and Drug Administration, 5600 Fishers Lane, Rockville, MD
20857
Health Resources Administration, 3700 East-West Hwy, Hyattsville,
MD 20782

Health Services Administration, 5600 Fishers Lane, Rockville, MD 20857
National Institutes of Health, 9000 Rockville Pike, Bethesda, MD 20205
Social Security Administration, 6401 Security Blvd, Baltimore, MD 21235

Regional Offices

John F. Kennedy Federal Building, Boston, MA 02203
20 Federal Plaza, New York, NY 10007
3535 Market Street, Philadelphia, PA 19101
101 Marietta Towers, NE Atlanta, GA 30323
300 S. Wacker Drive, Chicago, IL 60606
1200 Main Tower Building, Dallas, TX 75202
601 E. 12th Street, Kansas City, MO 64106
1961 Stout Street, Denver, CO 80202
50 United Nations Plaza, San Francisco, CA 94102
1321 2nd Avenue, Seattle, WA 98101

U.S. Department of Housing and Urban Development

Central Office
451 Seventh Street, SW,
Washington, DC 20410

Regional Offices

John F. Kennedy Federal Building, Boston, MA 02203
26 Federal Plaza, New York, NY 10007
Curtis Building 6th and Walnut Streets, Philadelphia, PA 19106
1800 Pennsylvania Avenue, Delaware Trust Plaza, Atlanta, GA 30303
300 S. Wacker Drive, Chicago, IL 60606
221 West Lancaster Avenue, Fort Worth, TX 76113
1103 Grant Avenue, Kansas City, MO 64106
450 Golden Gate Avenue, San Francisco, CA 94102
3003 Arcade Plaza Bldg, Seattle, WA 98101

U.S. Department of the Interior

Central Office
18th & C Streets, NW,
Washington, DC 20240 (202) 343-1100

Branch of Supply, Office of Administrative Services
National Park Service
Division of Personnel Management, Heritage Conservation and Recreation Service
Branch of Procurement, Bureau of Land Management

Division of Procurement and Property, Bureau of Reclamation
Contracts and Grants Management Division, Office of Water Research
   and Technology
Contracting and Grants Administration, Bureau of Indian Affairs
Division of Contracting and General Services, U.S. Fish and Wildlife
   Service
Division of Contracting and Property Management, National Park
   Service
1100 Ohio Drive, SW, Washington, DC 20242: Division of Contracting
   and Procurement, National Capital Region, National Park Service
1951 Constitution Avenue, NW, Washington, DC 20245:
Division of Support Services, Bureau of Indian Affairs
Branch of Contracts and Grants, Bureau of Indian Affairs
Commissioner of Indian Affairs
Eastern Area Director, Bureau of Indian Affairs

Bureau of Land Management

555 Cordova Street, Anchorage, AK 99501
Federal Building, Room 3022, Phoenix. AZ 85025
2800 Cottage Way, Sacramento, CA 95825
550 W. Fort Street, Boise, ID 83724
7981 Eastern Avenue, Silver Spring, MD 20910
222 E. 32nd Street, Billings, MT 59107
300 Booth Street, Reno, NV 89509
729 NE Oregon Street, Portland, OR 97208
136 E.S. Temple and 125 S. State Street, Salt Lake City, UT 84111
2120 Capitol Avenue, Cheyenne, WY 82001

Bureau of Indian Affairs

Phoenix Area Office, 3030 N. Central, Phoenix, AZ 85011
Navajo Area Office, POB 1060, Window Rock, AZ 86515
Palm Springs Area Office, 587 S. Palm Canyon Drive, Palm Springs,
   CA 92262
Area Office, 2800 Cottage Way, Sacramento, CA 95825
Minneapolis Area Office, 831 Second Avenue S., Minneapolis, MN
   55402
Billings Area Office, 316 N. 26th Street, Billings, MT 59101
Division of Facilities Engineering, 500 Gold Avenue, SW, Albu-
   querque, NM 87103
Southwestern Indian Polytechnic Institute, 1000 Indian School Road,
   NW, Albuquerque, NM 87103
Administrative Services Center, POB 2088, Albuquerque, NM 87103
Area Office, Albuquerque, NM 5301 Central Avenue, Albuquerque,
   NM 87108
Navajo Area Office, POB 1060, Gallup, NM 87301
Anadarko Area Office, Anadarko, OK 73005
Muskogee Area Office, Federal Building, Muskogee, OK 74401
Area Office, 1425 Irving Street, NE, Portland, OR 97208
Area Office, 115 4th Avenue, SE, Aberdeen, SD 57401

Division of Procurement and Contracting, 1000 2nd Avenue, Seattle, WA 98104

Bureau of Mines

Tuscaloosa Metallurgy Research Center, POB L, University, Tuscaloosa, AL 35486

Denver Mining Research Center, Building 20, Denver Federal Center, Denver, CO 80225

Avondale Metallurgy Research Center, 4900 LaSalle Road, Avondale, MD 20782

Twin Cities Mining Research Center, POB 1660, Twin Cities, MN 55111

Rolla Metallurgy Research Center, POB 280, Rolla, MO 65401

Boulder City Metallurgy Research Center, 500 Date Street, Boulder City, NV 89005

Reno Metallurgy Research Center, Reno, NV 89512

Eastern Field Operations Center, 4800 Forbes Avenue, Pittsburgh, PA 15213

Salt Lake City Metallurgy Research Center, 1600 E. 1st South Street, Salt Lake City, UT 84112

Spokane Mining Research Center, E. 315 Montgomery Avenue, Spokane, WA 99207

Geological Survey

Western Mapping Center, Water Resources Division, and Geologic Division, 345 Middlefield Road, Menlo Park, CA 94025

Topographic Division, Water Resources Division, and Geologic Division, Denver Federal Center, Denver, CO 80225

Topographic Division, 1459 Peachtree Street, NE, Atlanta, GA 30309

Topographic Division, Midcontinent Mapping Center, POB 133, Rolla, MO 65401

Branch of Procurement and Contracts, Eastern Region Office, 12201 Sunrise Valley Drive, Reston, VA 22092

Bureau of Reclamation

2800 Cottage Way, Sacramento, CA 95825, Regional Office (RO)

Building 20, Denver Federal Center, Denver, CO 80225 (RO)

550 W. Fort Street, Boise, ID 83724 (RO)

POB 2553, Billings, MT 59103 (RO)

POB 427, Boulder City, NV 89005 (RO)

Herring Plaza, Box H-4377, Amarillo, TX 79101 (RO)

Division of Management Services, 125 S. State Street, POB 11505, Salt Lake City, UT 84111

National Park Service

Division of Contracting and Property Management, 3401 Whipple Street, Atlanta, GA 30344

1895 Phoenix Road, Atlanta, GA 30349 (RO)

POB 728, Santa Fe, NM 87501 (RO)

143 S. 3rd Street, Philadelphia, PA 19106 (RO)
Contracting and Property Management Division, Pike Bldg, Seattle, WA 98101

U.S. Department of Justice

Central Office
10th Street & Constitution Avenue, NW,
Washington, DC 20530

Community Relations Service, 550 11th Street,NW, Washington, DC 20530
Federal Bureau of Investigation, 9th Street & Pennsylvania Avenue, NW, Washington, DC 20535
Bureau of Prisons, 320 First Street, NW, Washington, DC 20534
Immigration and Naturalization Service, 425 I Street, NW, Washington, DC 20536
Drug Enforcement Administration, 1405 I Street, NW, Washington, DC 20537
Office of Assistance, Research and Statistics, 633 Indiana Avenue, NW, Washington, DC 20531

U.S. Department of Labor

Central Office
200 Constitution Avenue, NW,
Washington, DC 20210

Occupational Safety and Health Administration and Employment Standards Administration, 200 Constitution Avenue, NW, Washington, DC 20210
Employment and Training Administration and Office of Job Corps, 601 D Street, NW, Washington, DC 20213
Bureau of Labor Statistics, 441 G Street, NW, Washington, DC 20212

U.S. Department of Transportation

Central Office
400 7th Street, SW,
Washington, DC 20590

Federal Highway Administration, Federal Railroad Administration, National Highway Traffic Safety Administration, Urban Mass Transportation Administration, Saint Lawrence Seaway Development Corporation, Coast Guard, and Research and Special Programs Administration, 400 7th Avenue, SW, Washington, DC 20590
Transportation Systems Center, Kendall Square, Cambridge, MA 02142

Federal Aviation Administration

800 Independence Avenue, SW, Washington, DC 20591
National Aviation Facilities Experimental Center, Atlantic City, NJ 08405
Aeronautical Center, 6400 S. MacArthur Blvd, Oklahoma City, OK

U.S. Coast Guard

400 7th Street, SW, Washington, DC 20590
Coast Guard Academy, New London, CT 06320
Training Center, Petaluma, CA 94952
Supply Center, 830 3rd Avenue, Brooklyn, NY 11232
Aircraft Repair and Supply Center, Elizabeth City, NC 27909

U.S. Department of the Treasury

Central Office
Main Treasury Building, 15th Street and Pennsylvania Avenue, NW, Washington, DC 20220
Bureau of Alcohol, Tobacco and Firearms, 1200 Pennsylvania Avenue, NW, Washington, DC 20226
U.S. Customs Service, 1301 Constitution Avenue, NW, Washington, DC 20229
Federal Law Enforcement Training Center, Glynco, GA 31520
United States Secret Service, 1800 G Street, NW, Washignton, DC 20223
Internal Revenue Service, 1111 Constitution Avenue, NW, Washington, DC 20224

Environmental Protection Agency

Central Office
401 M Street, SW,
Washington, DC 20460

Laboratories and Special Facilities

POB 3009, Montgomery, AL 36109
West Ridge University of Alaska, College, AK 99701
Sabine Island, Gulf Breeze, FL 32561
College Station Road, Athens, GA 30605
9311 Groh Road, Ann Arbor, MI 48105
6201 Congdon Blvd, Duluth, MN 55804
11640 Administration Drive, St. Louis, MO 63141
POB 15027, Las Vegas, NV 89114
Research Triangle Park, NC 27711
26 W. St. Clair Street, Cincinnati, OH 45268
POB 1198, Ada, OK 74820

200 SW 35th Street, Corvallis, OR 97330
South Ferry Road, Narragansett, RI 02882

General Services Administration

Central Office
18th and F Streets, NW,
Washington, DC 20405

Public Buildings Service and Automated Data and Telecommunications Service, 18th and F Streets, NW, Washington, DC 20405
National Archives and Records Service, 8th Street and Pennsylvania Avenue, NW, Washington, DC 20408
Federal Property Resources Service, 1755 Jefferson Davis Hwy, Arlington, VA 22209
Transportation and Public Utilities Service, 425 Eye Street, NW, Washington, DC 20406

Federal Supply Service

1941 Jefferson Davis Hwy, Arlington, VA 22209
7th and D Streets, SW, Washington, DC 20407
26 Federal Plaza, New York, NY 10007

National Aeronautics and Space Administration

Central Office
400 Maryland Avenue, SW,
Washington, DC 20546

Centers and Facilities

George C. Marshall Space Flight Center, Huntsville, AL 35812
Hugh L. Dryden Research Center, POB 273, Edwards, CA 93523
Ames Research Center, Moffet, CA 94035
Jet Propulsion Laboratory, 4800 Oak Grove Drive, Pasadena, CA 91103
John F. Kennedy Space Center, Cape Canaveral, FL 32899
Goddard Space Flight Center, Greenbelt, MD 20771
National Space Technology Laboratories, Bay St. Louis, MS 39520
Lewis Research Center, 21000 Brookpark Road, Cleveland, OH 44135
Lyndon B. Johnson Space Flight Center, Houston, TX 77058
Langley Research Center, Langley Station, Hampton, VA 23665
Wallops Flight Center, Wallops Island, VA 23337

National Science Foundation

Central Office
1800 G Street, NW, Washington, DC 20550

Office of Personnel Management

Central Office
1900 E Street, NW, Washington, DC 20415

Pension Benefit Guaranty Corporation

Central Office
2020 K Street, NW, Washington, DC 20006

U.S. Postal Service

Central Office
475 L'Enfant Plaza West, SW, Washington, DC 20260

Veterans Administration

Central Office
810 Vermont Avenue, NW, Washington, DC 20420

Office of Data Management and Telecommunications, 810 Vermont Avenue, NW, Washington, DC 20420

Data Processing Centers
941 N. Capitol Street, NE, Washington, DC 20421
11000 Wilshire Blvd, Los Angeles, CA 90013
Lock Box 66303, AMF O'Hare, Chicago, IL 60666
Federal Building, Fort Snelling, St. Paul, MN 55111
5000 Wissahickon Avenue, Philadelphia, PA 19101
1615 E. Woodward Street, Austin, TX 78772
Records Processing Center, POB 172, St. Louis, MO 63166

Chapter 11

DIRECTORY OF STATE AND LOCAL GOVERNMENT PROSPECTS

State and local governments are not the mirror image of the federal government in purchasing procedures and policies but do tend to a similar pattern, while also showing a tendency to emulate commercial purchasing practices in many respects.

All Public Procurement Tends to Maximize Competition

Like the many federal government procurement officials, most state and local government purchasing agents have shown an active interest in eliciting as many vendor applications as possible. That is, they tend to encourage and maximize competition among vendors for at least two reasons:

1. Competition has classically been the way to produce the best prices and best quality of goods and services. For purely selfish reasons of making the best buys, procurement officials value maximum competition.

2. Most states and local governments, like the federal government (and often in emulation of the lead provided by the federal government), have statutes requiring that the agencies encourage both opportunity and competition in their procurement functions.

The federal government spends a great deal of money and makes a considerable effort to help entrepreneurs learn how to become aware of and take advantage of opportunities to do business with federal agencies. (A later chapter will go into programs and facilities offered to achieve this.) Unfortunately and mysteriously, most of that money is wasted because the federal government is remarkably ineffectual at publicizing the help offered: Only the most fortunate or most persistent (and frequently only the most resourceful and tireless) entrepreneurs do finally learn how to do business successfully with federal agencies. That is, such determination and persistence are generally required to succeed in this market.

Unfortunately, the state and local governments are perhaps even less successful in making businesspeople generally aware of the opportunities to do business with their agencies. Many have information services and offer other help rivaling that of the federal government, but those services are helpful only when the individual succeeds in learning enough to seek out the help, learning where and how to begin uncovering the opportunities.

There are indications that many state and local governments are in the process of developing and, in many cases, revising or expanding their entire procurement systems and preparing information materials at the same time. A great many of the jurisdictions offer lists of commodities they buy and descriptive brochures of one kind or another, again following the example of the federal government. Some states and even local governments offer quite elaborate information packages, virtual starter kits for the vendor, while others have extremely little to offer, at least at this moment. (However, it is entirely possible that by the time you read this this situation will have greatly improved.)

Overall, the lists tend to resemble the federal listings, and in some cases, that of California, for instance, to be almost a carbon copy of the federal supply lists and classifications, even to the extent of using the same supply-group numbers and designations.

An Important Difference

One major difference between the federal procurement system and that of most states is that the federal system tends strongly to decentralize purchasing, while the state systems tend to the opposite direction. The mandatory use of centralized supply sources is the exception in the federal system; in many, if not most, states the authority of state agencies to buy independently is the exception, or is at least regarded as an exception, to the general rule. In many cases when purchase authority is delegated to other agencies of the state the authority is limited to certain, specific classes of procurement, such as professional services and items that are peculiar to the needs of that agency.

These are important exceptions, for the vendor, however, for most states and even many local governments have a large number of agencies, representing a proportionately large potential market in the state or local government. It is not at all unusual for a state to have as many as 300 or more agencies of various kinds, agencies which tend to parallel the federal agencies, including various departments, bureaus, commissions, and institutions. These are too numerous to list here, but they include at least the following classes:

Prisons and other correctional institutions	Hospitals and sanitariums
Highway/transportation departments	Colleges and universities
Insurance commissioners	Public school systems
Fish and wildlife departments	Agriculture departments

Assessments & taxation departments	Conservation departments
Bank commissioners	Aviation administrations
Income/general tax bureaus	Budget and fiscal planning offices
State department of education	Data processing divisions
	Port authorities

What State and Local Governments Buy

Like the federal government, many state governments tried to achieve some standardization in their procurement of computers and related services and supplies by establishing special offices or specialists on their purchasing staffs for the purpose of exercising some control over and standardization of the ADP systems—at least, a degree of compatibility among the systems used by different agencies. But the advent of inexpensive desktop computers has complicated that effort for the state and local governments, as it has for the federal government.

Following is a composite list of typical computer, communication, training, and other equipment, services, and supplies that are germane to the activities in today's computer industries. Note that this is a composite list, offering actual terms drawn from the commodity lists published by several state and local governments, so as to provide a cross section of typical relevant procurement, as listed by the states' purchasing offices. The various terms used are reported verbatim, although organized so as to fit into this single brief list. This results in some degree of redundancy in some cases, but the purpose of this list is to show the actual terms used by the various purchasing offices, as well as to identify what they buy relevant to computers and data processing. This is helpful in marketing because the customers often use other terms than those you yourself use to identify the goods, supplies, and services you sell. Note that most of the jurisdictions recognize the need for special technical consultants and for training.

Audiovisual equipment, supplies, repairs
Computer equipment, tapes
Computers, data- and word-processing machines, systems, accessories, and services
Consultant services
Data processing cards, paper, and posting fluids
Disks
Electronic data processing equipment, software, supplies, and support equipment
Office equipment—data processing furniture, machines, supplies
Office machines, equipment, and accessories
Office supplies not otherwise classified
Office machines and visible record equipment
Professional services (analytical disciplines)—computer software development, data processing analysis/consultants, telecommunications, management and training, and educational consultants

Professional staff services—consultants, data processing systems; consultants, telecommunications; data processing, programming; data processing, data entry and keypunch; data processing, training; data processing, equipment maintenance
Training aids

How and Where State and Local Governments Buy

Whereas federal government purchasing is largely decentralized (at least 15,000 federal procurement offices exist throughout the United States, with relatively few in Washington, DC), most state and local governments tend to concentrate their purchasing in capitals—the state capitals, the county seats, and the city and town halls. The first list offered here is one of the state governments' purchasing offices. Almost without exception each purchasing office requires vendors to register as bidders and to fill out suitable forms to get on the bidders lists. (In a few cases a registration fee is exacted.) And all strongly recommend, even urge, personal visits to the purchasing office, if possible, to meet personally with the various buyers. (Most of these purchasing offices employ staffs of buyers, each buyer assigned a group of items.)

In many cases the state purchasing office does centralized purchasing for all agencies in the state on term contracts and permits local governments to utilize those contracts to place their own orders. This benefits both the governments because both get the advantages of group buying. But it also benefits the vendors because they can thus utilize their contracts with the state to sell to the local governments. Therefore, in many cases it is the state government's purchasing office that opens doors to the local government markets. (Also, all state and local governments can utilize the federal supply contracts negotiated and listed as "Federal Supply Schedules.")

Using the Directory

Select the purchasing offices of immediate interest—for example, those of your own state and perhaps surrounding states, if their capitals are not too far—and try to visit the purchasing offices personally, if at all possible, and get acquainted with the appropriate buyers. In any case, register with the offices, by mail if necessary, and apply for inclusion on the bidders lists.

Directory of State Purchasing Offices

ALABAMA: Finance Department, Purchase & Stores Division, Room 125, Capitol Building, Montgomery, AL 36130, (205) 832-3580

Centralized purchasing, term contracts. Small purchases (under $500) may be made by informal bids. The office awards term contracts, permits other jurisdictions to place orders under those contracts.

ALASKA: Department of Administration, Division of General Services & Supply, Pouch C, Juneau, AK 99811, (907) 465-2253, and 330 East 4th Avenue, Suite A, Anchorage, AK 99501, (907) 272-1491

This office spends some $40+ million annually and welcomes new suppliers enthusiastically. The commodity index has about 35 supply classes, including furniture, machines, supplies, and services required for data processing applications. The state issues purchase orders, term contracts, and definite-quantity contracts. Small purchases are those under $300. Professional services are exempt from bidding, are negotiated, using proposals, with requests issued by using agencies, which are authorized to do at least some purchasing independently.

ARIZONA: Department of Administration, Finance Division, Purchasing Office, 1688 West Adams Street, Room 220, Phoenix, AZ 85007, (602) 255-5511

All purchases over $5,000 must be by formal sealed bids; those over $500 but not more than $2,500, may be by oral bids. And those less than $5,000 but more than $2,500 must be by written bids, although informal. The state purchasing office may enter into consortia to buy jointly with other political jurisdictions of the state, and these 12 Arizona agencies are authorized to buy independently:

Department of Corrections
Department of Education
Department of Public Safety
Northern Arizona University
Correctional Industries
Division of Military Affairs
State Compensation Fund
Department of Economic Security
Arizona State University
University of Arizona
Department of Health Services
Game and Fish Department

ARKANSAS: Office of State Purchasing, Department of Finance and Administration, POB 2940, Little Rock, AR 72203, (501) 371-1771.

Although this office buys for the state, many agencies may buy independently, to at least some extent. At least the following state agencies may be approached directly:

Arkansas Highway Department
Arkansas State University
Arkansas Tech University
East Arkansas Community College
West Arkansas Community College
North Arkansas Community College
University of Arkansas at Pine Bluff
Phillips County Community College

University of Arkansas
University of Arkansas Medical Science
University of Arkansas at Monticello
Henderson State University

Garland County Community College

Mississippi County Community College

University of Central Arkansas

Southern Arkansas University

CALIFORNIA: Office of Procurement, Department of General Services, 1823 14th Street, POB 1612, Sacramento, CA 95807, (916) 445-2500, and 107 S. Broadway, Los Angeles, CA 90012, (213) 620-5660

California furnishes an abundant package of procurement information on request, and the state's list of commodities, classification numbers, and system in general resemble the federal system rather closely. Like many other states, California delegates much buying authority to various state agencies: Although the state's purchasing office does buy a wide array of goods, it does not buy professional services, land, or buildings, nor does it negotiate leases, leaving these purchases to its delegates, the individual user agencies. Sealed bids are the usual method, and the small-purchase limit is normally $1,000.

Procurement regulations designate EDP equipment purchases as meriting special policies, and normally makes all such purchases via the proposal-and-negotiation method. Such supplies are listed as supply Group 70: EDP Equipment, Software, Supplies, and Support Equipment.

COLORADO: Department of Administration, Division of Purchasing, 1525 Sherman Street, R, 712, Denver, CO 80203, (303) 839-3261

This organization reports annual purchases of well over $200 million, but delegates separate purchasing authority to the state's Department of Highways, colleges and universities, and other state institutions. Formal, sealed bids are required for procurements over $1,500.

CONNECTICUT: Bureau of Purchases, 460 Silver Street, Middletown, CT 06457, (203) 344-2080

The State of Connecticut reports that it is a "multi-million dollar participant in the market place as a buyer of supplies, equipment, and services—including construction—to meet the needs of more than 300 budgeted agencies of the executive branch of State government." State law permits open-market purchases where the total value is less than $6,000. Larger purchases must be advertised and bid competitively. The Bureau of Purchases is part of Connecticut's Department of Administrative Services and is assigned major procurement responsibility, but purchasing authority is assigned to other bureaus of the Department: Bureau of Public Works, Bureau of Public Works, and Bureau of Information Services and Data Processing. The latter bureau lists the following items as those goods and services normally purchased:

Data communication equipment and services	Computers, all sizes
Disk controllers and drives	Plotters
Tape controllers and drives	Graphics equipment
Card reader/punch and associated controllers	Printers and associated controllers
Video display terminals	Word processing systems
Cabling for interconnection of equipment	Micrographics equipment and services
Systems software	Keyboard terminals
Applications software	Equipment and software maintenance

Information systems and DP
consultant services

DELAWARE: Administrative Services Department, Division of Purchasing, Governor Bacon Health Center, Delaware City, DE 19706, (302) 834-4512

The State of Delaware maintains centralized purchasing for common-use commodities, but delegates purchase authority to many other agencies of the state and also permits other agencies to buy independently by processing purchase requests through the Division of Purchasing, after direct contact with vendors.

FLORIDA: Department of General Services, Division of Purchasing, 613 Larson Building, Tallahassee, FL 32304, (904) 488-1194

Florida advises all corporations that wish to do business with the state to register with Florida's Secretary of State, and suggests calling (904) 488-9000 to get relevant information and request vendor applications.

The Division of Purchasing is made up of a Bureau of Procurement and a Bureau of Standards, the latter charged with developing specifications, as necessary. Both have relatively large staffs of specialists. However, the many agencies within the state each have some purchasing power of their own, and each such agency has an individual named as a purchasing agent or has assigned the purchasing responsibility to an administrative official.

GEORGIA: Department of Administrative Services, Purchasing & Supplies Division, 116 Mitchell Street, Room 504, Atlanta, GA 30335, (404) 656-3240

Purchasing for all agencies, with certain exceptions provided by law or departmental regulation, is done centrally by the division. Purchases between $100 and $5,000 may be made by informal bids, which may be oral and made via telephone. Larger procurements must be made by formal, sealed bids, with public bid openings. And local governments within the state may utilize the state's contracts for their own purchasing. The law also provides that any contractor with the state has the option to offer to do business with local governments under the same contract and/or terms as those the state government enjoys. As in the case of many other state governments, various state agencies may contract independently for professional services.

HAWAII: Department of Accounting and General Services, Purchasing and Supply Division, 1151 Punchbowl Street, POB 119, Honolulu, HI 96810, (808) 548-7428

The State of Hawaii does not envision its purchasing organization as making purchases for the entire state but rather as a service agency, assisting the various other state agencies in making procurements by soliciting bids, publishing price lists, and providing other services.

The state may issue purchase orders for procurements up to $8,000 but must negotiate formal contracts for larger purchases, which must also be advertised in two local newspapers for at least three days. (Purchases between $4,000 and $8,000 must be advertised for at least one day.)

IDAHO: Department of Administration, Division of Purchasing, 650 West State Street, Room 100, Boise, ID 83720, (208) 384-2465

Idaho has a comprehensive Registration Packet available for vendors who wish to register with the state. The Division of Purchasing has sole authority to contract for goods and services for the state, with certain specific exemptions of those other agencies authorized to buy independently.

In general the law requires that all purchases of more than $500 but less than $5,000 be made only after soliciting competitive bids from at least three registered vendors. Purchases of more than $5,000 require that at least 20 registered vendors be invited to bid. The law provides that where appropriate (as in the case of federal procurement procedures) proposals may be solicited, proposals evaluated, and contracts negotiated.

Idaho furnishes a lengthy commodities list, covering data processing equipment and services, the latter as consulting services in "data processing, computer, information systems, and programming," under supply group 94.

ILLINOIS: Department of Administrative Services, Office of Procurement, 810 Stratton Office Building, Springfield, IL 62706, (217) 782-2301

Illinois procurements of $2,500 or more require competitive sealed bids and advertising in an English-language newspaper designated as the "official newspaper," for such purposes, as required by Illinois law. The exceptions include the existence of emergency conditions of some sort that make normal competitive procurement impractical or when the item is available from only a single source, such as would be the case for a proprietary for which there is no suitable equivalent.

INDIANA: Department of Administration, Procurement Division, 100 N. Senate Avenue, 507 State Office Building, Indianapolis, IN 46204, (317) 232-3032

At the time the above information was furnished, Indiana had no formal brochures or other literature to furnish aspirants to their supplier lists, but explained a policy of sending inquirers a form letter and a registration form to fill out. Out-of-state firms must also register with Indiana's Secretary of State and a form is furnished for that purpose also. Purchases under $500 do not require competitive bids, as do those above that figure.

Indiana also uses negotiated procurement, after soliciting proposals and selecting contenders with whom to negotiate. Typically, those are two-step processes, where an unpriced proposal is submitted first, and then prices are solicited from those whose technical proposals are acceptable.

The Procurement Division may delegate purchasing authority to other state agencies and may also buy for local governments, open its contracts to local governments, and/or buy from the federal supply schedules, utilizing federal supply contracts for its own procurement.

IOWA: Department of General Services, Purchasing Division, Hoover State Office Building, Des Moines, IA 50319, (515) 281-5856

The State of Iowa furnishes a *Vendor Information Booklet* to assist suppliers in understanding Iowa's procurement policies and regulations. Under Iowa law the Department of General Services is charged with central procurement of all supplies and services for all state agencies, except as otherwise exempted specifically by law. Procurements are of both one-time purchases and term contracts, and of both definite- and indefinite-quantity types. In some cases local governments are offered the opportunity to order under the state's contracts to satisfy their own needs.

Formal (sealed and advertised) bids are required for all procurements of $15,000 or more, to include both newspaper advertising and Information for Bid (IFB) solicitations—mailed to registered vendors. Procurements between $2,500 and $14,999 need not be advertised but will be solicited from those on the Vendor's List. In both cases the bids will be opened publicly and awards made to the lowest responsive and responsible bidders.

For procurements less than $2,500 Requests for Quotations (RFQs) will be sent out to registered vendors and informal written bids can be accepted. And for those procurements under $500 oral bids are acceptable.

Requests for Proposals (RFPs) are used also when the sealed-bid procedure is inappropriate to the procurement, and the familiar processes of proposal evaluation, selection, and negotiation follow.

KANSAS: Department of Administration, Division of Purchasing, State Office Building, Topeka, KS 66612, (913) 296-2376

Kansas furnished little information regarding any aspect of its state purchasing and procurement functions, other than to identify its purchasing office. However, there may be some literature available by the time you read this, if it follows the general trend extant.

KENTUCKY: Finance and Administration Cabinet, Department for Administration, Division of Purchases, 348 Capitol Annex, Frankfort, KY 40601, (502) 564-4510

Procurements of over $1,000 are required to be made via sealed bids and public openings under Kentucky law. Procurements less than $1,000 may be made under small-purchase procedures, and procurements over $10,000 must be advertised in at least two widely circulated Kentucky newspapers.

Kentucky makes a comprehensive *Bidders Application Packet* available to applicants who wish to register as vendors and advises that it has a comprehensive manual of instructions for evaluating proposals, which the Division of Purchases often solicits for procurements requiring negotiation, rather than bids.

LOUISIANA: Division of Administration, State Purchasing, One American Place (Waterside Mall Entrance), Plaza West, POB 44095, Baton Rouge, LA 70804, (504) 342-4441

A request to the above office will bring you a copy of Louisiana's *Vendor's Guide, How to do Business with the State of Louisiana*, which furnishes detailed information about state government procurement. As do most other purchasing offices, this one urges personal visits by prospective suppliers and adds that it is helpful to bring along price lists, photographs, samples, specifications, and anything else that will help state purchasing officials review and evaluate the goods and services you offer.

Louisiana has a lengthy and highly detailed commodities list, describing some 200 supply classes and as many as 60 items within a class. Computers and computer-related goods and services are therefore covered under several classes of supply, such as consulting, leasing, maintenance, office equipment and supplies, and others.

Procurements expected to run over $5,000 must be made via bids solicited from at least eight vendors.

MAINE: Department of Finance and Administration, Bureau of Purchases, State Office Building, State House Station 9, Augusta, ME 04333, (207) 289-3521

Maine's Bureau of Purchases is empowered by law to do all purchasing for Maine's agencies, but may also delegate purchase authority to the agencies, if and as necessary and justified. Small purchase policy is limited to purchases not more than $250, and with written authorization to make the purchase such purchases may be made on the open market.

The commodities purchased regularly by the Bureau of Purchases are purchased on fixed schedules, described in the state's vendor brochure, *How to do Business with Maine*, issued by the Bureau. The brochure describes some 125 supply classes and anticipates that agencies will contract out independently for services.

MARYLAND: Department of General Services, Purchasing Bureau, 301 West Preston Street, Baltimore, MD 21201, (301) 383-3573

Maryland has four principal procurement authorities. The other three (other than that listed above, that is) are these:

Department of General Services
Department of Transportation
Department of Budget and Fiscal Planning

Advertising bids by the state purchasing bureaus in Maryland is done by publishing the announcements in the *Maryland Register*, an official state publication, analogous to the federal government's *Federal Register*. Subscriptions to the *Maryland Register* at the time of this writing are $50 per year and are ordered by addressing a request and check as follows:

Circulation Manager
MARYLAND REGISTER
Division of State Documents
POB 802, Annapolis, MD 21404

Procurements are made via competitive sealed bids, competitive negotiation, small-purchase procedures, and sole-source (non-competitive) procurement when justified. Contracts over $25,000 must be advertised in the *Maryland Register* for at least 30 days before the bid-opening date, but many contracts less than $25,000 must also be advertised. Contract awards must be listed in the *Maryland Register* also, to furnish leads for subcontracting opportunities.

A list of the state's purchasing agents for the school systems of each of Maryland's 24 counties and another listing of some 300 other state agencies, boards, and commissions are available on request.

MASSACHUSETTS: Purchasing Division. McCormack State Office Building, One Ashburton Place, Room 1011, Boston, MA, 02108, (617) 727-2882

The Commonwealth of Massachusetts has an active and well-organized procurement system, with a large number of vendors and customers in the commonwealth. The excellent vendor's manual offered suppliers, *How to do Business with the State*, is unusually well done and highly informative.

Massachusetts buys as most states do, with both single-purchase and term contracts. State agencies may issue purchase orders for purchases under $500; purchases above that amount must follow bid procedures. One basic, relevant policy is this: For soliciting professional services with a maximum obligation of $40,000 or more formal proposals are required, solicited from at least three qualified vendors.

Massachusetts maintains an active Business Service Center to assist suppliers. It is part of the Massachusetts Department of Commerce and is located at 100 Cambridge Street, Boston, Massachusetts 02202. A free hot line is available, too: 1-800-632-8181.

A lengthy list of state agencies (approximately 200) that are to at least some degree independent in their purchasing authority (and some of whom are entirely independent in purchasing authority) is available also.

MICHIGAN: Department of Management and Budget, Purchasing Division, Stevens T. Mason Building, 2nd Floor, POB 30026, Lansing, MI 48909, (517) 373-0330

A vendor's guide brochure is available from the above office, and it is quite complete in the information it offers, despite its modest size. A commodity list of some 1,000 items in over 50 supply groups is also available to vendors.

Purchases of $4,000 or more must be made by formal, sealed bids; those of lesser amount may be on an "open bid" or informal basis. That is, the latter kind of bid may be opened immediately on receipt, and does not require the formality of public opening at a preannounced time and place. Both types of bid are solicited by an Request for Quotation (RFQ).

Term contracts are used for most commodities, and a list of contracts is published for the use of all state agencies, which are instructed to order from those for appropriate procurements. For procurement of items not covered by the existing contracts the agencies must order through the Purchasing Division (unless the agency is specifically exempted), except for purchases not more than $400. Among the several buying units is one (Unit 9) designated specifically for data processing. However, certain relevant items, such as books, tab cards, office furniture, magazines, office machines, office supplies, and paper, are listed for other units.

MINNESOTA: Department of Administration, Division of Procurement, 50 Sherburn Avenue, St. Paul, MN 55155, (612) 296-6152

Small purchases in Minnesota are those up to $500. Above that amount newspaper advertising and sealed bids and/or negotiations are required to make procurements. Although the Division of Procurement does buy for the state's agencies, many of the state's agencies do buy independently and/or make purchase requests to the Division of Purchasing, identifying specific sources of supply for the requested purchases. (This makes it advisable to market directly to these agencies, of course.)

MISSISSIPPI: Commission of Budget and Accounting, Division of Purchase Supervision, 902 Walter Sillers Building, Jackson, MS 39202, (601) 354-7107

Mississippi does not operate a central purchasing office as such, but advises that the above-named office supervises purchasing by the agencies and institutions within the state. The division includes among its functions such tasks as coordinating and consolidating purchasing or arranging for cooperative purchasing to take advantages of the benefits that can be derived therefrom, and ensuring that pertinent Mississippi statutes are observed when making purchases. These include the requirement that purchases over $1,500 must be advertised and made by formal competitive methods. Purchases of less than $500 may be made by small-purchase procedures, and those between $500 and $1,500 may be made without advertising if at least two competitive written bids are obtained.

A procurement manual was being written at the time this information was provided and should be available by the time you read this.

MONTANA: Department of Administration, Purchasing Division, Mitchell Building, Room 165, Helena, MT 59620, (406) 449-2575

Montana reports annual spending by the Purchasing Division for supplies and services in excess of $52 million. (Whether this does or does not include the various procurement budgets of all the state agencies served by the Purchasing Division is not made clear.) In-state suppliers are given a 3-point preference over out-of-state suppliers, a practice followed in several states, although not always announced in brochures.

Procurements of $2,000 or more must be advertised in three in-state newspapers, at least one of them a daily publication. Bids under that amount do not require advertising, but both must be by sealed bids and public openings.

State agencies may make competitive purchases of less than $200 for items not available under existing state term contracts. Term contracts are normally entered into for computer magnetic tape, continuous paper, tab cards, and other related items.

NEBRASKA: Department of Administrative Services, State Purchasing Bureau, 301 Centennial Mall, South, POB 94847, Lincoln, NE 68509

Nebraska offers a publication, *Nebraska Procurement Manual for Vendors*, and invites all interested vendors to compete for its business. Vendors must register for inclusion on bid lists to receive solicitations, although they may make bids without being formally registered, the manual advises; that is, notices of all goods and services required are posted at offices of the State Purchasing Bureau and vendors may visit and examine these listings and postings.

The procedures are typical, favoring formal, sealed bids and/or negotiation for all except small purchases.

NEVADA: Department of General Services, Purchasing Division, 205 Blasdel Building, Carson City, NV 89701, (702) 885-4070

Nevada reports annual expenditures of over $35 million for central purchasing. Procurements are advertised in local newspapers and solicitations sent out to those on appropriate bidders' lists. The figure cited does not include the procurement budgets of the various state agencies, which must place their procurement orders through the Purchasing Division.

NEW HAMPSHIRE: Department of Administration and Control, Division of Purchase and Property, State House Annex, Concord, NH 03301, (603) 271-2700

New Hampshire offers a comprehensive *Manual of Procedure* to prescribe purchasing procedures to purchasing division personnel and to vendors who wish to do business with the state. The manual covers New Hampshire procurement law and regulations, purchasing procedures and requirements, commodities normally purchased, and other useful data, such as names and telephone numbers of buyers in the division.

Purchases of $500 or more are generally made by sealed bids, with formal public openings and awards to the lowest responsible bidders. Procurements under $500 may be made by soliciting quotations and selecting an awardee.

Many commodities are bought on term contracts, and these are scheduled for various times throughout the year.

NEW JERSEY: Department of the Treasury, Purchase Bureau, CN 230, State House, Trenton, NJ 08625, (609) 292-4700

The Purchase Bureau reports an annual procurement budget of over $425 million to buy supplies and services for all the state's agencies. As in the case of other states, local governments may utilize state term contracts for their own purchasing. In fact, the state reports that some 1,427 user agencies had made such cooperative purchases at the time this information was supplied, representing additional expenditures of some $460 million through state contracts.

As in many other states, vendors are required to register by filling out a bidders' application form, available from the Purchase Bureau on request.

Purchases over $2,500 must be made via the advertised and sealed-bid processes, using local newspapers to make the announcements of solicitation. Purchases under this amount may be made by telephone requests to registered vendors. Out-of-state corporations wishing to do business with the Bureau must register as foreign corporations with the New Jersey Secretary of State.

Other agencies may buy independently, issuing their own purchase orders against the existing term contracts, and under some circumstances may get authority from the Purchase Bureau to make completely independent procurements, using competitive bidding procedures.

NEW MEXICO: Department of Finance and Administration, Purchasing Division, Lamy Building, Santa Fe, NM 87503, (505) 827-2626

New Mexico has a brochure for you, *How to do Business with the State of New Mexico*, several forms for registering as a vendor and applying for inclusion on bidders lists, and information that the state charges a $58 registration fee to cover the costs of issuing solicitations.

In-state suppliers are given a 5-point preference over out-of-state suppliers. Single purchases up to $1,000 may be made by small-purchase procedures, purchases to $1,500 using only three oral bids, and purchases over $1,500 up to $2,500 only under sealed bids. Large purchases require advertising in three newspapers in the state.

A lengthy commodity list is supplied on request, which includes as a supply class: 58 Data Processing Equipment and Supplies and lists under this class the following specific items:

02 Cards, tabulating	04 Data processing accessory equipment
06 Data processing machine supplies	08 Data Processing Machines and systems
10 Data processing machines and systems—RENTL only	12 Data processing services
14 Maintenance and repairs	

NEW YORK: Standards and Purchase Group, Office of General Services, 41st Floor, Tower Building, Empire State Plaza, Albany, NY 12242, (518) 474-6262

New York State's brochure, *How to Sell to New York State*, says, "The State is a good customer. It knows what it wants and it maintains strict standards of quality to protect the taxpayer. It pays promptly, and otherwise maintains a good relationship with its vendors." The brochure reports annual purchases ". . . of over $650 million worth of commodities for State agencies, political subdivisions, private non-profit educational institutions," and others authorized by law. (The figure may be a bit low for today, since it is not a recent one and does not include all state purchasing.)

The state buys in much the same manner that most states do, with term contracts for common-use commodities, special one-time purchases, and open-market purchasing in cases where such purchasing is authorized by law. For purchases up to $500 small-purchase procedures may be used. Purchases ranging from $500 to $1,000 require three bids, and those from $1,000 to $1,500 require five bids. Above that figure special authorization is required.

Typically, the central purchasing authority does all buying of commodities for state agencies and institutions, but for small purchases buying authority may be released to the agency, where justified. However, the agencies all negotiate on their own for services, and you must approach the many agencies and institutions directly to sell services. (A list of well over 500 such agencies and institutions is available.)

The commodity list furnished is lengthy and includes the following items:

Computers/scientific (only)	Computer, micro
Computer, mini	Computer ribbons
Furniture, computer	Micro computers
EDP, labels (unprinted)	Ribbons, computer and computer printer
Ribbons, tabulating and key punch	

NORTH CAROLINA: Department of Administration, Division of Purchase and Contract, 116 West Jones Street, Raleigh, NC 27611, (919) 733-3581

The North Carolina purchasing program employs seven purchasing teams, a purchasing consulting group, a data processing group, and a staff group. Team number 6 buys consulting services and team number 7 buys data processing equipment. Included on that team is one individual whose responsibility is described as "Purchases by local municipalities & other non-state agencies." The Division also has its own internal data processing group.

All purchases in excess of $2,500 must be advertised and made competitive, and RFPs are issued to contract for technical and professional services, such as consulting.

NORTH DAKOTA: Office of Management and Budget, Purchasing Division, State Capitol, Bismarck, ND 58505, (701) 224-2680

Although buying for one of the less-populous states and with a relatively small procurement budget, the Purchasing Division of North Dakota's state government is well organized and operates with well-defined procedures. As in most states, in-state vendors are given preference over out-of-state vendors. Advertising methods are not specified, however, and the principal method of soliciting bids is by mailing invitations out to registered vendors.

Sealed bids may be formal or informal, the distinction being cost: Informal bids without bonds are acceptable for purchases of $1,000 to $5,000. Bids in excess of this must be made via formal procedures, and they require bid bonds of 5 percent and performance bonds of 25 percent. Bids of less than $1,000 may be made orally, by telephone, with written confirmation to follow. Other state agencies are empowered to do their own separate purchasing.

OHIO: Department of Administrative Services, State Purchasing, 364 S. Fourth Street, Columbus, OH 43216, (614) 466-8218

A request to Ohio's purchasing office brings an abundance of information about the purchasing system. Among the basic policies and regulations are these: Purchases of $5,000 or more must be by formal, sealed bids, solicited by mailing bid sets to registered vendors and posting notices on a bulletin board in a public area of the purchasing offices. Purchase authority may be delegated to other agencies, and some agencies are exempt by statute and are thus authorized to buy independently.

The state has been divided into 12 bid districts, and a map of the districts is furnished, with the various state agencies and institutions of each district identified. Eleven of the bid districts are actual geographic areas, but the 12th is a hypothetical subdivision and actually represents the state as a whole, and is identified as the "district" to be served when the purchase is for the state as a whole, rather than for some geographic subdivision.

OKLAHOMA: State Board of Public Affairs, Central Purchasing, State Capitol Building, Room 306, Oklahoma City, OK 73105, (405) 521-2115

Oklahoma's purchasing office furnishes a 236-page manual to vendor applicants, most of which is devoted to listing over 7,000 commodities and services in 191 supply classes, listed both by supply classes and in an alphabetical index. The manual's title is *How to Sell to the State of Oklahoma*, with the subtitle *Partners in Procurement*. Except for those agencies exempted specifically by statute, the purchasing office buys all commodities for the state. However, that the purchasing office considers itself to be the agent of other state agencies, performing a service for them, is clearly indicated by the graphic device on the cover of the manual, three meshing gears, labeled "Agency," "Vendor," and "Central Purchasing."

Four procurement methods are used: open market bids, annual and semiannual term contracts, formal competitive bids (for one-time purchases), and small purchases under emergency conditions, of not more than $750. (Emergency purchases may run to $2,000, if the governor certifies the need in writing.)

Among those who may buy independently are the State Transportation Commission, all state educational institutions, the Department of Corrections, and the University Hospital. However, the purchase of professional services is exempt from the general requirements for competitive bids and awards to low bidders, but the published regulations are less than crystal-clear on exactly what procedures must be followed, and the logical inference is that negotiated procurement methods may be used here.

RHODE ISLAND: Department of Administration, Division of Purchases, 289 Promenade Street, Providence, RI 02908, (401) 277-2321

A brochure titled *A Guide on How to Sell to the State of Rhode Island* is provided to inquirers. The brochure explains the following procurement procedures and policies:

> Formal Bids: Sealed bids with stated opening date and time for public opening in the division's bid room.
> Informal Bids: As above but for small purchases, not necessarily formal public bid openings
> Telephone Bids: Emergency procurements where situation precludes usual procedures.

SOUTH CAROLINA: Budget and Control Board, Division of General Services, Materials Management Office, 800 Dutch Square Boulevard, Suite 150, Columbia, SC 29210, (803) 758-6060

The Materials Management Office spends some $200+ million annually for goods and services for the state agencies. Specifically exempt from procurement via this office and authorized to make purchases independently are the following agencies of the state:

> South Carolina Department of Corrections, Division of Prison Industries
> South Carolina State Ports Authority
> South Carolina Public Railways Commission
> South Carolina Public Service Authority

Procurement policies and statutes provide for both formal, sealed bids, with awards to the lowest bidders, and for negotiated procurement. In-state vendors are given preference, where they are competitive with out-of-state bidders, and contract forms used are fixed-price, cost-reimbursement, one-time purchase, annual supply term contracts, and even multiyear term contracts.

TENNESSEE: Department of General Services, Purchasing Division, C2-211 Central Service Building, Nashville, TN 37219, (615) 741-1035
The State of Tennessee lists thousands of items purchased annually, and furnishes its commodity lists on microfiche. However, it also offers a vendor's guide, *Rule of the Department of General Services Purchasing Division*. The Purchasing Division has supply responsibility, as well as purchasing authority, for the entire state. However, other agencies and institutions may negotiate their own contracts for the purchase of professional services, and the following state agencies and institutions are authorized generally to use the services of the Purchasing Division or to buy autonomously, as they wish:

The General Assembly of the State
The University of Tennessee
The State University and Community College System
The State Technical Institutes

The local governments within the state may purchase through the Purchasing Division also, for both one-time purchases and for term contracts, and/or may utilize the state's contracts to place their own orders.
Purchases not over $2,000 must be by competitive bid, but may be made informally by written or verbal (telephone) means. Purchases above that amount must be made through formal, sealed bids, with public openings and awards to lowest responsible and responsive bidders. Purchases up to $300 are classed as small purchases.

TEXAS: State Purchasing and General Services Commission, Lyndon Baines Johnson State Office Building, POB 13047, Capitol Station, Austin, TX 78711, (512) 475-2211
Except for certain professional and consulting services and a few other exclusions, the commission is the purchasing agent for the entire state. In general, formal competitive is required, under one of the following options:
Open Market Purchases: Bids invited for fixed-quantity, fixed- price purchase, with award to lowest responsive and responsible bidder.
Term Contract Purchase: Supply contract, usually for one year, for common-use commodities at fixed prices, but indefinite quantity. (State agencies issue purchase orders under the basic contract, in much the same manner as the federal supply contracts known as GSA "schedules.")
Multiple Award Contract Purchases: Variant of Term Contract Purchase, wherein there is to be more than one level of performance or more than one supply service, and separate contracts are awarded for each level or service.

UTAH: Department of Administrative Services, Division of Purchasing, 147 State Capitol Building, Salt Lake City, UT 84114, (801) 533-4620
Utah advises that its procurement budget is more than $150 million, exclusive of highway funds, and offers vendors a guidance publication, *Procurement regulations*. Purchases expected to be in excess of $8,000 are

advertised each Monday in the legal-notices columns of the *Salt Lake Tribune* and the *Deseret News*. The favored method of procurement is via formal sealed bids, with public openings and awards to the lowest bidders. However, Utah also uses a multistep sealed-bid method, consisting of unpriced technical proposals followed by sealed bids from those whose proposals were found acceptable, so Utah issues RFPs as well as invitations to bid.

Small purchases are those under $8,000, and are made according to these guidelines:

To $500: Made through expedited procedures, not clearly defined because the regulation simply directs that the contracting official may "adopt operational procedures."

$500 to $2,000: Minimum of two bids, which may be made by telephone.

$2,000 to $8,000: Minimum of two bids, written.

On any of these purchases, up to $5,000, purchase authority may be delegated to the requesting agency.

VERMONT: Agency of Administration, Purchasing Division, 7 School Street, Montpelier, VT 05602, (802) 828-2211

Vermont furnished no information, other than to identify its purchasing office.

VIRGINIA: Department of General Services, Division of Purchases and Supply, 805 East Broad Street, POB 1199, Richmond, VA 23209, (804) 786-3845

Virginia's central purchasing office provides a guidance publication, *Vendor's Manual*, and reports an annual procurement budget of over $400 million, spent to buy some 5,000 individual items of supply in approximately 100 supply classes, and extends a welcome to all prospective new suppliers. The office also recommends that sales efforts be directed to the Director of Purchasing, Virginia's Department of Highways and Transportation (1221 E. Broad Street, Richmond, VA 23219, (804) 786-2801) because that agency does its own purchasing.

The purchasing office reports that it does not buy services for the other state agencies and institutions, although the commodities list does include such items as printing and bookbinding, and in general small purchases (those under $500) do not require their authorization. Moreover, computers and related equipment are purchased for the state through Virginia's Department of Management Analysis and Systems Development. Too, Virginia's publicly operated colleges and universities are exempt and may buy independently with their own purchase orders. General guidelines include these:

Purchases less than $200: Small purchases, may be noncompetitive where justified.

$200 to $500: Informal quotations/bids, verbally or in writing.

$500 to $5,000: May be by unsealed bids on special Virginia form.

$5,000 up: Must be formal, sealed bids.

Other Virginia agencies that make at least some of their purchases independently include these:

Agriculture and Commerce Department	Conservation Department
Economic Development Department	Public Utilities Division
Insurance Division	Consumer Affairs Office
Labor & Industry Department	Arts and Humanities Commission
Taxation Department	

WASHINGTON: Department of General Administration, Purchasing Division, 216 General Administration Building AX-22, Olympia, WA 98504, (206) 753-0900

The Purchasing Division has an annual procurement budget of well over $100 million, but many of the state's agencies and institutions buy independently. The Purchasing Division buys from approximately 10,000 vendors registered with it. (Registration is required, to be placed on the bidders list.)

The Division is divided into four purchasing groups, with Contract Group A and Contract Group B buying items and services relevant to computers and data processing. However, a special file of prequalified individuals and organizations is maintained for the procurement of a variety of technical and professional services, and the following are the relevant contacts to make, in regard to computers and data processing:

For management services: Management Services, Office of Financial Management, 101 House Office Building AL-01, Olympia, WA 98504, (206) 753-5448

For data processing services and equipment: Data Processing Authority, 2604 12th Court, SW FV-11, Olympia, WA 98504

For software and maintenance: Room 25, Office Building 2, Olympia, WA 98504, (206) 753-7277

WEST VIRGINIA: Department of Finance and Administration, Purchasing Division, Capitol Station, POB 5280, Charleston, WV 25311

West Virginia's purchasing office furnishes a small but informative booklet, *Selling to the State of West Virginia*, upon request. The staff of the Division includes a roster of buyers, each of whom is assigned a "File Number." Bids for commodities are solicited via Request for Quotations (RFQs), and Request for Proposals (RFPs) are used to solicit problem-solving and other special services. Purchases over $2,000 must be advertised in the newspaper of the county where the procuring agency is located. Most procurements are made by State Purchase Order, but such purchases as those of consulting and other technical/professional services are made via contracts, which the state refers to as "Agreements."

WISCONSIN: Department of Administration, State Bureau of Procurement, 101 South Webster Street, 6th Floor, POB 7867, Madison, WI 53707

The procurement bureau of Wisconsin uses an automated bidders list and procurement management system, spending over $300 million annually to purchase goods and services for the state. As in the case of other states, many of the state's agencies are authorized to make their purchases independently, and the bureau furnished a list of about 100 such agencies and institutions, along with an extensive commodity list.

WYOMING: Department of Administration and Fiscal Control, Purchasing and Property Control Division, Emerson Building, Room 301, Cheyenne, WY 82002, (307) 777-7523

Wyoming's *Vendor's Guide*, available from the office listed here, advises the reader that Wyoming has five separate purchasing authorities. In addition to the centralized purchasing by the bureau listed here, purchasing authority is extended to the following agencies of the state:

> The Judicial Districts throughout the state
> The Legislative Branch, in Cheyenne
> The Highway Department, in Cheyenne
> The University of Wyoming, in Laramie

The bureau employs seven buyers, one of whom is assigned the purchase of data processing equipment and related supplies. Most purchases are made by state purchase orders, and solicitations are issued in both general forms, invitations to bid, and requests for proposals, and some preference is given to in-state vendors, except when the purchase is made with federal funds.

Miscellaneous Jurisdictions

The following are procurement offices for other United States jurisdictions, local governments that are not states, counties, cities, towns, or townships.

DISTRICT OF COLUMBIA: Bureau of Material Management, Department of General Services, 613 G Street, NW, Washington, DC 20001, (202) 629-5014

AMERICAN SAMOA: Department of Purchases, Government House, Pago Pago, Samoa 96799 (684)633-4116

GUAM: Procurement and Supply, Department of Administration, Agana, Guam 96910

PUERTO RICO: Purchases and Supply Services, Department of Treasury, Box 2112, San Juan, PR 00903 (809) 723-2789

VIRGIN ISLANDS: Department of Property and Procurement, Government House, St. Thomas, Virgin Islands 00801 (809) 774-0828

Chapter 12

DIRECTORY OF CITY AND COUNTY GOVERNMENT PROSPECTS

The needs of the cities and counties parallel those of the states generally, as do the procurement systems. And in many cases the city and county procurement budgets rival those of the states in size and diversity as well.

A Few Relevant Statistics

There are approximately 125 major urban or metropolitan areas, large cities surrounded by heavily populated suburbs in the United States. There are some 2,500 municipalities of over 10,000 population and approximately 7,000 municipalities of over 2,500 population. And there are also more than 3,000 counties in the United States. Without counting the towns and townships of less than 2,500 population we can count in excess of 12,500 governments within our national borders, all of which purchase goods and services every day. With the enormous procurement budget of the federal government, we are talking about an annual government procurement of goods and services that can be counted in the hundreds of billions of dollars. In numerals, which are somewhat more expressive in helping us to grasp the enormous size of this overall procurement budget, it would look something like this: $550,000,000,000. And a large part of that total, probably about one-half, or something in excess of $250,000,000,000, represents the annual procurement of goods and services by the local governments or over 99 percent of those jurisdictions the Census Bureau refers to as "governmental units."

Obviously, while it is possible to list the major customers of the federal and state governments of our country and provide some fairly detailed guidance information about each, it would be impractical to attempt to present information at that level of detail for all those cities, towns, townships, and counties and still have a book of manageable size. But it is not necessary to do so. Instead, in this chapter there are listed a number of those city/county jurisdictions, with details of their procurement systems and potential as markets, serving as examples of what you may expect typically in such jurisdictions. This chapter therefore begins with presentations of city/county markets on the level of detail followed generally for the states in the preceding chapter and then goes on to list the key addresses for the remaining cities and counties.

Philosophically, at Least, the Systems are Similar

In general, cities and counties follow the same overall pattern to be found among the various state governments: Procurement is primarily by sealed bids as the procurement method of choice. (Purchasing officials usually favor this method whenever it is appropriate and practical to use it because it is the most competitive method and therefore the most effective way to persuade bidders to offer their best prices.) Negotiated procurement is resorted to when circumstances make sealed bids impractical, as when technical competence is at least as much a consideration as cost in influencing the final selection. Most cities and counties, like most cities and states, employ a philosophy of centralized procurement, but recognize the inevitability of authorizing many agencies to do at least some of their purchasing autonomously. The City of Oakland, California, for example, has a centralized purchasing office and a rather comprehensive and complete central purchasing organization, but delegates purchasing authority to 11 agencies in the city nevertheless.

Those agencies most likely to have some independent spending authority for other than routine procurements, such as office supplies and furniture, include highway or public roads agencies (also called transportation departments in many jurisdictions), school districts, utilities (when publicly owned), and airports, although there are many others often found to be authorized at least some independent purchasing authority. This includes public libraries, police departments, fire departments, port authorities, and others whose needs are likely to be so highly specialized as to be virtually unique within that government. Obviously, this will vary considerably, from one local government to another, as it does from one state government to another, as local conditions and local concerns vary.

In counties the purchasing bureau, by whatever name it may be called, is generally found at the county seat, the county's capital, and in cities the purchasing office is generally found in the city hall. Names and ideas about organizational assignments vary widely and a purchasing function may be assigned to someone and/or some office with a title that does not directly suggest the purchasing function. In some cases, for example, purchasing is the responsibility of someone called "Chief of Administration" or "Manager of Services." Generally speaking, if you do not know the formal name of the purchasing office or purchasing official, a letter or inquiry addressed to "Purchasing Office" or "Purchasing Officer" will generally be routed to the proper office and individual.

Some Typical City/County Purchasing Systems

Following are somewhat detailed descriptions of several city and county purchasing organizations and their systems, intended to serve as examples of what you are likely to find in most of the approximately 21,000 cities, towns, townships, and counties of the United States (not to mention the remaining 59,000 "governmental units" the U.S. Census Bureau identifies). But while the examples here are typical, bear in mind that there is also a wide range of differences among all these 21,000 government entities. As in the case of the state governments some of these jurisdictions are quite generous in accommodating your needs, and will offer you extensive literature to help you market your goods and services to their governments, while others will have extremely little to offer as organized information or even reasonably detailed definition of their procurement and purchasing policies. And, as in the case of the states, the amount and scope of the information made available has no apparent relationship to the size of the government or the volume of their annual purchasing. For example, New York and Texas (especially Texas, which not only furnished little information, but was not very cooperative in furnishing even that little) furnished less help than did some relatively small states, such as Massachusetts, which was quite generous and gracious with its help.

In some cases a simple request will bring you all the information you could possibly want, while in other cases you will have to dig extensively to get the information you need. However, each jurisdiction does buy, of course, and they are spending public money, which means that you have a legal right to get information about their purchasing and to participate in bidding for their business.

The lists furnished here are therefore offered as starting points to begin your marketing to these governments and to serve you as examples of what you can expect and/or may pursue in other cities and counties. Bear in mind, in the meanwhile, that most of the literature furnished to me in researching this field—guidance brochures, procurement manuals, commodity lists, procurement regulations, and other such literature—was developed before the advent of the desktop/personal microcomputers, and did not anticipate the changes in computer procurement that would result from this revolutionary development. Be alert, therefore, for relevant deviations from some of the prescribed practices.

OAKLAND, CALIFORNIA: Purchasing Department, 7101 Edgewater Drive, Oakland, CA 94621, (415) 273-3521

The City of Oakland Purchasing Department buys for the following agencies:

Office of Public Works	Office of General Services
Office of Parks and Recreation	Office of Community Development
Social Services Department	Housing Department
Library Department	Oakland Museum
Police Department	Fire Department
Data Processing Department	Finance Department

On the other hand, all the following agencies buy independently, and each of them has its own purchasing department, which you should contact directly:

Oakland Unified School District
Oakland Housing Authority
Bay Area Rapid Transit System (BART)
Pacific Gas & Electric Co. (gas and electricity)
County of Alameda (general incl. hospitals)

Oakland/Alameda County Coliseum
Port of Oakland and Airport
East Bay Municipal Utility District (Water)
Alameda-Contra Costa Transit (bus transportation)
East Bay Regional Park District

Oakland Scavenger Co.

The Oakland purchasing organization has as its objective maximizing competition and making awards to the lowest responsible bidders. For purchases less than $1,000, Requests for Quotations (RFQs) are sent out to vendors and oral bids (usually via telephone) are accepted. Above that amount, up to $15,000, written bids are required. And for purchases in excess of $15,000 the procurement is advertised in local newspapers, formal specifications are mailed to vendors, and bids are opened publicly every Monday at 2.00 P.M. by the City Clerk in Room 306, Oakland City Hall, 14th and Washington Streets.

JACKSONVILLE, FLORIDA: Department of Central Services, Purchasing Division, 220 East Bay Street, Jacksonville, FL 32202, (904) 633-2704

Under Jacksonville's form of government the Purchasing Division buys for the city, the county, the Duval County School Board, and for several other agencies of the jurisdiction. There are three groups of buyers constituting the purchasing staff, and purchases in excess of $8,000 must be made by formal sealed bids. Procedures are not specifically defined by statute for smaller purchases, although a series of Purchasing Bulletins have been issued, describing decisions and prescribing procedures to be followed.

MILWAUKEE, WISCONSIN: Central Board of Purchases, Room 607, City Hall, 200 East Wells Street, Milwaukee, WI 53202, (414) 278-3501

Milwaukee classifies bids over $20,000 as "Formal Bids," and those under that figure as "Informal Bids." Formal Bids are also referred to as "Class A Purchases" and must be awarded by the Central Board of Purchases after using formal sealed bids to find the lowest responsible bidder. The Informal Bids, which are those under $20,000 and referred to also as "Class B Purchases," must also be subjected to the formal sealed bid process, but awards may be made by the City Purchasing Agent.

Preference, in case of tie bids, is given to those who manufacture their goods in the city, those who manufacture in the County of Milwaukee, or are otherwise "local," rather than "foreign" bidders, in an order of priority prescribed by the City.

Other Class B purchases are informal bids referred to as "Buyer Bids," for purchases expected to cost less than $1,000. In these purchases the buyer may make awards and telephone bids may be accepted, under these guide-lines:

$100 to $1,000:   Three or more quotes from vendors
$35 to $100:   Quote from one or more vendors
$35 or less: Petty-cash expenditure (no quote required)

Emergency purchases may run between $1,000 and $20,000, and require that quotes be solicited from at least three vendors.

TULSA, OKLAHOMA: Department of Purchasing, 200 Civic Center, Room 1023, Tulsa, OK 74103, (918) 581-5511
Tulsa spends on the order of $20 million or more annually for centralized purchasing, using formal sealed bids after advertising in the *Tulsa Legal News*, when the purchase is expected to be over $4,000. Informal bids are solicited from at least three sources for procurements less than this.

DALLAS, TEXAS: Department of Purchasing, City Hall, 1500 Marilla Street, Dallas, TX 75201, (214) 670-3326
The Dallas centralized purchasing office spends some $40 million annu-ally for goods and services, exclusive of construction contracts. Purchases in excess of $2,000 must be advertised in one of the city's daily newspapers. The Director of Purchasing may approve purchases up to $2,000. The City Manager may approve purchases up to $10,000. And the City Council must approve larger purchases. Moreover, the City Council must also approve the advertising notices when the purchase is to be in excess of $100,000.
The Dallas commodity list covers more than 1,000 items of goods and services, many of the latter in technical/professional categories of many kinds.

SAN DIEGO, CALIFORNIA: Purchasing Department, City Opera-tions Building, 1222 1st Avenue, San Diego, CA 92101, (714) 236-6210
San Diego's annual budget for centralized purchasing is approximately $45 million. The Purchasing Department operates with a staff of eight buyers and an assistant purchasing agent, who buy from a commodity list of several hundred commodity supply groups. All purchases of $5,000 or more are advertised in the San Diego *Daily Transcript*, the City's official newspaper, and bid competitively.

NEW YORK CITY: Department of General Services, Office of Vendor Relations, Room 1919, Municipal Building, 1 Centre Street, New York, NY 10007, (212) 566-3062
New York City, not surprisingly, is a market for a wide array of goods and services, spending more than $350 million annually in such procure-ments. The City furnishes vendor-applicants a brochure, *How to do Business with New York City, A Vendor's Guide*, and urges vendors to apply to the address listed here for a form issued to register and qualify you as a vendor and place your name on the bidder's list. The publication assures the reader that New York City is constantly seeking new and additional sources of supply and is most receptive to offers from vendors.

Two kinds of contracts are offered: Formal Contracts are used for purchases of $10,000 or more, and Open Market Contracts are used for smaller purchases. In some cases, prebid conferences are held.

In addition to being placed on the bidder's list to receive bid solicitations by mail you may subscribe to New York City's official publication, *The City Record*, which lists bid proposals from all the city agencies and/or you may visit the Bid Room (Room 1911, Municipal Building), where copies of all bid proposals are posted for your inspection.

Local (New York City) vendors are given a preference of up to 5 percent in determining the lowest bid. (To qualify for this the vendor must have a New York City business address and be a New York taxpayer.)

At least nine other city agencies do their own purchasing, independently, and it is advisable to market to these agencies directly and separately:

Board of Education
44th Road & Vernon Blvd
Long Island City, NY 11101

Board of Higher Education
535 East 80th Street
New York, NY 10021

Transit Authority
25 Chapel Street
Brooklyn, NY 11201

Port of New York Authority
1 World Trade Center, Suite 73N
New York, NY 10048

Housing Authority
250 Broadway, Room 707
New York, NY 10007

Health and Hospitals Corporation
125 Worth Street
New York, NY 10013

Triboro Bridge & Tunnel Authority
Randall's Island
New York, NY 10035

Off-Track Betting Corp.
1501 Broadway
New York, NY 10036

Bureau of Water Resources Development
1250 Broadway
New York, NY 10001

CLEVELAND, OHIO: Department of Finance, Division of Purchasing, Room 128, City Hall, 601 Lakeside Avenue, Cleveland, OH 44114, (216) 664-2620

The City of Cleveland spends approximately $200 milllion annually for centrally purchased goods and services. All purchases expected to exceed $3,500 must be advertised in the *City Record*.

WASHINGTON, DC: Department of General Services, Bureau of Materiel Management, 613 G Street, NW, Room 1001, Washington, DC 20001, (202) 727-1000

Washington's commodity list identifies about 250 supply classes and about 6,000 individual items of goods and services purchased by the City, for an estimated annual total of approximately $300 million (exclusive of about $300 million more for construction contracts).

Many of the City's agencies buy independently, and each of the following has its own designated purchasing agent:

Office of Consumer Protection
Office of Administrative Services, Personnel Office
Office of Inspector General
Council of the District of Columbia
Department of Licenses, Investigations, and Inspections
DC Court of Appeals, DC Courthouse
Office of Business and Economic Development
Board of Education, DC Public Schools
Department of Housing and Community Development
Material Support and Contracts Division
DC National Guard, USPFODC
Public Defender Services
Public Library
Office of the People's Counsel
Department of Recreation
University of the District of Columbia
DC Commission on Judicial Disabilities and Tenure
DC Bail Agency
Executive Office of the Mayor
Rental Accommodation Office
Department of Transportation
Armory Board

Office of Human Rights
Office of Emergency Preparedness

Office of the City Administrator
Board of Appeals and Review
Office of Documents

Office of the Corporation Counsel

Department of Corrections

Board of Elections

Department of Environmental Services
Department of Finance and Revenue

DC Court System
Fire Department
Department of General Services
Department of Employment Services
Board of Public Employee Relations
Metropolitan Police Department

Department of Insurance

Board of Parole
Commission for Women
Office of the Surveyor
Office of the District of Columbia Auditor
Public Service Commission
Metropolitan Police Department

MEMPHIS, TENNESSEE: Division of Finance & Administration, Purchasing Agent, Room 304, City Hall, 125 North Main Street, Memphis, TN 38103, (901) 528-2683

Purchases over $2,000 for the City of Memphis must be made by formal contracts, after advertising notices are run for three days in the *Memphis Daily News*, with solicitations also mailed to appropriate vendors. Purchases under $500 may be made informally, after verbal (telephone) solicitations and quotes, or informally by written quotations for purchases between these two figures. Several agencies are authorized to buy independently, including the City School System; City of Memphis hospitals; the Memphis Light, Gas, and Water Division; and all Shelby County government agencies, including the Sheriff's Department, the City/County Health Department, and the Library System.

Municipalities

Following is a list of about 800 municipalities, most of them over 25,000 population. The list is alphabetical, by states and municipalities, with population figures noted for each municipality, following the zip code. Where street addresses are given they are generally those of city or town halls. Address inquiries to the city or town and purchasing offices or purchasing agents at the addresses or box numbers given, with requests for information. However, as in the case of the state purchasing offices, most purchasing agents recommend making visits to meet the buyers personally, and you should follow up inquiries with visits when possible.

Alabama

Anniston 36201 (32,000)
POB 670

Bessemer 35020 (33,000)
1800 3rd Avenue North

Birmingham 3203 (301,000)
City Hall

Decatur 35602 (38,000)
POB 488

Dothan 36301 (37,000)
POB 2128

Florence 35630 (34,000)
POB 98

Gadsden 35902 (54,000)
POB 267

Huntsville 35804 (138,000)
308 Fountain Row

Mobile 36601 (190,000)
POB 1827

Montgomery 36102 (133,000)
POB 1111

Prichard 36610 (42,000)
POB 10427

Tuscaloosa 35401 (66,000)
2201 University Blvd

Alaska

Anchorage 99701 (15,000)
Pouch 6-650

Fairbanks 99701 (15,000)
410 Cushman Street

Juneau 99801 (14,000)
155 S. Seward Street

Arizona

Flagstaff 86001 (26,000)
POB 1208

Glendale 85311 (36,000)
POB 1556

Mesa 85201 (63,000)
POB 1466

Phoenix 85003 (582,000)
251 West Washington Street

Scottsdale 85251 (68,000)
3939 Civic Center Plaza

Tempe 85281 (63,000)
POB 5002

Tucson 85703 (263,000)
POB 5547

Yuma 85364 (29,000)
180 First Street

Arkansas

El Dorado 71730 (25,000)
City Hall

Fayetteville 72701 (31,000)
Drawer F

Fort Smith 72901 (63,000)
POB 1908

Little Rock 72201 (132,000)
500 West Markham Street

North Little Rock 72114 (60,000)
3rd and Main Streets

Pine Bluff 71601 (57,000)
200 East 8th Street

California

Alameda 94501 (71,000)
Oak and Santa Clara Streets

Alhambra 91801 (62,000)
111 South First Street

Anaheim 92803 (43,000)
POB 3222

Arcadia 91006 (43,000)
240 West Huntington Drive

Bakersfield 93301 (70,000)
City Hall

Baldwin Park 91706 (47,000)
1 Civic Center

Bellflower 90706 (51,000)
9838 East Belmont

Berkeley 94704 (117,000)
2180 Milvia Street

Beverly Hills 90210 (33,000)
450 North Crescent Drive

Buena Park 90620 (64,000)
6650 Beach Boulevard

Burbank 91502 (89,000)
275 East Olive Avenue

Carson 90745 (71,000)
21919 South Avalon Boulevard

Chula Vista 92012 (68,000)
POB 1087

Comptom 90224 (79,000)
600 North Alameda Avenue

Concord 94519 (85,000)
1950 Parkside Drive

Costa Mesa 92626 (73,000)
POB 1200

Covina 91723 (30,000)
125 East College Street

Culver City 90230 (35,000)
POB 507

Cypress 90630 (31,000)
5275 Orange Avenue

Downey 90241 (88,000)
8425 Second Street

El Cajon 9202 (52,000)
200 East Main Street

El Monte 91734 (70,000)
11333 Valley Boulevard

Escondido 92025 (54,000)
100 Valley Boulevard

Fairfield 94533 (44,000)
1000 Webster Street

Fountain Valley 92708 (32,000)
10200 Slater Avenue

Fremont 94538 (101,000)
39700 Civic Center drive

Fresno 93721 (166,000)
2326 Fresno Street

Fullerton 92632
303 West Commonwealth Avenue

Gardena 90247 (41,000)
1700 West 162nd Street

Garden Grove 92640 (123,000)
11391 Acacia Parkway

Glendale 91205 (133,000)
613 East Broadway

Glendora 91740 (31,000)
249 East Foothill Boulevard

Hawthorne 90250 (53,000)
4460 West 126th Street

Hayward 94541 (93,000)
22300 Foothill Boulevard

Huntington Beach 92648 (116,000)
POB 190

Huntington Park 90255 (34,000)
6550 Miles Avenue

Inglewood 90301 (90,000)
1 Manchester Boulevard

La Habra 90631 (41,000)
Civic Center

La Mesa 92041 (39,000)
8130 Allison Avenue

La Mirada 90638 (31,000)
13700 La Mirada Boulevard

La Puente 91744 (31,000)
15900 East Main Street

Lakewood (0714 (83,000)
5050 Clark Avenue

Livermore 94550 (38,000)
2250 First Street

Lodi 95240 (32,000)
221 West Pine Street

Long Beach 90802 (359,000)
333 West Ocean

Los Angeles 90012 (2,816,000)
200 North Spring Street

Lynwood 90262 (43,000)
11330 Bullis Road

Manhattan Beach 90262 (35,000)
1400 Highland Avenue

Merced 95340 (30,000)
POB 2068

Modesto 96353 (30,000)
POB 642

Monrovia 91016 (30,000)
415 South Ivy Avenue

Montebello 90640 (43,000)
1600 Beverly Boulevard

Monterey Park 91745 (49,000)
320 West Newmark Avenue

Mountain View 94042 (51,000)
POB 10

Napa 94558 (36,000)
POB 660

National City 92050 (43,000)
1243 National Avenue

Newport Beach 92663 (49,000)
3300 Newport Boulevard

Norwalk 90650 (92,000)
12700 Norwalk Boulevard

Novata 94947 (31,000)
POB 578

Oakland 94621 (362,000)
7101 Edgewater Drive

Oceanside 92054 (40,000)
706 3rd Street

Ontario 91761 (64,000)
222 South Euclid Avenue

Orange 92666 (77,000)
300 East Chapman Avenue

Oxnard 93030 (71,000)
225-305 West Third Street

Pacifica 94044 (36,000)
170 Santa Maria Avenue

Palm Springs 92262 (50,000)
POB 1786

Palo Alto 94301 (56,000)
250 Hamilton Avenue

Paramount 90723 (35,000)
16420 Colorado Avenue

Pasadena 91009 (113,000)
100 North Garfield Avenue

Petaluma 94951 (25,000)
Post and English Streets

Pico Rivera 90660 (54,000)
6615 Passons Boulevard)

Pleasantown 94566 (32,000)
200 Bernal Avenue

Pomona 91766 (87,000)
POB 660

Rancho Palos Verdes 90274 (40,000)
30940 Hawthorne Boulevard

Redlands 92373 (36,000)
POB 280

Redondo Beach 90277 (56,000)
425 Diamond Street

Redwood City 94064 (56,000)
POB 468

Richmond 94804 (79,000)
27th Street and Barrett Avenue

Riverside 92522 (155,000)
3900 Main Street

Rosemead 91770 (41,000)
8838 East Valley Boulevard

Sacramento 95814 (254,000)
915 I Street

Salinas 93901 (59,000)
200 Lincoln Avenue

San Bernardino 92418 (104,000)
300 North D. Street

San Bruno 94066 (39,000)
567 El Camino Real

San Buenaventura 93001 (56,000)
POB 99

San Diego 92101 (697,000)
1222 First Avenue

San Francisco 94102 (716,000)
400 Van Ness Avenue

San Gabriel 91778 (30,000)
POB 130

San Jose 95110 (446,000)
801 North First Street

San Leandro 94577 (69,000)
835 East 14th Street

San Mateo 94403 (79,000)
330 West 20th Avenue

San Rafael 94901 (39,000)
1400 Fifth Avenue

Santa Ana 92701 (157,000)
20 Civic Center Plaza

Santa Barbara 93102 (88,000)
POB P-P

Santa Clara 95050 (88,000)
1500 Warburton Avenue

Santa Cruz 95060 (32,000)
809 Center Street

Santa Maria 93454 (33,000)
110 East Cook Street

Santa Monica 90401 (88,000)
1685 Main Street

Santa Rosa 95403 (50,000)
POB 1678

Seaside 93955 (36,000)
440 Harcourt Avenue

Simi Valley 93065 (56,000)
3200 Cochran Street

South Gate 90280 (57,000)
8650 California Avenue

South San Francisco 94080 (47,000)
POB 711

Stockton 95202 (108,000)
425 North El Dorado Street

Sunnyvale 94086 (95,000)
456 West Olive Avenue

Thousand Oaks 91360 (36,000)
401 West Hillcrest Drive

Torrance 90503 (135,000)
3031 Torrance Boulevard

Upland 91786 (33,000)
POB 460

Vallejo 94590 (67,000)
555 Santa Clara Street

Visalia 93277 (35,000)
707 West Acequia Street

Walnut Creek 94596 (40,000)
1445 Civic Drive

West Covina 91790 (68,000)
POB 1440

Westminster 92683 (60,000)
8200 Westminster Avenue

Whittier 90602 (73,000)
13230 Penn Street

Colorado

Arvada 80002 (47,000)
8101 Ralson Road

Aurora 80012 (75,000)
1470 Emporia Street

Boulder 80302 (67,000)
POB 791

Colorado Springs 80901 (135,000)
POB 1575

Denver 80202 (515,000)
1437 Bannock Street

Englewood 80110 (34,000)
3400 South Eluti

Fort Collins 80522 (43,000)
POB 580

Grand Junction 81501 (20,000)
POB 968

Greeley 80632 (39,000)
Civic Center Complex

Lakewood 80228 (93,000)
44 Union Boulevard

Northglenn 80233 (32,000)
10701 Melody Drive

Pueblo 81001 (97,000)
One City Hall Plaza

Wheat Ridge 80033 (30,000)
POB 610

Connecticut

Bridgeport 06604 (157,000)
45 Lyon Terrace B

Bristol 06010 (55,000)
111 North Main Street

Danbury 06810 (51,000)
155 Deer Hill Avenue

East Hartford 06108 (58,000)
740 Main Street

Enfield 06082 (46,000)
820 Enfield Street

Fairfield 06430 (56,000)
610 Old Post Road

Greenwich 06830 (60,000)
Greenwich Avenue

Groton 06340 (39,000)
295 Meridian Street

Hamden 06518 (49,000)
2372 Whitney Avenue

Hartford 06103 (158,000)
550 Main Street

Manchester 06040 (48,000)
41 Center Street

Meridien 06450 (56,000)
142 East Main Street

Middletown 06457 (37,000)
POB 141

Milford 06460 (51,000)
River Street

New Britain 06051 (83,000)
27 West Main Street

New Haven 06508 (130,000)
City Hall

New London 06320 (32,000)
181 Captain's Walk

Norwalk 06856 (79,000)
41 North Main Street

Norwich 06360 (41,000)
City Hall

Southington 06489 (31,000)
Main Street

Stamford 06904 (109,000)
429 Atlantic Street

Stratford 06497 (50,000)
2725 Main Street

Torrington 06790 (32,000)
140 Main Street

Trumbull 06611 (31,000)
5866 Main Street

Wallingford 06492 (36,000)
350 Center Street

Waterbury 06702 (108,000)
236 Grand Street

West Hartford 06107 (68,000)
28 South Main Street

West Haven 06516 (53,000)
355 Main Street

Delaware

Dover 19901 (17,000)
POB 475

Wilmington 19801 (80,000)
800 French Street

District of Columbia

Washington 20004 (757,000)
14th and E Streets, NW

Florida

Clearwater 33618 (52,000)
POB 4748

Coral Gables 33134 (42,000)
405 Biltmore Way

Daytona Beach 32015 (45,000)
POB 551

Fort Lauderdale 33302 (140,000)
POB 14250

Gainesville 33602 (65,000)
POB 490

Hialeah 33011 (102,000)
POB 40

Hollywood 33022 (107,000)
POB 2207

Jacksonville 32202 (529,000)
220 East Bay Street

Key West 33040 (28,000)
POB 1550

Lakeland 33802 (42,000)
City Hall

Melbourne 32901 (40,000)
900 East Strawbridge Avenue

Miami 333133 (335,000)
3500 Pan American Drive

Miami Beach 33139 (87,000)
505 17th Street

North Miami 33161 (35,000)
776 NE 125th Street

North Miami Beach 33162 (31,000)
17011 NE 19th Avenue

Orlando 32801 (99,000)
400 South Orange Avenue

Panama City 32401 (32,000)
9 Harrison Avenue

Pensacola 32521 (60,000)
POB 12910

Pompano Beach 33061 (38,000)
POB 1300

St. Petersburg 33731 (216,000)
POB2842

Sarasota 33577 (40,000)
1565 First Street

Tallahassee 32304 (72,000)
City Hall

Tampa 33602 (278,000)
315 East Kennedy Boulevard

Titusville 32780 (31,000)
555 South Washington Avenue

West Palm Beach 33402 (57,000)
POB 3366

Georgia

Albany 31702 (73,000)
POB 447

Athens 30601 (44,000)
City Hall

Atlanta 30303 (497,000)
68 Mitchell Street, SW

Augusta 30902 (60,000)
Municipal Building

Columbus 31902 (154,000)
POB 1340

East Point 30344 (39,000)
2777 East Point Street

Macon 31202 (122,000)
City Hall

Rome 30161 (31,000)
POB 1433

Savannah 31402 (118,000)
POB 1027

Valdosta 31601 (32,000)
POB 1125

Warner Robbins 31093 (33,000)
POB 1488

Hawaii

Honolulu 96813 (325,000)
530 South King Street

Idaho

Boise 83702 (75,000)
POB 500

Idaho Falls 83401 (36,000)
POB 220

Lewiston 83501 (26,000)
1134 F Street

Pocatello 83201 (40,000)
POB 4169

Illinois

Alton 62002 (40,000)
101 East Third Street

Arlington Heights 60005 (65,000)
333 South Arlington Heights Road

Aurora 60504 (74,000)
44 East Downer Place

Belleville 62220 (42,000)
101 South Illinois Street

Berwyn 60402 (53,000)
6700 West 26th Street

Bloomington 61701 (40,000)
109 East Olive street

Calumet City 60409 (33,000)
204 Pulaski Road

Champaign 61820 (57,000)
102 North Neill Street

Chicago 60602 (3,367,000)
121 North LaSalle Street

Chicago Heights 60411 (41,000)
1601 Chicago Road

Cicero 60650 (67,000)
4937 West 25th Street

Danville 61832 (43,000)
402 North Hazel Street

Decatur 62523 (90,000)
707 East Wood Street

De Kalb 60115 (33,000)
200 South Fourth Street

Des Plaines 60018 (57,000)
1412 Miner Street

Downers Grove 60515 (33,000)
801 Burlington Avenue

East St. Louis 62201 (70,000)
7 Collinsville Avenue

Elgin 60120 (56,000)
150 Dexter Court

Elmhurst 60126 (51,000)
119 Schiller Street

Evanston 60204 (80,000)
2100 Ridge Avenue

Galesburg 61401 (36,000)
City Hall

Granite City 62040 (40,000)
2000 Edison Avenue

Harvey 60426 (35,000)
15320 Broadway

Highland Park 60035 (32,000)
1707 St. Johns Avenue

Hoffman Estates 60172 (32,000)
1200 North Gannon Drive

Joliet 60435 (80,000)
150 West Jefferson Street

Kankakee 60901 (31,000)
385 East Oak Street

Lombard 60148 (36,000)
48 North Park Avenue

Maywood 60153 (30,000)
115 South Fifth Avenue

Moline 61265 (46,000)
619 16th Street

Mount Prospect 60056 (46,000)
100 South Emerson Street

Niles 60648 (31,000)
7601 Milwaukee Avenue

Normal 61761 (31,000)
124 North Street

North Chicago 60064 (47,000)
1850 Lewis Avenue

Oak Lawn 60453 (60,000)
5252 West James Street

Oak Park 60301 (63,000)
Village Hall Plaza

Park Forest 60466 (31,000)
200 Forest Boulevard

Park Ridge 60068 (42,000)
505 Park Place

Pekin 61554 (31,000)
City Hall

Peoria 61602 (127,000)
419 Fulton Street

Quincy 62301 (45,000)
507 Vermont Street

Rockford 61104 (147,000)
425 East State Street

Rock Island 61201 (50,000)
1528 Third Avenue

Schaumberg 60193 (37,000)
101 Schaumberg Court

Skokie 60067 (69,000)
5127 Oakton Street

Springfield 62701 (92,000)
Municipal Building

Urbana 61801 (33,000)
400 South Vine Street

Waukegan 60085 (65,000)
106 North Utica Street

Wheaton 60187 (31,000)
303 West Wesley Street

Wilmette 60091 (32,000)
1200 Wilmette Avenue

Indiana

Anderson 46011 (71,000)
POB 2100

Bloomington 47401 (43,000)
Municipal Building

East Chicago 46514 (43,000)
4527 Indianapolis Boulevard

Elkhart 46514 (43,000)
Municipal Building

Evansville 47708 (139,000)
302 Civic Center Complex

Fort Wayne 46802 (178,000)
City-County Building

Gary 46902 (175,000)
City Hall

Hammond 46320
5925 Calumet Avenue

Indianapolis 46204 (745,000)
200 East Washington Street

Kokomo 46901 (44,000)
City Building

Lafayette 47901 (45,000)
20 North Sixth Street

Marion 46952 (40,000)
City Hall

Michigan City 46360 (39,000)
Warren Building

Mishawaka 46544 (36,000)
First and Church Streets

Muncie 47305 (69,000)
City Hall

New Albany 47150 (38,000)
City-County Building

Richmond 47374 (44,000)
50 North Fifth Street

South Bend 46601 (126,000)
227 West Jefferson Boulevard

Terre Haute 47807 (70,000)
17 Harding Avenue

Iowa

Ames 50010 (40,000)
Fifth and Kellog Streets

Burlington 52601 (32,000)
4th and Washington Streets

Cedar Falls 50613 (34,000)
220 Clay Street

Cedar Rapids 52401 (111,000)
City Hall

Clinton 52732 (35,000)
POB 337

Council Bluffs 51501 (60,000)
209 Pearl Street

Davenport 52801 (98,000)
226 West Fourth Street

Des Moines 50307 (201,000)
First and Locust Streets

Dubuque 52001 (62,000)
13th and Central Avenue

Fort Dodge 50501 (31,000)
813 First Avenue South

Iowa City 52240 (47,000)
410 East Washington Street

Mason City 50401 (30,000)
19 South Delaware Avenue

Ottuma 52501 (30,000)
105 East Third Street

Sioux City 51102 (86,000)
POB 447

Waterloo 50705 (76,000)
City Hall

Kansas

Hutchinson 67501 (37,000)
125 East Avenue B

Kansas City 666101 (168,000)
Civic Center Plaza

Lawrence 66044 (46,000)
POB 708

Leavenworth 66048 (25,000)
Fifth and Shawnee

Overland Park 66212 (77,000)
8500 Santa Fe Drive

Salina 67401 (38,000)
300 West Ash Street

Wichita 67202 (277,000)
455 North Main Street

Kentucky

Bossier City 71010 (42,000)
635 Barksdale Boulevard

Bowling Green 42101 (36,000)
POB 130

Covington 41011 (53,000)
City-County Building

Lexington 40507 (108,000)
Municipal Building

Louisville 40202 (361,000)
601 West Jefferson Street

Owensboro 42301 (50,000)
4th and St. Ann Streets

Paducah 42001 (32,000)
POB 891

Louisiana

Alexandria 71301 (42,000)
POB 71

Baton Rouge 70821 (166,000)
POB 1471

Houma 70360 (31,000)
City Hall

Lafayette 70501 (69,000)
733 Jefferson Street

Lake Charles 71201 (56,000)
POB 1178

Monroe 71201 (56,000)
POB 123

New Iberia 70560 (30,000)
POB 11

New Orleans 70112 (593,000)
1300 Perdido Street

Shreveport 71163 (182,000)
POB 1109

Maine

Augusta 04330 (22,000)
One Cony Street

Bangor 044012 (33,000)
73 Harlow Street

Biddeford 04005 (20,000)
POB 586

Lewiston 04240 (42,000)
Pine Street

Portland 04111 (65,000)
389 Congress Street

Sanford 04073 (16,000)
267 Main Street

Waterville 04901 (18,000)
City Hall

Maryland

Annapolis 212030,000)
166 Duke of Gloucester Street

Baltimore 21202 (906,000)
100 Holliday Street

Bowie 20715 (35,000)
Tulip Grove Drive

College Park 20740 (26,000)
4500 Knox Road

Cumberland 21502 (30,000)
City Hall

Hagerstown 21740 (36,000)
City Hall

Rockville 20850 (42,000)
111 Maryland Avenue

Massachusetts

Arlington 02174 (54,000)
730 Massachusetts Avenue

Attleboro 02703 (33,000)
29 Park Street

Beverly 01915 (38,000)
191 Cabot Street

Billerica 01821 (32,000)
Concord Road

Boston 02201 (641,000)
City Hall, Government Center

Braintree 02185 (35,000)
One J. F. Kennedy Memorial Drive

Brockton 02401 (89,000)
45 School Street

Brookline 02146 (59,000)
City Hall

Cambridge 022139 (100,000)
795 Massachusetts Avenue

Chelmsford 01824
One North Road

Chelsea 02150 (31,000)
City Hall

Chicopee 01013 (67,000)
City Hall

Everett 02149 (42,000)
484 Broadway

Fall River 02720 (97,000)
123 Main Street

Fitchburg 01420 (43,000)
718 Main Street

Framingham 01701 (64,000)
Memorial Building

Haverhill 01830 (46,000)
4 Summer Street

Holyoke 0140 (50,000)
536 Dwight Street

Lawrence 01840 (67,000)
200 Common Street

Leominster 01453 (33,000)
City Hall

Lexington 02173 (32,000)
1625 Massachusetts Avenue

Lowell 01853 (94,000)
City Hall

Lynn 01901 (90,000)
City Hall Square

Malden 02148 (56,000)
200 Pleasant Street

Medford 02155(64,000)
85 George P. Hassett Drive

Melrose 02176 (33,000)
562 Main Street

Methuen 01844 (35,000)
90 Hmpshire Street

Natick 01760 (31,000)
City Hall

New Bedford 02740 (102,000)
133 William Street

Newton 02159 (91,000)
1000 Commwealth Avenue

Northampton 01060 (30,000)
210 Main Street

Norwood 02062 (31,000)
Municipal Building

Peabody 01960 (48,000)
24 Lowell Street

Pittsfield 01201 (57,000)
City Hall

Quincy 02169 (88,000)
1305 Hancock Street

Revere 01970 (41,000)
City Hall

Salem 01970 (41,000)
93 Washington Street

Somerville 02144 (89,000)
Highland Avenue

Springfield 01103 (164,000)
36 Court Street

Taunton 02780 (44,000)
15 Summer Street

Waltham 02154 (62,000)
City Hall

Watertown 02072 (39,000)
149 Main Street

Westfield 01085 (31,000)
59 Court Street

Weymouth 02189 (55,000)
75 Middle street, East Weymouth

Woburn 01801 (37,000)
10 Common Street

Worcester 01608 (177,000)
Main Street

Michigan

Allen Park 48101 (41,000)
16850 Southfield Road

Ann Arbor 48107 (100,000)
100 Fifth Avenue

Battle Creek 49014 (39,000)
POB 1717

Bay City 48706 (49,000)
301 Washington Avenue

Burton 48519 (33,000)
4303 South Center Road

Dearborn 48126 (104,000)
3615 Michigan Avenue

Dearborn Heights 48127 (80,000)
6045 Fenton Street

Detroit 48226 (1,511,000)
912 City-County Building

East Detroit 48021 (46,000)
23200 Gratiot Avenue

East Lansing 48823 (48,000)
410 Abbott Road

Farmington Hills 48024 (51,000)
Mile Road

Ferndale 48220 (31,000)
300 East Nine Mile Road

Flint 48502 (193,000)
1101 South Saginaw

Garden 48135 (42,000)
6000 Middlebelt Road

Grand Rapids 49503 (198,000)W
300 Monroe, NW

Highland Park 48203 (35,000)
30 Gerald Avenue

Inkster 48141 (39,000)
2121 Inkster Road

Jackson 49201 (45,000)
132 West Washington Avenue

Kalamazoo 49006 (86,000)
41 West South Street

Lansing 48933 (132,000)
125 West Michigan Avenue

Lincoln Park 48146 (53,000)
1355 Southfield Road

Livonia 48154 (110,000)
33001 Five Mile Road

Madison Heights 48071 (39,000)
300 West Thirteen Mile Road

Menominee 49858 (11,000)
City Hall

Midland 48640 (35,000)
202 Ashman

Muskegon 49443 (45,000)
933 Terrace Street

Oak Park 48273 (37,000)
3600 Oak Park Boulevard

Pontiac 48058 (85,000)
450 East Widetrack Drive

Portage 49081 (34,000)
7800 Shaver Road

Port Huron 48060 (36,000)
201 McMorran Boulevard

Roseville 48066 (61,000)
29777 Gratiot Avenue

Royal Oak 48068 (85,000)
POB 64

Saginaw 48601 (92,000)
1315 South Washington Avenue

St. Clair Shores 48081 (88,000)
277600 Jefferson Street

Southfield 48076 (69,000)
6000 Evergreen Road

Southgate 48195 (34,000)
13763 Northline Road

Sterling Heights 48078 (61,000)
40555 Utica Road

Taylor 48084 (70,000)
23555 Goddard Road

Troy 48084 (39,000)
500 West Big Beaver Road

Warren 48093 (179,000)
29500 Van Dyke Avenue

Westland 48185 (87,000)
36601 Ford Road

Wyandotte 48192 (41,000)
3131 Briddle Avenue

Wyoming 49509 (57,000)
1151 28th Street, SW

Minnesota

Austin 55912 (25,000)
500 Fourth Avenue NE

Bloomington 55431 (82,000)
2215 West Old Shakopee Road

Brooklyn Center 55430 (35,000)
6301 Shingle Creek Parkway

Coon Rapids 55433 (31,000)
1313 Coon Rapids Boulevard

Crystal 55422 (31,000)
4141 Douglas Drive North

Duluth 55802 (101,000)
403 City Hall

Edina 55424 (49,000)
4801 West 50th Street

Mankato 56001 (31,000)
202 East Jackson Street

Minneapolis 55415 (434,000)
350 South Fifth Street

Minnetonka 55343 (36,000)
14600 Minnetonka Boulevard

Richfield 55423 (47,000)
6700 Portland Avenue South

Rochester 55901 (54,000)
City Hall

Roseville 55113 (35,000)
2701 North Lexington Avenue

St. Cloud 56301 (40,000)
City Hall

St. Louis Park 55416 (49,000)
5005 Minnetonka Boulevard

St. Paul 55102 (310,000)
15 West Kellog Boulevard

Mississippi

Biloxi 39533 (48,000)
POB 429

Greenville 38701 (40,000)
POB 897

Gulfport 39501 (41,000)
POB 1780

Hattiesburg 39401 (38,000)
POB 1898

Jackson 39205 (154,000)
POB 17

Laurel 39440 (24,000)
City Hall

Meridian 39301 (45,000)
POB 1430

Missouri

Cape Girardeau 63701 (31,000)
402 Chesley Drive

Columbia 65201 (59,000)
POB N

Florissant 63031 (66,000)
955 Rue St. Francois

Independence 64050 (112,000)
103 N. Main Street

Jefferson City 65101 (32,000)
240 East High Street

Joplin 64801 (39,000)
City Hall

Kansas City 64106 (507,000)
414 East 12th Street

Kirkwood 63122 (32,000)
139 S. Kirkwood Road

Raytown 64133 (34,000)
10000 East 59th Street

St. Charles 64501 (32,000)
11th and Federal Streets

St. Joseph 64501 (73,000)
City Hall

St. Louis 63103 (622,000)
1206 Market Street

Springfield 65802 (120,000)
830 Boonville

University City 63130 (62,000)
6801 Delmar Boulevard

Montana

Billings 59103 (62,000)
POB 1178

Great Falls 59403 (60,000)
POB 1609

Helena 59601 (23,000)
Civic Center

Nebraska

Grand Island 68801 (31,000)
POB 1968

Lincoln 68508 (150,000)
555 South 10th Street

North Platte 69101 (19,000)
POB 1329

Omaha 68102 (347,000)
County Civic Center

Nevada

Carson City 89701 (18,000)
813 North Carlson Street

Las Vegas 89101 (126,000)
400 Stewart Street

North Las Vegas 89030 (48,000)
2200 Civic Center Drive

Reno 89505 (73,000)
POB 1900

Sparks 89431 (24,000)
431 Prater Way

New Hampshire

Concord 03301 (30,000)
City Hall

Manchester 03101 (88,000)
904 Elm Street

Nashua 03060 (56,000)
229 Main Street

New Jersey

Atlantic City 08401 (48,000)
Tennessee and Bacharach

Bayonne 07002 (73,000)
630 Avenue C

Belleville 07109
152 Washington Avenue

Bergenfield 07621 (33,000)
198 North Washington Avenue

Bloomfield 07003 (52,000)
Municipal Building

Brick Township 08723 (35,000)
401 Chamber Bridge Road

Bridgewater Township 08807 (30,000)
POB 6300

Camden 08101 (103,000)
6th and Market Streets

Cherry Hill Township 08002 (64,000)
820 Mercer Street

Clifton 07102 (82,000)
1187 Main Avenue

Dover Township 08753 (44,000)
POB 728

East Brunswick Township 08816 (34,000)
One Jean Walling Civic Center

East Orange 07017 (75,000)
44 City Hall Plaza

Edison Township 08817 (67,000)
Plainfield and Woodbridge Avenues

Elizabeth 07201 (113,000)
West Scott Plaza

Ewing Township 08618 (33,000)
1872 Pennington Road

Fairlawn 07410 (38,000)
Fairlawn Avenue

Fort Lee 07024 (31,000)
309 Main Street

Franklin Township 08873
475 De Mott Lane

Garfield 07026 (31,000)
Outwater Lane

Gloucester Township 080
POB 8

Hackensack 07602 (36,000)
65 Central Avenue

Hamilton Township 08609
2090 Greenwood Avenue

Hoboken 07030 (45,000)
First and Washington St

Irvington 07111 (60,000)
Civic Square

Jersey City 07302 (261,000)
City Hall, Grove Street

Kearny 07032 (38,000)
400 Kearny Avenue

Linden 07036 (41,000)
North Wood Avenue

Long Branch 07740
344 Broadway

Middleton Township 07748 (55,000)
King's Highway

Montclair 07042 (44,000)
647 Bloomfield Avenue

Newark 07102 (382,000)
City Hall

New Brunswick 08903
78 Bayard Street

North Bergen Township 07047 (48,000)
4233 Kennedy Boulevard

Nutley 07110 (32,000)
Public Safety Building

Old Bridge Township 08857 (51,000)
Box 70C, RD 1

Orange 07050 (33,000)
29 North Day Street

Parsippany-Troy Hills 07054 (55,000)
1001 Parsippany Boulevard

Passaic 07055 (55,000)
101 Passaic Avenue

Paterson 07505 (145,000)
155 Market Street

Pennsauken Township 08110 (36,000)
5605 North Crescent Boulevard

Perth Amboy 08861 (38,798)
260 High Street

Piscataway Township 08854 (36,000)
455Hoes Lane

Plainfield 07061 (47,000)
515 Wachtung Avenue

Sayreville 08872 (33,000)
167 Main Street

Teaneck Township 07666
Municipal Building

Trenton 08608 (105,000)
319 East State Street

Union Township 07083 (53,000)
1976 Morris Avenue

Union City 07087 (59,000)
3715 Palisade Avenue

Vineland 08360 (47,000)
7th and Wood Streets

Wayne Township 07470 (49,000)
475 Valley Road

Westfield 07090 (34,000)
425 East Broad Street

West New York 07093 (40,000)
428 60th Street

West Orange 07052 (44,000)
66 Main Street

Willingboro Township 08046 (43,000)
Salem Road

Woodbridge Township 07095 (99,000)
One Main Street

New Mexico

Albuquerque 87102 (244,000)
400 Marquette Avenue

Las Cruces 89001 (38,000)
POB 760

Roswell 88201 (34,000)
POB 1838

Santa Fe 87501 (41,000)
POB 909

New York

Albany 12207 (115,000)
City Hall

Auburn 13021 (35,000)
24 South Street

Binghamton 13901 (64,000)
City Hall

Buffalo 14202 (463,000)
65 Niagara Square

Elmira 14901 (40,000)
Lake and Church Streets

Freeport 11520 (40,000)
46 North Ocean Avenue

Hempstead 11551 (39,000)
99 Nichols Court

Jamestown 14701 (40,000)
Municipal Building

Long Beach 11561 (33,000)
City Hall

Mount Vernon 10500 (73,000)
City Hall

Newburgh 12550 (26,000)
93 Broadway

New Rochelle 10801 (75,000)
515 North Avenue

New York 10007 (7,868,000)
80 Centre Street

Niagara Falls 14302 (86,000)
745 Main Street

North Tonawanda 14120 (36,000)
216 Payne Avenue

Poughkeepsie 12602 (32,000)
Memorial Square

Rochester 14614 (296,000)
Church and Fitzhugh Streets

Rockville Center 11570 (27,000)
College Place

Rome 13440 (50,000)
207 North James Street

Schenectady 12305 (78,000)
City Hall

Syracuse 13202 (197,000)
City Hall

Troy 12181 (63,000)
City Hall

Utica 13502 (92,000)
One Kennedy Place

Valley Stream 11580 (40,000)
123 South Central Avenue

Watertown 13601 (50,000)
Municipal Building

White Plains 10601 (50,000)
225 Main Street

Yonkers 10701 (204,000)
City Hall

North Carolina

Asheville 28807 (58,000)
POB 7148

Burlington 27215 (36,000)
POB 1358

Chapel Hill 27514 (32,000)
306 North Columbia Street

Charlotte 28202 (241,000)
600 East Trade Street

Durham 27702 (95,000)
POB 2251

Fayetteville 28302 (54,000)
POB 437

Gastonia 28052 (47,000)
POB 1748

Greensboro 27402 (144,000)
PO Drawer W-2

High Point 27261 (63,000)
POB 230

Raleigh 27602 (121,000)
POB 590

Rocky Mount 27801 (34,000)
POB 1180

Salisbury 28144 (23,000)
POB 479

Wilmington 28401 (46,000)
POB 1810

Wilson 27893 (31,000)
POB 10

Winston-Salem 27102 (133,000)
POB 2511

North Dakota

Bismarck 58501 (35,000)
POB 1578

Fargo 58102 (53,000)
201 Fourth Street

Grand Forks 58201 (39,000)
POB 1518

Ohio

Akron 44308 (275,000)
166 South High Street

Barberton 44203 (33,000)
576 West Park Avenue

Bedford Heights 44146 (13,000)
5661 Perkins Road

Brook Park 44142 (31,000)
6161 Engle Road

Canton 44702 (110,000)
City Hall

Cincinnati 45202 (453,000)
800 Central Avenue

Cleveland 44114 (751,000)
601 East Lakeside Avenue

Cleveland Heights 44118 (61,000)
2953 Mayfield Road

Columbus 43215 (540,000)
90 West Broad Street

Cuyahoga Falls 44222 (50,000)
2310 Second Street

Dayton 45402 (244,000)
104 West Third Street

East Cleveland 44112 (40,000)
14340 Euclid Avenue

Elyria 44035 (53,000)
328 Broad Street

Euclid 44123 (72,000)
585 East 222nd Street

Fairborn 45324 (32,000)
44 West Hebble Avenue

Findlay 45840 (36,000)
119 Court Place

Garfield Heights 44125 (41,000)
5555 Turney Road

Hamilton 45011 (68,000)
Two High Street

Kettering 45429 (70,000)
3600 Shroyer Road

Lakewood 44107 (70,000)
12650 Detroit Avenue

Lancaster 43130 (33,000)
104 East Main Street

Lima 45801 (54,000)
219 East Market Street

Lorain 44052 (78,000)
200 West Erie Avenue

Mansfield 44902 (55,000)
30 North Diamond Street

Maple Heights 44137 (34,000)
5353 Lee Road

Marion 43302 (39,000)
685 Delaware Avenue

Massillon 44646 (33,000)
City Hall

Mentor 44060 (37,000)
8500 Civic Center Boulevard

Middletown 45042 (49,000)
City Building

Newark 43035 (42,000)
40 West Main Street

North Olmstead 44070 (35,000)
5206 Dover Center Road

Norwood 45212 (30,000)
Montgomery and Elm Avenues

Parma 44129 (100,000)
6611 Ridge Road

Sandusky 44870 (33,000)
202 Meigs Street

Shaker Heights 44120 (36,000)
3400 Lee Road

Springfield 45501 (82,000)
City Building

Steubenville 43952 (31,000)
123 South Third Street

Toledo 43624 (384,000)
525 Erie Street

Upper Arlington 43221 (39,000)
3600 Tremont Road

Warren 44483 (63,000)
391 Mahoning NW

Youngstown 44503 (140,000)
City Hall

Zanesville 43701 (33,000)
401 Market Street

Oklahoma

Bartlesville 74003 (30,000)
POB 699

Enid 73701 (44,000)
POB 1768

Lawton 73501 (74,000)
4th and A Streets

Midwest City 73110 (48,000)
100 North Midwest Boulevard

Muskogee 74401 (37,000)
POB 19278

Norman 73069 (52,000)
POB 370

Oklahoma City 73102 (366,000)
200 NW Fifth Street

Stillwater 74074 (31,000)
POB 631

Tulsa 74103 (332,000)
200 Civic Center

Oregon

Corvallis 97330 (35,000)
501 SW Madison Avenue

Eugene 97401 (96,000)
777 Pearl Street

Medford 97501 (28,000)
411 West Eighth Street

Portland 97204 (382,000)
1220 SW Fifth Avenue

Salem 97301 (68,000)
555 Liberty SE

Pennsylvania

Allentown 18101 (110,000)
435 Hamilton Street

Altoona 16603 (63,000)
13th Avenue and Twelfth Street

Bethel Park 15102 (35,000)
5100 West Library Avenue

Bethlehem 18018 (73,000)
10 East Church Street

Chester 19013 (56,000)
Fifth and Welsh Streets

Easton 18042 (30,000)
650 Ferry Street

Erie 16501 (129,000)
Municipal Building

Harrisburg 17101 (68,000)
City Hall

Hazelton 18201 (30,000)
City Hall

Johnstown 15901 (42,000)
Main and Market Streets

Lancaster 17604 (58,000)
120 North Duke Street

McKeesport 15132 (38,000)
201 Lysle Boulevard

Mount Lebanon 15228 (40,000)
710 Washington Road

New Castle 16101 (39,000)
230 North Jefferson Street

Norristown 19404 (38,000)
East Airy Street

Philadelphia 19107 (1,949,000)
23 North Juniper Street

Pittsburgh 15219 (520,000)
510 City-County Building

Reading 19601 (88,000)
Eighth and Washington Streets

Scranton 18503 (104,000)
Municipal Building

State College 16801 (34,000)
118 South Fraser Street

Wilkes-Barre 18701 (59,000)
40 East Market Street

Williamsport 17701 (38,000)
454 Pine Street

York 17405 (50,000)
50 West King Street

Puerto Rico

Bayamon 00619 (148,000)
Maceo and Degetau Streets

Caguas 00625 (163,000)
City Hall

Ponce 00731 (128,000)
POB 1709

San Juan 00905 (453,000)
POB 4355

Rhode Island

Cranston 02910 (73,000)
869 Park Avenue

East Providence 02914 (48,000)
60 Commercial Way

Newport 02840 (35,000)
City Hall

Pawtucket 02860 (77,000)
City Hall

Providence 02903 (179,000)
25 Dorrance Street

Warwick 02864 (84,000)
3275 Post Road

Woonsocket 02895 (47,000)
169 Main Street

South Carolina

Charleston 29401 (67,000)
City Hall

Columbia 29217 (114,000)
POB 147

Greenville 29602 (61,000)
POB 2207

North Charleston 29406 (54,000)
POB 5817

Rockhill 29730 (34,000)
POB 11706

Spartanburg 29303 (45,000)
480 North Church Street

South Dakota

Aberdeen 57401 (26,000)
POB 1299

Rapid City 57701 (44,000)
22 Main Street

Sioux Falls 57102 (72,000)
24 West Ninth Street

Tennessee

Chattanooga 37402 (119,000)
City Hall, Municipal Building

Clarksville 17040 (32,000)
City Hall

Jackson 38301 (40,000)
312 East Main Street

Johnson City 337601 (34,000)
Municipal-Safety Building

Kingsport 37660 (32,000)
225 West Center Street

Knoxville 37902 (175,000)
City Hall

Memphis 38103 (624,000)
125 North Main Street

Nashville 37201 (448,000)
107 Court House

Texas

Abilene 79604 (90,000)
POB 60

Amarillo 79186 (127,000)
POB 19171

Arlington 76010 (91,000)
POB 2880

Austin 78701 (252,000)
124 West Eight Street

Baytown 77520 (44,000)
POB 424

Beaumont 77704 (116,000)
POB 3287

Brownsville 78520 (53,000)
POB 911

Bryan 77801 (34,000)
POB 1000

Corpus Christi 78408 (205,000)
POB 9277

Dallas 75201 (844,000)
1501 Marilla Street

Denton 76201 (40,000)
215 East McKinney

El Paso 79901 (322,000)
500 East San Antonio Street

Fort Worth 76102 (393,000)
1000 Throckmorton

Galveston 77550 (62,000)
POB 779

Garland 75040 (81,000)
POB 40189

Grand Prairie 75050 (51,000)
POB 11

Harlingen 78550 (34,000)
POB 2207

Houston 77002 (1,233,000)
900 Brazos Street

Irving 75061 (97,000)
POB 3008

Killeen 76541 (36,000)
400 North Second Street

Laredo 78040 (69,000)
City Hall

Longview 75601 (46,000)
POB 1952

Lubbock 79457 (149,000)
POB 2000

McAllen 78501 (38,000)
POB 220

Mesquite 75149 (55,000)
POB 137

Midland 79701 (59,000)
POB 1152

Odessa 79760 (78,000)
POB 4398

Pasadena 77506 (89,000)
1211 East Southmore

Plano 75074 (44,000)
POB 358

Port Arthur 77640 (57,000)
POB 1089

Richardson 75080 (49,000)
POB 309

San Angelo 76901 (6FL
POB 1751

San Antonio 78205 (654,000)
Military Plaza, POB 9066

Temple 76501 (33,000)
Municipal Building

Texarkana 75501 (30,000)
POB 1967

Texas City 77590 (39,000)
POB 2608

Tyler 75701 (58,000)
POB 2039

Victoria 77901 (41,000)
104 West Juan Linn Street

Waco 76703 (95,000)
POB 1370

Wichita Falls 76307 (98,000)
POB 1431

Utah

Bountiful 84010 (28,000)
745 South Main Street

Ogden City 84401 (69,000)
Municipal Building

Provo 84601 (53,000)
POB 799

Salt Lake City 84111 (176,000)
300 City and County Building

Vermont

Burlington 05401 (38,000)
City Hall

Montpelier 05602 (9,000)
Main Street

Virginia

Alexandria 22314 (111,000)
125 North Royal Street

Charlottesville 22902 (39,000)
POB 911

Chesapeake 23320 (90,000)
POB 15225

Danville 14541 (46,000)
Municipal Building

Hampton 23669 (121,000)
22 Lincoln Street

Lynchburg 24505 (54,000)
POB 60

Newport News 23607 (138,000)
2400 Washington Avenue

Norfolk 23501 (308,000)
City Hall Building

Petersburg 23803 (45,000)
City Hall

Portsmouth 23705 (11,000)
POB 820

Richmond 23219 (250,000)
900 East Broad Street

Roanoke 24011 (92,000)
Municipal Building

Suffolk 23434 (45,000)
POB 1858

Virginia Beach 23456 (172,000)
Municipal Center

Washington

Bellevue 98009 (61,000)
POB 1768

Bellingham 98225 (39,000)
210 Lottie Street

Bremerton 98310 (35,000)
239 Fourth Street

Everett 98201 (54,000)
City Hall

Richland 99352 (28,000)
POB 190

Seattle 98104 (531,000)
600 Fourth Avenue

Spokane 99201 (171,000)
North 221 Wall Street

Tacoma 98402 (155,000)
County-City Building

Vancouver 98660 (42,000)
210 East 13th Street

Yakima 98901 (46,000)
129 North Second Street

West Virginia

Charleston 25717 (74,000)
POB 1659

Morgantown 26505 (29,000)
389 Spruce Street

Parkersburg 26101 (44,000)
POB 1348

Wheeling 26003 (48,000)
City-County Building

Wisconsin

Appleton 54911 (57,000)
POB 1857

Beloit 53511 (36,000)
Municipal Center

Brookfield 53005 (32,000)
2000 North Calhoun Road

Eau Claire 54701 (45,000)
203 South Farwell Street

Fond du Lac 54935 (36,000)
POB 150

Green Bay 54301 (88,000)
Jefferson Street

Janesville 53545 (46,000)
18 North Jackson Street

Kenosha 53140 (79,000)
625 52nd Street

La Crosse 54601 (51,000)
City Hall

Madison 53709 (173,000)
210 Monona Avenue

Manitowoc 54220 (33,000)
817 Franklin Street

Menomonee Falls 53051 (32,000)
POB 100

Milwaukee 53202 (717,000)
200 East Wells Street

Oshkosh 54901 (53,000)
POB 1130

Racine 53403 (95,000)
730 Washington Avenue

Sheboygan 53081 (48,000)
828 Center Avenue

Superior 54880 (32,000)
1407 Hammond Avenue

Waukesha 53186 (40,000)ield Street

Wausau 54401 (33,000)
407 Grant Street

Wauwatosa 53213 (59,000)
7725 West North Avenue

West Allis 53214 (72,000)
7525 West Greenfield Avenue

Wyoming

Casper 82601 (39,000)
City-County Building

Cheyenne 82001 (41,000)
City-County Building

Counties and Their Governments

States are too large to be governed from a single headquarters or capital and so are divided into counties, with only 3 counties in the tiny State of Delaware, but 254 counties in Texas. And in California there is one county that is larger in area than Belgium and several other European countries. And just as each state has a capital city, so each county has a county seat in one of its cities or towns, which serves as the capital of the county and in which the county government is housed.

In many cases counties do as significant an amount of purchasing as do many busy cities. This is certainly true in the Washington, DC, suburban county where this is being written (Montgomery County, Maryland), for example. This is a prosperous county, with a great deal of industrial and business activity, and a large population living in a large number of bedroom communities. A great deal of this population, business, and industry lies in large, unincorporated areas of the county, such as the well-known and sprawling area called Silver Spring, Maryland. Virtually everything unincorporated in this part of the county is referred to as Silver Spring, and there is even a "downtown" Silver Spring, where there is a very citylike section of stores, restaurants, broad sidewalks, and other urban features. However, since there is actually no city or town of Silver Spring, the entire area depends on the Montgomery County government to patrol its streets, fight its fires, and provide all the other services a built-up community needs. That, plus the fact that Montgomery County is a rather large and prosperous county (with one of the largest per capita income levels in the country), makes it inevitable that purchasing is a major activity of the county government from its seat in Rockville, Maryland.

The nearby County of Fairfax, Virginia, is another excellent example. It has its own Purchasing and Supply Management Agency, which is reasonably typical of government purchasing organizations. A few illlustrative details of purchasing organization and practices of Fairfax County, whose county seat is in Fairfax, Virginia, are presented here as an example of county purchasing. It is easy to see the resemblance philosophically and functionally to the purchasing organizations and practices of the state and other local governments.

Fairfax County Procurement System The County of Fairfax, Commonwealth of Virginia, operates its Purchasing and Supply Management Agency at 4100 Chain Bridge Road, Fairfax, Virginia 22030. The agency offers vendors a *Vendor's Guide,* which lists as personnel and organizational units connected with purchasing a Director of the Agency, a Deputy Director, a Commodity Buying Section, and a Projects and Contracts Section, among other offices, staff, and functions. Vendors must register to get on bidders lists and will then be invited to bid and/or submit proposals (for the county issues both invitations to bid and requests for proposals) in competition for contracts and purchase orders. Formal bids are classified as those larger than $5,000, and solicitations for both formal bids and proposals will be advertised in a local newspaper. Informal bids may be invited via RFQs, and oral (telephone) quotes may be accepted for those kinds of bids.

County Listings and Their Use

County governments tend to centralize their functions in a County Courthouse, and in most counties the Chief Executive tends to bear some title such as County Executive or County Supervisor. In the following listings three items are furnished: the name of the county; the city, town, or township that is the county seat; and the zip code for the County Courthouse, or other building in which county government offices are located. The listings are alphabetical by state and city or town, as in earlier listings. For example, this is the first listing:

Alabama
Calhoun, Anniston 36201
   This tells you that the county seat of Calhoun County, Alabama, is at Anniston, Alabama 36201, and you may address the county government along the following lines if you do not have a local telephone directory available to get a specific street address, with reasonable certainty that your request for information will usually find its way to the right office or official:

County Purchasing Agent   County Purchasing Office
County Courthouse   or: Calhoun County Government
Calhoun County   Anniston, AL 36201
Anniston, AL 36201

Of course, you should also watch for announcements in newspaper classified columns under the heading Bids and Proposals, if you have access to the newspapers published in the county.
   The listings that follow are by no means represented as a complete listing of all counties in the United States but are of approximately 500 counties. It would not serve any good purpose to list all 3,021 counties, for not all are suitable prospects. Those which are listed here are those which justify being called "major" counties, either because they do a great deal of buying directly or were otherwise deemed suitable for inclusion here. (Note that many counties bear the same name as the city or town that serves as the county seat.)
   Surprisingly often, too, the city or town that serves as the county seat is also the state capital and/or the site of important federal facilities that are good market targets, which is itself a good reason for inclusion here.

Alabama

Calhoun, Anniston 36201
Dallas, Selma 36701
Houston, Dothan 36301
Jefferson, Birmingham 36701
Macon, Tuskeegee 36083
Madison, Huntsville 35801
Mobile, Mobile 36602
Montgomery, Montgomery 36102
Morgan, Decatur 35601
Russell, Phenix City 36837
Tuscaloosa, Tuscaloosa 35401

Alaska

Fairbanks North Star, Fairbanks 99701
Anchorage, Anchorage 99510
Greater Juneau, Juneau 99801
North Slope, Barrow 99723

Arizona

Coconino, Flagstaff 86001
Maricopa, Phoenix 85007
Pima, Tucson 85701
Yuma. Yuma 85364

Arkansas

Benton, Bentonville 72712
Craighead, Jonesboro 72401
Garland, Hot Springs 71901
Jefferson, Pine Bluff 71601
Mississippi, Blytheville 72315
Pulaski, Little Rock 72201
St. Francis, Forrest City 72335
Sebastian, Fort Smith 72901
Washington, Fayetteville 72701

California

Alameda, Oakland 94612
Butte, Oroville 95965
Contra Costa, Martinez 94553
Fresno, Fresno 93721
Humboldt, Eureka 95501
Imperial, El Centro 92243
Kern, Bakersfield 93301
Los Angeles, Los Angeles 90012
Marin, San Rafael 94902

Merced, Merced 95340
Monterey, Salinas 93901
Orange, Santa Ana 92701
Riverside, Riverside 92501
Sacramento, Sacramento 95814
San Bernardino, San Bernardino 95801
San Diego, San Diego 92101
San Francisco, San Francisco 94102
San Joaquin, Stockton 95202
San Luis Obispo, San Luis Obispo 93401
San Mateo, Redwood City 94063
Santa Barbara, Santa Barbara 93101
Santa Clara, San Jose 95110
Santa Cruz, Santa Cruz 95060
Shasta, Redding 96001
Solano, Fairfield 94533
Sonoma, Santa Rosa 95402
Stanislaus, Modesto 95352
Tulare, Visalia 93227
Ventura, Ventura 93001
Yolo, Woodland 96596

Colorado

Adams, Brighton 80601
Arapahoe, Littleton 80120
Boulder, Boulder 80302
Denver, Denver 80203
El Paso, Colorado Springs 80902
Jefferson, Golden 80401
Larimer, Fort Collins 80521
Mesa, Grand Junction 81501
Pueblo, Pueblo 81003
Weld, Greeley 80631

Connecticut

Fairfield, Bridgeport 06430
Hartford, Hartford 06115
Litchfield, Litchfield 06759
Middlesex, Middletown 06457
New Haven, New Haven 06510
New London, New London 06320
Tolland, Rockville 06066
Windham, Putnam 06280

Delaware

Kent, Dover 19901
New Castle, Wilmington 19801

Sussex, Georgetown 19947

Florida

Alachua, Gainesville 32601
Bay, Panama City 32401
Brevard, Titusville 32780
Broward, Fort Lauderdale 33301
Dade, Miami 33132
Duval, Jacksonville 32202
Escambia, Pensacola 32502
Hillsborough, Tampa 33602
Lee, Fort Myers 33902
Leon, Tallahassee 32304
Manatee, Bradenton 33505
Monroe, Key West 33040
Okaloosa, Crestview 32536
Orange, Orlando 32801
Palm Beach, West Palm Beach 33401
Pinellas, Clearwater 33516
Polk, Bartow, 33830
St. Lucie, Fort Pierce 33450
Sarasota, Sarasota 33577
Volusia, De Land 32720

Georgia

Bibb, Macon 31201
Chatham, Savannah 31401
Cobb, Marietta 30060
De Kalb, Decatur 30030
Dougherty, Albany 31702
Fulton, Atlanta 30303
Houston, Warner-Robins 31093
Muscogee, Columbus 31902
Richmond, Augusta 30902
Whitfield, Dalton 30720

Hawaii

Hawaii, Hilo 96720
Honolulu, Honolulu 96813
Kauia, Lihue 96766
Maui, Wailuku 96793

Idaho

Ada, Boise 83702
Bannock, Pocatello 83201
Bonneville, Idaho Falls 83401
Canyon, Caldwell 83605

Kootenai, Coeur d'Alene 83814
Nez Perce, Lewiston 83501
Twin Falls, Twin Falls 83301

Illinois

Champaign, Urbana 61801
Cook, Chicago 60602
Du Page, Wheaton 60187
Kane, Geneva 60134
Kankakee, Kankakee 60901
Knox, Galesburg 61401
Lake, Waukegan 60085
La Salle, Ottawa 61350
McHenry, Bloomington 61701
Macon, Decatur 62525
Madison, Edwardsville 62025
Peoria, Peoria 61602
Rock Island, Rock Island 61201
St. Claire, Belleville 62222
Sangamon, Springfield 62706
Tazewell, Pekin 61554
Vermilion, Danville 61832
Will, Joliet 60434
Winnebago, Rockford 61104

Indiana

Allen, Fort Wayne 46802
Delaware, Muncie 47302
Elkhart, Goshen 46526
Lake, Crown Point 46307
La Porte, La Porte 46350
Madison, Anderson 46011
Marion, Indianapolis 46204
Monroe, Bloomington 47401
Porter, Valparaiso 46383
St. Joseph, South Bend 40601
Tippecanoe, Lafayette 47902
Vanderburg, Evansville 47708
Vigo, Terre Haute 47808
Wayne, Richmond 47374

Iowa

Black Hawk, Waterloo 50705
Cerro Gordo, Mason City 50401
Clinton, Clinton 52732
Des Moines, Burlington 52601
Dubuque, Dubuque 52201

Johnson, Iowa City 52240
Linn, Cedar Rapids 52401
Polk, Des Moines 50307
Pottawattamie, Council Bluffs 51501
Scott, Davenport 52801
Story, Nevada 50201
Woodbury, Sioux City 51101

Kansas

Douglas, Lawrence 66044
Johnson, Olathe 66061
Leavenworth, Leavenworth 66048
Reno, Hutchinson 67501
Riley, Manhattan 66502
Saline, Salina 67401
Sedgwick, Wichita 67202
Shawnee, Topeka 66603

Kentucky

Boyd, Catlettsburg 41129
Campbell, Newport 41071
Davies, Owensboro 42301
Fayette, Lexington 40507
Hardin, Elizabethtown 42701
Jefferson, Louisville 40202
Kenton, Covington 41011
McCracken, Paducah 42001
Madison, Richmond 40475
Pike, Pikeville 41501
Warren, Bowling Green 42101

Louisiana *

Acadia, Crowley 70526
Bossier, Benton 71006
Caddo, Shreveport 71101
Calcasieu, Lake Charles 70601
East Baton Rouge, Baton Rouge 70801
Jefferson, Gretna 70053
Lafayette, Lafayette 70501
Orleans, New Orleans 70112
Ouchita, Monroe 71201
Rapides, Alexandria 71301
St. Landry, Opelousas 70570
St. Mary, Franklin 70538

---

*In Louisiana, counties are generally called
"parishes."

St. Tammany, Covington 70433
Tangipahoa, Amite 70422
Terrebone, Houma 70360

Maine

Androscoggin, Auburn 04210
Aroostook, Houlton 04730
Cumberland, Portland 04111
Kennebec, Augusta 04330
Penobscot, Bangor 04401
York, Alfred 04002

Maryland

Allegany, Cumberland 21502
Anne Arundel, Annapolis 21401
Baltimore, Baltimore 21202
Carroll, Westminster 21157
Frederick, Frederick 21701
Harford, Bel Air 21014
Howard, Ellicott City 21043
Montgomery, Rockville 20850
Prince Goerges, Upper Marlboro 20870
Queen Annes, Centreville 21617
Washington, Hagerstown 21740

Massachusetts

Barnstable, Barnstable 02630
Berkshire, Pittsfield 01201
Bristol, Taunton 02780
Essex, Salem 01970
Hampden, Springfield 01101
Hampshire, Northampton 01060
Middlesex, Concord 01742
Norfolk, Dedham 002026
Plymouth, Plymouth 02360
Suffolk, Boston 02201
Worcester, Worcester 01601

Michigan

Bay, Bay City 48706
Berrien, St. Joseph 49085
Calhoun, Marshall 49086
Genesee, Flint 48502
Ingham, Mason 48854
Jackson, Jackson 49201
Kalamazoo, Kalamazoo 49003
Kent, Grand Rapids 49502

Macomb, Mt. Clemens 48043
Monroe, Monroe 48161
Muskegon, Muskegon 49440
Oakland, Pontiac 48053
Ottawa, Grand Haven 49417
Saginaw, Saginaw 48601
Washtenaw, Ann Arbor 48108
Wayne, Detroit 48226

Minnesota

Anoka, Anoka 55303
Dakota, Hastings 55033
Hennepin, Minneapolis 55415
Olmstead, Rochester 55901
Ramsey, St, Paul 55802
St. Louis, Duluth 56301
Washington, Stillwater 55082

Mississippi

Forrest, Hattiesburg 39401
Harrison, Gulfport 39501
Hinds, Jackson 39201
Jackson, Pascagoula 39567
Lauderdale, Meridian 39301
Washington, Greenville 38701

Missouri

Boone, Columbia 65201
Buchanan,St. Joseph 64501
Clay, Liberty 64068
Greene, Springfield 65802
Jackson, Kansas City 64106
Jefferson, Hillsboro 63050
St, Charles, St. Charles 63301
St. Louis, Clayton 63105

Montana

Cascade, Great Falls 59401
Flathead, Kalispell 59901
Gallatin, Bozeman 59715
Lewis and Clark, Helena 59601
Missoula, Missoula 59801
Silver Bow, Butte 59701
Yellowstone, Billings 59101

Nebraska

Douglas, Omaha 68102
Hall, Grand island 68801
Lancaster, Lincoln 68509
Sarpy, Papillon 68046

Nevada

Clark, Las Vegas 89114
Ormsby, Carson City 89701
Washoe, Reno 89501

New Hampshire

Cheshire, Keene 03431
Grafton, Woodsville 03785
Hillsborough, Nashua 03060
Merrimack, Concord 03301
Rockingham, Exeter 03833
Strafford, Dover 03820

New Jersey

Atlantic, Mays Landing 08330
Bergen, Hackensack 07602
Burlington, Mt. Holly 08060
Camden, Camden 08101
Cape May, Cape May 08210
Cumberland, Bridgeton 08302
Essex, Newark 07102
Gloucester, Woodbury 08096
Hudson, Jersey City 07302
Mercer, Trenton 08625
Middlesex, New Brunswick 08903
Monmouth, Freehold 07728
Morris, Morristown 07960
Ocean, Toms River 08753
Passaic, Paterson 07505
Somerset, Somerville 08876
Union, Elizabeth 07207

New Mexico

Bernalillo, Albuquerque 87102
Chaves, Roswell 88201
Dona Ana, Las Cruces 88001
Lea, Lovington 88260

McKinley, Gallup 87301
Otero, Alamogordo 88310
San Juan, Aztec 87410
Santa Fe, Santa Fe 87501

New York

Albany, Albany 12207
Broome, Binghamton 13901
Bronx, Bronx 10451
Chatauqua, Mayville 14757
Chemung, Elmira 14902
Dutchess, Poughkeepsie 12602
Erie, Buffalo 14202
Jefferson, Watertown 13601
Kings, Brooklyn 11201
Monroe, Rochester 14614
Nassau, Mineola 11501
New York, New York 10007
Niagara, Lockport 14094
Oneida, Utica 13503
Onondaga, Syracuse 13202
Orange, Goshen 10924
Oswego, Oswego 13126
Queens, Jamaica 11434
Rensselaer, Troy 12180
Richmond, St. George 10301
Rockland, New City 10956
Saint Lawrence, Canton 13617
Saratoga, Ballston Spa 12020
Schenectady, Schenectady 12307
Suffolk, Riverhead 11901
Ulster, Kingston 12401
Westchester, White Plains 10601

North Carolina

Alamance, Graham 27253
Buncombe, Newton 28658
Cleveland, Shelby 28150
Craven, New Bern 28560
Cumberland, Fayetteville 28301
Davidson, Lexington 27292
Durham, Durhan 27702
Forsyth, Winston-Salem 27101
Gaston, Gastonia 28052
Guilford, Greensboro 27402
Mecklenburg, Charlotte 28202
New Hanover, Wilmington 28401
Onslow, Jacksonville 28540

Pitt, Greenville 27834
Robeson, Lumberton 28358
Rowan, Salisburg 28144
Wake, Raleigh 27611

North Dakota

Burleigh, Bismarck 58501
Cass, Fargo 58102
Grand Forks, Grand Forks 58201
Ward, Minot 58701

Ohio

Allen, Lima 45802
Ashtabula, Jefferson 44047
Butler, Hamilton 45012
Clark, Springfield 45501
Clermont, Batavia 45103
Columbiana, Lisbon 44432
Crawford, Bucyrus 44820
Cuyahoga, Cleveland 44114
Erie, Sandusky 44870
Fairfield, Lancaster 43130
Franklin, Columbus 43215
Greene, Xenia 45385
Hamilton, Cincinnati 45202
Jefferson, Steubenville 43952
Lake, Painesville 44077
Licking, Newark 43055
Lorain, Elyria 44035
Lucas, Toledo 43624
Mahoning, Youngstown 44503
Medina, Medina 44256
Miami, Troy 45373
Montgomery, Dayton 45402
Muskingum, Zanesville 43360
Portage, Ravenna 44266
Richland, Monsfield 44902
Ross, Chillicothe 45601
Stark, Canton 44702
Summit, Akron 44308
Trumbull, Warren 44482
Warren, Lebanon 45036
Wayne, Wooster 44691
Wood, Bowling Green 43402

Oklahoma

Cleveland, Norman 73069
Garfield, Enid 73701

Oklahoma, Oklahoma City 73105
Payne, Stillwater 74074
Tulsa, Tulsa 74103

Oregon

Clackmas, Oregon City 97045
Douglas, Roseburg 97470
Jackson, Medford 97501
Lane, Eugene 97401
Marion, Salem 97310
Multnomah, Portland 97205
Washington, Hillsboro 97123

Pennsylvania

Adams, Gettysburg 17325
Allegheny, Pittsburgh 15219
Beaver, Beaver 15009
Berks, Reading 19601
Blair, Hollidaysburg 16648
Bucks, Doylestown 18901
Butler, Butler 16001
Cambria, Ebensburg 15931
Centre, Bellefonte 16823
Chester, West Chester 19380
Cumberland, Carlisle 17013
Dauphin, Harrisburg 17101
Delaware, Media 19063
Erie, Erie 16501
Fayette, Uniontown 15401
Franklin, Chambersburg 15723
Lackawanna, Scranton 18503
Lancaster, Lancaster 17602
Lawrence, New Castle 16101
Lebanon, Lebanon 17042
Lehigh, Allentown 18101
Luzerne, Wilkes-Barre 18703
Lycoming, Williamsport 17701
Mercer, Mercer 16137
Montgomery, Norristown 19404
Northampton, Easton 18042
Northumberland, Sunbury 17801
Philadelphia, Phildelphia 19107
Schuylkill, Pottsville, 17901
Somerset, Somerset 15501
Venango, Franklin 16323
Washington, Washington 15301
Westmoreland, Greensburg 15601
York, York 17405

Rhode Island

Kent, East Greenwich 02818
Newport, Newport 02840
Providence, Providence 02903
Washington, West Kingston 02892

South Carolina

Aiken, Aiken 29801
Anderson, Anderson 29621
Charleston, Charleston 29401
Florence, Florence 29501
Greenville, Greenville 29601
Lexington, Lexington 29072
Orangeburg, Orangeburg 29115
Spartanburg, Spartanburg 29301
Sumter, Sumter 29150

South Dakota

Hughes, Pierre 57501
Minnehaha, Sioux Falls 57102
Pennington, Rapid City 57701

Tennessee

Davidson, Nashville 37210
Hamilon, Chattanooga 37402
Knox, Knoxville 37902
Shelby, Memphis 38103
Sullivan, Blountville 37617

Texas

Bell, Belton 76513
Bexar, San Antonio 78205
Brazoria, Angleton 77551
Cameron, Brownsville 78520
Dallas, Dallas 75201
El Paso, El Paso 79901
Galveston, Galveston 77550
Harris, Houston 77002
Jefferson, Beaumont 77704
Lubbock, Lubbock 79404
McLennan, Waco 76887
Nueces, Corpus Christi 78401
Potter, Amarillo 79101
Reeves, Pecos 79772
Smith, Tyler 75701
Tarrant, Fort Worth 76102
Taylor, Abilene 79601

Travis, Austin 78767
Wichita, Wichita Falls 76301

Utah

Davis, Farmington 84025
Salt Lake, Salt Lake City 84110
Utah, Provo 84601
Weber, Ogden 84401

Vermont

Chittenden, Burlington 05401
Rutland, Rutland 05701
Washington, Montpelier 05602

Virginia

Arlington, Arlington 22210
Fairfax, Fairfax 22030
Henrico, Richmond 23219
Prince Willam, Manassas 22110
Virginia Beach, Virginia Beach 73458

Washington

Clark, Vancouver 98660
King, Seattle 98101
Pierce, Tacoma 98402
Snohomish, Everett 98201
Spokane, Spokane 99201
Thurston, Olympia 98501
Walla Walla, Walla Walla 99362
Whatcom, Bellingham 98225
Yakima, Yakima 98901

West Virginia

Harrison, Clarksburg 26301
Kanahwa, Charleston 25301
Monongalia, Morgantown 26505
Ohio, Wheeling 26003
Wood, Parkersburg 26105

Wisconsin

Brown, Green Bay 54301
Dane, Madison 53701
Eau Claire, Eau Claire 54701
Fond du Lac, Fond du Lac 54935
Kenosha, Kenosha 53140
La Crosse, La Crosse 54601
Manitowoc, Manitowoc 54220
Marathon, Wausau 54401
Milwaukee, Milwaukee 53202
Outagamie, Appleton 54911
Racine, Racine 53403
Rock, Janesville 53545
Sheboygan, Sheboygan 53081
Waukesha, Waukesha 53186
Winnebago, Oshkosh 54901

Wyoming

Albany, Laramie 82070
Laramie, Cheyenne 82001
Natrona, Casper 82601

Chapter 13

SOCIOECONOMIC (SPECIAL HELP) PROGRAMS

There are many varieties and sources of help available to most small businesses, but they are not well publicized. Knowledge of the programs and sources is therefore of special importance.

The Government Will Help You Sell to the Government

Prior to the postwar period following World War II the government of the United States did not have a formal or comprehensive set of procurement regulations, nor was federal purchasing a really great economic force prior to that war. However, while the end of the war brought about some slackening in federal expenditures, spending for postwar weapons systems remained high, with typical surges later as the United States became engaged in later wars in Korea and Vietnam. But other programs were launched, and it was soon obvious that federal spending was never going to revert to prewar levels, but would remain relatively high indefinitely.

That brought about formal procurement regulations, which have continued to evolve over the years, reflecting a trend to unification of procurement regulations. Where there were formerly several different sets of regulations and myriad memoranda and bulletins directing procurement policies and practices, a uniform set of procurement regulations, the Federal Acquisition Regulations (FAR) has finally evolved. But concurrent with this order of magnitude increase in federal procurement budgets and formalization of federal procurement practices, there has come also an awakening national social conscience with many programs developed to pursue liberal goals.

Ultimately, the legislators recognized that modern purchasing power of the federal government is such a great economic force that government procurement alone has a great ability to influence the economy of the country. This has led to a succession of socioeconomic programs linked to federal buying power, in which goals generally are to encourage and nourish free enterprise and small business growth, and to afford greater equality of economic opportunity for all.

The Small Business Administration

Among the earliest efforts to use the federal purchasing power for socioeconomic benefits was the formation of the Small Business Administration (SBA) in 1953, under the Small Business Act. The SBA operates a variety of programs in carrying out its missions, which are to aid small business generally and minority- and women-owned business especially in a variety of ways. These are the general types of programs and activities SBA carries out, and they were being threatened with abolition by the federal government early in 1985:

1. Financing of enterprises through a variety of loans, loan guarantees, and other programs.
2. Special preference, where possible and practicable, and special help in winning government contracts and in carrying them out successfully.
3. Special services, such as consulting and training in general business functions.
4. Publications, many free, others at nominal cost.

Among its functions SBA sets the standards that determine what qualifies a venture as a small business. The general language of the law is that to qualify as a small business the company must not be in a dominant position within its industry, so SBA must determine what size determines dominance or nondominance within each industry and how that may be measured. The standards therefore vary from one industry to another so that there are many standards of small-business size. Some are based on annual sales in dollars, some on number of employees, and some on other factors.

To help small businesses win government contracts, some contracts are set aside for small businesses only; larger businesses cannot bid for them. In addition, small businesses are entitled automatically to progress payments on government contracts and are also entitled to enlist SBA aid when they are having difficulties of any kind, such as finding the financing necessary to handle a contract or to demonstrate qualifying "financial responsibility" and financial capability to a contracting officer. Similarly, if in bidding for a contract it becomes necessary to demonstrate qualifying technical capability to a contracting officer, a small business may seek assistance from SBA in an SBA certification of technical capability.

The Small Business Administration also operates a special program for minorities, the so-called 8(a) program, to help minority entrepreneurs succeed in winning government contracts by certifying minority firms as qualifying under that clause—8(a)—of the law and exempting them from normal competition for many awards set aside as 8(a) contracts. (The competition, when and if there is any for such contracts, is technical only, not cost, and is confined to certified minority firms only.)

The Small Business Administration operates approximately 100 offices throughout the United States, with the central or headquarters office in Washington, DC. (Other offices are Regional or District offices.) Following is a list of those offices:

ALABAMA
Birmingham 35205
908 S. 20th Street, Room 202
ALASKA
Anchorage 99501
1016 W. 6th Avenue, Suite 200
Fairbanks 99701
Federal Building & Courthouse
ARIZONA
Phoenix 85004
112 N. Central Avenue
ARKANSAS
Little Rock 72202
611 Gaines Street, Suite 900
CALIFORNIA
Fresno 93712
1229 N. Street
Los Angeles 90071
350 S. Figueroa Street
Sacramento 95825
2800 Cottage Way, Room 2535
San Diego 92188
880 Front Street, Room 4-S-38
San Francisco 94102
*450 Golden Gate Avenue
211 Main Street, 4th Floor
COLORADO
Denver 80202
*1405 Curtis Street, 22nd Floor
721 19th Street
CONNECTICUT
Hartford 06103
1 Financial Plaza
DELAWARE
Wilmington 19801
844 King Street, Room 5207
DISTRICT OF COLUMBIA
Washington 20416
**1441 L Street, NW
Washington 20417
1030 15th Street, NW

FLORIDA
Coral Gables 33134
2222 Ponce de Leon Boulevard
Jacksonville 32202
400 West Bay Street, Room 261
Tampa 33607
700 Twiggs Street
West Palm Beach 33402
701 Clematis Street
GEORGIA
Atlanta 30309
*1375 Peachtree Street, NE
1720 Peachtree Street, NW
GUAM
Agana 96910
Pacific Daily News Building
HAWAII
Honolulu 96850
300 Ala Moana, Box 50207
IDAHO
Boise 83702
1005 Main Street
ILLINOIS
Chicago 60604
*219 South Dearborn Street
Springfield 62701
1 North Old State Capital Plaza
INDIANA
Indianapolis 46204
575 North Pennsylvania Street
IOWA
Des Moines 50309
210 Walnut Street, Room 749
KANSAS
Wichita 67202
110 East Waterman Street
KENTUCKY
Louisville 40202
600 Federal Plaza, Room 188
LOUISIANA
New Orleans 70113
1001 Howard Avenue, 17th Floor

*Regional Office

**Central (Headquarters) Office

Shreveport 71101
500 Fannin Street
 MAINE
Augusta 04330
40 Western Avenue, Room 512
 MARYLAND
Baltimore/Towson 21204
LaSalle Road
 MASSACHUSETTS
Boston 02114
*60 Batterymarch, 10th Floor
Boston 02203
150 Causeway Street
Holyoke 01050
302 High Street, 4th Floor
 MICHIGAN
Detroit 48226
477 Michigan Avenue
Marquette 49855
540 West Kave Avenue
 MINNESOTA
Minneapolis 55402
12 South 6th Street
 MISSISSIPPI
Biloxi 39530
111 Fred Haise Boulevard
Jackson 39201
200 East Pascagoula Street
 MISSOURI
Kansas City 64106
*911 Walnut Street, 23rd Floor
1150 Grande Avenue
St. Louis 63101
1 Mercantile Center
 MONTANA
Helena 59601
301 South Park, Drawer 10054
 NEBRASKA
Omaha 68102
Empire State Building, 2nd Floor
 NEVADA
Las Vegas 89101
301 East Stewart Street
Reno 89505
50 South Virginia Street, Room 213
 NEW HAMPSHIRE
Concord 03301
55 Pleasant Street, Room 213

NEW JERSEY
Camden 08104
1800 East Davis Street
Newark 07102
970 Broad Street, Room 1635
 NEW MEXICO
Albuquerque 87110
5000 Marble Avenue, NE
 NEW YORK
Albany 12210
99 Washington Avenue, Room 301
Buffalo 14202
111 West Huron Street, Room 1311
Elmira 14904
1051 South Maine Street
Melville 11746
425 Broad Hollow Road
New York 1007
*26 Federal Plaza, Room 29-118
26 Federal Plaza, Room 3100
Rochester 14614
100 State Street, Room 601
Syracuse 13260
100 South Clinton Street
 NORTH CAROLINA
Charlotte 28202
230 South Tryon Street
Greenville 27834
215 South Evans Street, Room 206
 NORTH DAKOTA
Fargo 58102
65 72nd Avenue North, Room 218
 OHIO
Cincinnati 45202
550 Main Street, Room 5028
Cleveland 44199
1240 East 9th Street, Room 317
Columbus 43215
85 Marconi Boulevard
 OKLAHOMA
Oklahoma City 73102
200 NW 5th Street, Room 670
 OREGON
Portland 97205
1220 SW 3rd Ave, Federal Building
 PENNSYLVANIA
Harrisburg 17101
100 Chestnut Street

*Regional Office

Philadelphia/Bala-Cynwyd 19004
*1 Bala-Cynwyd Plaza
Pittsburgh 15222
1000 Liberty Avenue Room 1401
Wilkes-Barre 18702
20 North Pennsylvania Avenue
  PUERTO RICO
Hato Rey 00919
Chardon and Bolivia Streets
  RHODE ISLAND
Providence 02903
40 Fountain Street
  SOUTH CAROLINA
Columbia 29201
1801 Assembly Street, Room 131
  SOUTH DAKOTA
Rapid City 57701
515 9th Street, Room 246
Sioux Falls 57102
101 S. Maine Avenue
  TENNESSEE
Knoxville 37902
502 South Gay Street, Room 307
Memphis 38103
167 North Main Street, Room 211
Nashville 37219
404 James Robertson Parkway
  TEXAS
Corpus Christi 78408
3105 Leopard Street
Dallas 75202
1100 Commerce St, Room 3C36
Dallas 75235
*1729 Regal Rox, Room 230
El Paso 79901
4100 Rio Bravo, Suite 300
Harlingen 78550
222 E. Van Buren Street

Houston 77002
500 Dallas Street
1 Allen Center
Lubbock 79401
1205 Texas Avenue, Room 712
Marshall 75670
100 South Washington Street
San Antonio 78206
727 East Durango, Room A-513
  UTAH
Salt Lake City 84138
125 South State Street
  VERMONT
Montpelier 06502
  VIRGINIA
Richmond 23240
  VIRGIN ISLANDS
St. Thomas 00801
Veterans Drive, U.S. Federal Building
  WASHINGTON
Seattle 98104
*710 2nd Avenue, 5th Floor
915 2nd Avenue, Room 1744
Spokane 99210
Court House Building, Room 651
  WEST VIRGINIA
Charleston 25301
Charleston National Plaza
Clarksburg 26301
109 North 3rd Street
  WISCONSIN
Eau Claire 54701
500 South Barstow Street
Madison 53703
212 East Washington Avenue
Milwaukee 53202
517 East Wisconsin Avenue
  WYOMING
Casper 82602
100 East B Street

*Regional Office

Small Business Innovative Research (SBIR) Program

The Small Business Administration (SBA) also operates the SBIR program mandated by Congress under a special act to encourage greater utilization of small business in creative work. Small Business Administration is, at the time of this writing, having an information brochure about this program prepared, which should be available by the time you read this.

General Services Administration

The General Services Administration (GSA) operates a network of Business Service Centers throughout the United States. The purpose of each of these centers is to assist vendors who wish to pursue government contracts. Each center has a supply of helpful literature and counselors who will meet with you to answer questions and provide guidance. The locations of these centers are as follows:

300 North Los Angeles Street
Los Angeles, CA 90012

1500 East Bannister Road
Kansas City, MO 64131

525 Market Street
San Francisco, CA 9410

26 Federal Plaza
New York, NY 10007

Denver Federal Center, Building 41
Denver, CO 80225

600 Arch Street
Philadelphia, PA 19106

7th & D Streets, SW
Washington, DC 20407

819 Taylor Street
Fort Worth, TX 76102

1776 Peachtree Street, NW
Atlanta, GA 30309

515 Rusk Street, FOB Courthouse
Houston, TX 77002

230 South Dearborn Street
Chicago, IL 60604

915 2nd Avenue
Seattle, WA 98174

John W. McCormack P.O. & Courthouse
Boston, MA 02109

Minority Business Development Agency

The Minority Business Development Agency (MBDA) is an organization within the U.S. Department of Commerce whose mission is to support the development of minority-owned businesses. This organization has changed direction in recent years (marked by the change from the former name, the Office of Minority Business Development [OMBD] to the present name). Where the original organization tended to support any kind of enterprise, the current organization tends to encourage the growth of minority-owned high-technology enterprises. In any case, the program consists primarily of supporting a number of nonprofit centers (roughly 100 in number, at this time) around the country. A request must be made of the organization in Washington, DC, for an up-to-date list of their contractors and centers. The central office address is as follows:

Minority Business Development Agency
U.S. Department of Commerce
14th Street & Constitution Avenue
Washington, DC 20230

Field and Regional offices of MBDA are as follows:

MBDA, Department of Commerce
2940 Valley Bank Center, Suite 2490
Phoenix, AZ 85073

MBDA, Department of Commerce
14 NE 1st Avenue, Room 1100
Miami, FL 33132

MBDA, Department of Commerce
450 Golden Gate Ave, Room 15045
San Francisco, CA 94102

MBDA, Department of Commerce
1371 Peachtree St, NW, Suite 505
Atlanta, GA 30309

MBDA, Department of Commerce
1730 K Street, NW
Washington, DC 20006

MBDA. Department of Commerce
55 East Monroe Street, Suite 1440
Chicago, IL 60603

MBDA, Department of Commerce
600 South Street, Room 901
New Orleans, LA 70130

MBDA, Department of Commerce
600 Arch Street
Philadelphia, PA 19106

MBDA, Department of Commerce
441 Stuart Street, 10th Floor
Boston, MA 02116

MBDA, Department of Commerce
United American Bank Blding, #714
Memphis, TN 38103

MBDA, Department of Commerce
505 Marquette Street
Albuquerque, NM 87101

MBDA, Department of Commerce
1412 Main Street, Room 1702
Dallas, TX 75202

MBDA, Department of Commerce
26 Federal Plaza
New York, NY 10007

MBDA, Department of Commerce
727 East Durango St., Room B-412
San Antonio, TX 78206

Small Business Utilization Offices

All federal agencies are required to maintain small business utilization functions, with individuals appointed to act as advocates for small business interests and to influence in all ways possible the utilization of small business in satisfying federal needs, directly and indirectly. That means making direct contract awards to small businesses, where possible, and assisting small business in winning subcontracts from the large prime contractors to the government. When making calls on any agency, it is always a good idea to talk to the contracting officer and any small-business representatives who are available. In agencies doing a large amount of procurement there is likely to be an individual or even an office of several individuals charged with the responsibility. In agencies doing only occasional or relatively small amounts of procurement the small-business representative may well be the agency's contracting officer wearing another hat. However, the function is required to exist, by law, and it is often well worth the time and effort to spend a few minutes with the small-business representative and/or contracting officer.

The Department of Defense (DOD) is especially active in utilizing small businesses as suppliers because DOD accounts for such a significantly large portion of the overall federal procurement budget that it is in DOD's own interest to maximize competition and support a maximum number of suppliers. (One major consideration of military procurement is the maintenance of the maximum industrial base to be ready with near-instant support in event of an emergency.) Of course, the law also requires small-business utilization, and DOD is unquestionably by far the largest customer in the federal establishment, so it follows that DOD would have the most highly developed system of small-business-utilization specialists.

Federal Procurement Literature

Virtually every federal agency publishes some kind of pamphlet, brochure, or booklet (depending on the volume of their procurements) describing their needs and usual items of purchase, and other information relevant to their procurement systems and practices. Those agencies accounting for large portions of federal procurement, such as the military services, publish relatively thick manuals describing their needs and systems. These larger manuals are offered for sale by the Government Printing Office. However, a great many of the agencies will furnish their manuals free of charge upon request, and it is a good idea to collect as many of these manuals and brochures as possible. (Some of the major publications of this type will be listed in an appendix, together with other suggested literature.)

State Government Programs

Like the federal government, many state governments and even local governments have instituted programs to support minority entrepreneurs, small businesses, and local businesses in a variety of ways. The programs fall into several categories:

> Loans and loan-guarantees
> Counseling and consultative assistance
> Preferences in government procurement
> Handling complaints
> Legislative activity for future programs

Table 13-1 reports on the latest general status of such programs for those states which have adopted or are in the process of adopting programs at the time this is being written. However, the adoption of programs is in somewhat of a state of flux, and is changing rather rapidly, so some of the information offered here may be dated by the time you read this. It is therefore highly advisable to make direct inquiry of all local purchasing offices, departments of commerce, business development agencies, or other state and local agencies that may be charged with such responsibilities and determine what the status of such programs is at the time. In the meanwhile, this information is helpful in gaining a general knowledge of the types of programs you may find in any state or local government which is of interest to you, and of which you make inquiry.

Table 13-1 is a general guide. However, wherever details are available further information is offered in addition to that in the table, in text following the figure. This includes identification of the state offices to contact for details and/or services. The major programs are indicated in the table. The

Table 13-1   State Socioeconomic Programs

State	Loan	Procurement Preference	Assistance Office	Complaint Handling	Other
ALABAMA		X			
ALASKA	X		X		
ARIZONA		X	X	X	
ARKANSAS			X	X	X
CALIFORNIA	X	X	X		X
COLORADO			X		X
CONNECTICUT	X	X	X	X	X
FLORIDA			X	X	X
GEORGIA		X			X
HAWAII	X				
ILLINOIS	X	X	X	X	X
INDIANA		X		X	X
IOWA				X	X
KANSAS		X			X
KENTUCKY	X	X	X	X	X
LOUISIANA		X	X	X	
MAINE	X				X
MARYLAND	X	X	X		
MASSACHUSETTS	X	X	X	X	X
MICHIGAN	X	X	X	X	X
MINNESOTA	X	X	X	X	X
MISSISSIPPI	X	X	X		X
MISSOURI	X	X			X
MONTANA	X	X	X	X	X
NEBRASKA			X		
NEW HAMPSHIRE	X				
NEW JERSEY	X		X	X	X
NEW MEXICO			X	X	X
NEW YORK		X	X	X	X
NORTH CAROLINA		X			X
NORTH DAKOTA	X				X
OHIO	X		X	X	X
OKLAHOMA	X				X
OREGON			X	X	X
PENNSYLVANIA		X	X	X	X
RHODE ISLAND	X			X	X
TENNESSEE	X		X		X
TEXAS	X	X	X		X
UTAH			X	X	X
VERMONT	X		X		
VIRGINIA			X		
WASHINGTON		X	X	X	X
WEST VIRGINIA			X	X	X
WISCONSIN		X		X	X
PUERTO RICO	X				
VIRGIN ISLANDS	X		X		

"other" column refers to legislative programs, advisory boards, and other types of assistance or support than the ones listed.

Some Additional Details

Following are additional details of each state's programs, on the basis of whatever information is available at this time. Once again, it is advisable to verify this information, which may very well be completely outdated by the time you read this.

Alabama.   Alabama gives preference for small business, which is defined as one with fewer than 50 employees or less than $1 million in gross annual receipts. The Department of Industrial Relations is authorized to render a variety of services to help small businesses win state contracts. Contact Office of State Planning, 3734 Atlanta Highway, Montgomery 36130.

Alaska.   Alaska has several loan programs, all of them rather comprehensive and well defined, and including both direct loans from the state and bank-participation loans, wherein the state and the bank are co-lenders. Alaska also operates a small business assistance office. Contact the Division of Economic Enterprise, Department of Commerce and Economic Development, 675 7th Avenue, Station A, Fairbanks 99701.

Arizona.   Little information on Arizona's socioeconomic programs is available at this moment. Contact Arizona's Office of Economic Planning and Development, 1700 West Washington, Room 400, Phoenix 85007.

Arkansas.   Arkansas has established a small-business office. Contact Arkansas's Small Business Assistance division, Arkansas Department of Economic Development, One State Capitol Mall, Little Rock 72201.

California.   California offers a comprehensive set of socioeconomic programs, including loan programs and a Small Business Procurement Office to give procurement preference to small business in the state. Requirements are that the business be located in California and not dominant in the relevant industry, to qualify for such preference. (Of course, you may always bid for state contracts without qualifying for preference.) Contact the Small Business Procurement Office, Department of General Services, 1823 14th Street, Sacramento 95807.

Colorado.   Colorado has a Small Business Council and also provides a number of other services to small business. Contact The Small Business Assistance Center, University of Colorado, Campus Box 434, Boulder 80309; and the Colorado Department of Local Affairs, Division of Commerce and Development, 1313 Sherman Street, Room 500, Denver 80203.

Connecticut.   Connecticut has a definite small-business set-aside requirement and defines small businesses as those which have been domiciled and doing business in the state for at least one year and whose annual revenues are not in excess of $1 million for the previous fiscal year. Contact the Office of Small Business Affairs, Department of Economic Development, State Office Building, Hartford 06115.

Florida.   Contact the Office of Business Assistance, Executive Office of the Governor, Tallahassee 32301.

Georgia.   Georgia defines small business as having fewer than 100 employees or less than $1 million in gross annual receipts. An advisory council of small business representatives offers counsel on procurement matters to Georgia's Department of Administrative Services.

Hawaii.   Hawaii uses the federal (SBA) definition of small business as its own and operates a loan program also. Contact the Department of Planning and Economic Development, 250 South King Street, Honolulu 96813.

Illinois.   Illinois has a Department of Commerce and Community Affairs within which is included the Illinois Office of Business Services. This office incorporates the duties and services formerly provided by the old Small Business Information Office. Contact the Illinois Office of Business Services, 180 North LaSalle Street, Chicago 60701; and/or the Small Business Coordinator, Department of Administrative Services, Stratton Office Building, Room 802, Springfield 62707.

Indiana.   Indiana now has a Small Business Ombudsman office to help small business in a variety of ways, including help in bidding for state contracts. Contact Ombudsman Office, 503 State Office Building, Indianapolis 46204.

Iowa.   Iowa operates an Office of Ombudsman and a legislative program for small business. Address inquiries to Iowa Citizens' Aide Office, State Capital, Des Moines 50319.

Kansas.   Kansas establishes as a goal the setting aside for small business of at least 10 percent of state purchases, and has a legislative program as well. Among several other criteria, businesses must meet standards of numbers of employees and/or annual dollar volume set for different industries to qualify as small business in the state.

Kentucky.   Kentucky has a small business office to oversee and manage its small business programs, which includes small business set-asides in state procurement. Contact the Small Business Development Section, Small and Minority Business Development Division, Kentucky Department of Commerce, Capital Plaza, Frankfort 40601.

Louisiana.   Louisiana has a small business set-aside program and defines small business according to standards of numbers of employees and annual volume, which vary for different types of enterprises. Contact the Louisiana Department of Commerce, Office of Commerce and Industry, POB 44185, Baton Rouge 70804.

Maine.   Contact the Maine Development Foundation, One Memorial Circle, Augusta 04333.

Maryland.   In-state small business in Maryland gets a 5 percent preference over out-of-state bidders for state contracts. Contact the Office of Business Liaison and the Office of Business and Industrial Development, Department of Economic and Community Development, 1748 Forest Drive, Annapolis 21401. An Office of Minority Business Enterprise is located at the same address.

Massachusetts.   Massachusetts operates a broad spread of small-business programs and other programs for business generally, including general assistance to small business in winning both state and federal contracts and offering a extensive consultative assistance. Contact the Division of Small Business Assistance, Department of Commerce and Development, 100 Cambridge Street, Boston 02202. Also contact the Business Information Center/Network (BIC/NET) and Business Service Center within the same Department and at the same address. Also Massachusetts Technology Development Corporation, 131 State Street, Boston 02109 and Massachusetts Business Development Corporation, One Boston Place, Boston 02108.

Michigan.   Michigan offers a variety of business-assistance programs, including help in winning state contracts. For small- and minority-business assistance programs contact the Business Enterprise Specialist, Purchasing Division, Department of Management and Budget, Mason Building, 2nd Floor, Lansing 48909 and the Small Business Development Division, Office of Economic Development, Michigan Department of Commerce, POB 30225, Lansing 48909.

Minnesota.   Minnesota has as a goal the awarding of 20 percent of the state's procurement dollars to small business, which it defines as one with not more than 20 employees nor more than $1 million in annual revenues. The program is administered by the Department of Economic Development, 480 Cedar Street, St. Paul 55101.

Mississippi.   Mississippi operates a broad spread of programs for small business, including publications, consultation, training, and procurement preference, and has a number of offices with related functions in different areas of the state. Contact the Small Business Assistance Division, Agricultural and Industrial Board, Agriculture and Commerce Department, 301 Walter Sillers Building, Jackson 39205.

Missouri.   Little information is available currently about Missouri's small business programs (relevant legislation was pending at the time of this writing), but the state advises that small businesses should seek assistance from the program of Existing Business Assistance, Division of Community and Economic Development, Jefferson City 65102.

Montana.   Montana includes within its small business programs one that pledges that "all agencies will insure that a fair proportion of the state government's total purchases and contracts for property and services are placed with small business concerns." Contact the Office of Commerce and Small Business Development, Governor's Office, Room 212, Capitol Station, Helena 59601.

New Jersey.   New Jersey has a small business assistance office with rather a general and broadly defined mission to aid small business. Contact the New Jersey Department of Labor and Industry, John Fitch Plaza, Trenton 08625.

New Mexico.   New Mexico has no specific program for small business, but vendors are invited to contact Existing Industry Liaison, Economic Development Division, Santa Fe 85703.

New York.   New York's several small business programs include one offering help in winning state contracts. Contact the Division of Ombudsmen and Small Business Services, 230 Park Avenue, New York 10017.

North Carolina.   North Carolina has a small business program, but without any specific dollar or percentage goals. Contact the Business Assistance Division, North Carolina Department of Commerce, 430 North Salisbury Street, Raleigh 27611.

Ohio.   Contact the Office of Small Business Assistance, Ohio Department of Economic and Community Development, Columbus 43215.

Oregon. Contact Small Business Office, Director for Business/Government Relations, Department of Economic Development, Salem 97310.

Pennsylvania.   Pennsylvania does not have a special small business program but takes the position that all businesses should have all possible assistance and services from the state. There is, however, a Small Business Service Center, South Office Building, Room G-13, Harrisburg 17120.

Tennessee.   Contact Small Business Information Center, Department of Economic & Community Development, 107 Andrew Jackson State Office Building, Nashville 37219.

Texas.   Texas has a small business procurement program, among others, which has the goal of awarding at least 10 percent of the state's procurement dollars to small business, defined as those with fewer than 100 employees or less than $1 million in annual revenues. Contact the Purchasing and General Services Commission, 1711 San Jacinto Street, Austin 78701.

Utah.   Utah has a small business office. Contact the Business Development Coordinator, No. 2 Arrow Press Square, Suite 260, 165 South West Temple, Salt Lake City 84101.

Vermont.   Contact Vermont Economic Opportunity Office, Montpelier 05602.

West Virginia.   West Virginia sets general goals for awards to small business, which is defined by using federal SBA standards. Contact Small Business Service Unit, Governor's Office of Economic and Community Development, Building 6, Suite B-564, Capitol Complex, Charleston 25305.

Wisconsin. Wisconsin includes a small business procurement program. Contact Small Business Ombudsman, Department of Business Development, Madison 53702.

Local Government Programs

Many local governments—those of counties, cities, towns, and townships—operate similar programs of preference for and general assistance to small-business and minority enterprises. Inquiry should be made of the purchasing offices in these jurisdictions to ensure that you learn of and can take advantage of such programs for which you qualify.

Chapter 14

THE REFERENCE FILE

If it is wisdom to know what you don't know, the essence of education must be to learn where and how to find out what you wish to know.

The Power of Knowledge

That we live in an increasingly complex world, that we have had an explosion of information over the past few decades (concurrent with and directly linked to the growth of the computer era) and that information is power, are all modern platitudes. They are, in fact, accepted premises, and do not need even to be argued. And this final chapter is itself an acknowledgement of those premises.

Although much of the preceding pages consisted of narrative, in a large sense this entire work is a reference book. Yet there are many miscellaneous items of reference information which are only indirectly related to marketing to all the agencies of the federal, state, and local governments, but which are of great significance to marketers nevertheless, and which can make important contributions to success in marketing. What you will find in these concluding pages, therefore, is a potpourri of items, such as listings of various kinds, checklists, guides, and sundry other kinds of information whose very existence you may not have even suspected.

Relevant Publications and Why They Are Useful

Publications that are relevant to the interests of those who market to government agencies fall into several classes, including these:

1. Those publications which are concerned with the procurement process itself, some designed to proliferate ideas among procurement specialists, including purchasing agents, contracting officers, lawyers specializing in procurement/contract laws, and others linked to these interests. These might be classified as "procurement publications."

2. Those publications which are directed to the marketers to bring them news, ideas, and sundry service articles intended to help them win contracts from government agencies. These might be referred to generally as "marketing publications."
3. There is a kind of hybrid, including those publications of the governments themselves, which are addressed to the marketers, but have the dual purpose of explaining the procurement systems while also intended to help marketers win government business; that is, they are both "procurement" and "marketing" publications.

The following list includes all three general types, with a few notes included, in some cases, to provide more detailed information about the publications. These publications are useful in at least two ways. Their obvious value lies in providing insights into government procurement philosophies, principles, and procedures, all necessary knowledge for the marketer. But there is a less obvious use that is at least as valuable and possibly even more so: Much of success in marketing to government agencies lies in the ability to write persuasive proposals, and many of the publications cited here contain valuable material for proposals. For that reason, even in those cases where the publication deals with the purchase of other items than those related to computers and computer services, they often offer useful ideas and input for proposals and should be part of the reference library of any organization seriously engaged in writing proposals.

The listings offered here are by no means exhaustive but are starter lists, to which you should add items, as you discover them. Too, if you write to all major federal agencies and ask for information about their purchasing and procurement activities, you will get a great many useful publications to add to your library of materials.

Newsletters

Government Sales Strategist, 10076 Boca Entrada Boulevard, Boca Raton, FL 33433.

Contracting Intelligence, 100 Northfield Street, Greenwich, CT 06830.

Federal Contracts Report, The Bureau of National Affairs, 1231 25th Street, NW, Washington, DC 20037.

NATaT's National Community Reporter, National Association of Towns and Townships, 1522 K Street, NW, Suite 730, Washington, DC 20005.

Off the Shelf, Coalition for Common Sense in Government Procurement, 1990 M Street, NW, Suite 570, Washington, DC 20036.

Small Business News, Smaller Business Association of N.E., 69 Hickory Drive, Waltham, MA 02154.

From the State Capitals, 321 Sunset Avenue, Asbury Park, NJ 07712.

Government Procurement Newsletter, Carnegie Press, 100 Kings Road, Madison, NJ 07940.

Government Training News, Carnegie Press, 100 Kings Road, Madison, NJ 0940.

Of Consuming Interest, Federal-State Reports, 5203 Leesburg Pike, Suite 1201, Falls Church, VA 22041.

Minority Contracting Reports & Reference File, WHM Publishing Co., 6073 Arlington Boulevard, Falls Church, VA 22044.

Government Purchasing Outlook, Executive Publications, Inc., 1725 K Street, NW, Washington, DC 20006.

Local Government Funding Report, Government Information Services, 725 National Press Building, Washington, DC 20045.

Public Works News, POB 578, Glen Echo, MD 20768.

State Headlines, Council of State Governments, POB 11910, Lexington, KY 40578.

Government Procurement Newsletter, 235 National Press Building, Washington, DC 20045.

Federal Funding News, National Association of State Mental Health Program Directors, 1001 3rd Street, SW, Suite 115, Washington, DC 20024

City Hall Digest, POB 309, Seabrook, MD 20801.

Books, Manuals, and Miscellaneous Publications   Quarterly reports compiled by Office of Information Resources Management/GSA, based on data from the Federal Procurement Data Center reporting on federal procurement, with a great deal of amplifying and ancillary information on many aspects of federal purchasing and procurement. An essential for the alert marketer to federal agencies. Contact the Federal Procurement Data Center, GSA, Suite 900, 4040 Fairfax Drive, Arlington, VA 22203.

U.S. Government Purchasing and Sales Directory, U.S. Small Business Administration, Washington, DC 1977.

United States Government Manual, annual publication, Government Printing Office, Washington, DC 20402 or any GPO bookstore.

Government Contracts: Proposalmanship and Winning Strategies, Holtz, Herman R., Plenum Publishing Corp., New York 1979.

The $100 Billion Market: How to do Business with the U.S. Government, Holtz, Herman R. AMACOM, New York 1980.

Directory of State Small Business Programs, U.S. Small Business Administration, Washington, DC 1980.

How to Sell to the Government, Cohen, William, John Wiley & Sons, New York 1981.

The Winning Proposal: How to Write it, Holtz, Herman R. and Schmidt, Terry, McGraw-Hill Book Co., New York 1981.

Directory of Federal Purchasing Offices, Holtz, Herman, John Wiley & Sons, New York 1981.

How to do Business with the Defense Logistics Agency and

An Identification of Commodities Purchased by the Defense Logistics Agency, DLA Small Business Advisor, Cameron Station, Alexandria, VA 22314.

Model Procurement Code for State and Local Governments, American Bar Association, Washington, DC 1979. Provides clear insight into basics of most government procurement policies, regulations, and practices. Especially useful to newcomers to government marketing. Single copies available. Order from Coordinating Committee on a

Model Procurement Code, American Bar Association, 1700 K Street, NW, Suite 601, Washington, DC 20006.

Purchase Manual, Guilford County, NC, and *Centralized Purchasing Manual*, Rockingham County, VA. Order from National Association of Counties, Home Rule Team: 1735 New York Avenue, NW, Washington, DC 20006.

Study of Selected Local Procurement Systems: Opportunities for Improvement in Local Government Purchasing (Part 1) and

Checklist and Guidelines for Evaluating Local Procurement Systems: Opportunities for Improvement in Local Government Purchasing (Part 2), U.S. General Accounting Office, August 1978. Single copies of both these documents, Part 1 and Part 2, available free from U.S. General Accounting Office, Document Handling and Information Services Facility, POB 6015, Gaithersburg, MD 20877. (You may apply, also, to have your name placed on their general distribution list for announcements of other reports which GAO publishes regularly.)

Purchasing for Local Governments, Institute of Government, University of Georgia 1976, 75 pp. Also *Cooperative Purchasing: A Guide for Local Governments*, by Jerry A. Singer, Institute of Government, University of Georgia 1977, 68 pp. Order from Publications Office, Institute of Government, Terrell Hall, University of Georgia, Athens, GA 30602.

"Contracting Out Public Services," National League of Cities 1979. Cassette tape. Reference No. 9017-430. Available from Eastern Audio Associates, Inc., 9505 Berger Road, Columbia, MD 21046.

A Purchasing Guide for Small Local Governments, Southeast Georgia Area Planning and Development Commission, May 1979, 33 pp, Publication HUD-PDR 441. Order from HUD User, POB 280, Germantown, MD 20767.

Standardization of Equipment and Products for Government Agency Purchasing, Urban Consortium, Washington, DC 1977, 40 pp, Publication IB/77-076. Order from Publications Distribution Section, Public Technology, Inc., 1140 Connecticut Avenue, NW, Washington, DC 220036.

Government for Sale: Contracting Out; the New Patronage, John D. Hanrahan, American Federation of State, County, and Municipal Employees, 1977. Order from AFSCME, 1625 L Street, NW, Washington, DC 20036.

"How Much Do Government Services Really Cost?" *Urban Affairs Quarterly*, September 1979, Vol. 15, No. 1, pp 23-40. Order from Sage Publications, 275 Beverly Drive, Beverly Hills, CA 90212.

Interlocal Service Delivery: A Practical Guide to Intergovernmental Agreements/ Contracts for Local Officials, National Association of Counties Research Foundation 1977, 84 pp. Order from Publications Desk, NACo, 1735 New York Avenue, NW, Washington, DC 20006.

Product Information Network (PIN) for local and state governments. Service of McGraw-Hill, includes reports, bulletins, other information. Contact George Finnegan, Director, Venture Development,

McGraw-Hill, Inc., 1221 Avenue of the Americas, New York, NY 10020.

Relevant Associations

There are thousands of associations of all kinds in the United States. Some of them are trade associations or otherwise of interest to people seeking to do business with governments and their agencies. Those associations that are deemed to be of probable interest to you are listed here.

American Chamber of Commerce Executives, 1133 15th Street, NW, Suite 620, Washington, DC 20005.

Council of State Chambers of Commerce, 499 South Capitol Street, Washington, DC 20003.

American Society for Public Administration, 1225 Connecticut Avenue, NW, Washington, DC 20036.

United States Conference of Mayors, 1620 Eye Street, NW, Washington, DC 20006.

International City Management Association, 1140 Connecticut Avenue, NW, Washington, DC 20036.

National Association of Counties, 1753 New York Avenue, Washington, DC 20006.

National Institute on Governmental Purchasing, Crystal Square Building #3, Suite 101, 1735 Jefferson Davis Highway, Arlington, VA 22202.

National Association of State Purchasing Officials, POB 11910, Lexington, KY 40578.

National Association of Towns and Townships, 1522 K Street, NW, Suite 730, Washington, DC 20005.

Coalition for Common Sense in Government Procurement, 1990 M Street, NW, Suite 570, Washington, DC 20036.

National Association of County Administrators, 1735 New York Avenue, NW, Washington, DC 20006.

National Association of City Planning Directors, 1735 New York Avenue, NW, Washington, DC 20006.

American Society for Hospital Purchasing and Materials Management, 840 North Lake Shore Drive, Chicago, IL 60611.

Society for Marketing Professional Services, 1437 Powhaten Street, Alexandria, VA 22314.

National Purchasing Institute, POB 20549, Houston, TX 77025. National Association of Purchasing Management, 11 Park Place, New York, NY 10007.

National Contract Management Association, 2001 Jefferson Davis Highway, Arlington, VA 22202.

More on Proposals and Strategies

Despite the fairly lengthy chapter on proposal writing, there is much more still left unsaid than has been said on the subject so far in these pages. But proposal writing is among the most important aspects of marketing to government: 85 percent of all procurement dollars spent by the federal government are spent in negotiated procurements, and those almost invariably involve proposal competitions. Ergo, at least a few of the most critical points must be covered in these last few pages.

"Unncessarily Elaborate Proposals."   More than a few proposal writers find themselves dismayed and puzzled by the admonition often found in RFPs against "unnecessarily elaborate" proposals, since the government never offers any definition of what the term "unnecessarily elaborate" means. That makes it somewhat difficult for proposers to comply without harming their own causes. And it is a matter for serious concern since the RFP often states flatly that such extravagance will be considered to be evidence of a lack of cost consciousness. However, an explanation of the origin and reason for the injunction should set the matter straight enough and explain the government's concern:

In the years following World War II, and especially in the fifties, our military organizations generally were awarding thousands of large contracts, some of them even huge contracts, to develop a variety of expensive new weapons and support systems, such as high-speed aircraft, missiles, radar, and computers. Many of the contracts were cost-plus, which all but ensured that the contractor not only would undertake nearly-zero risk in signing these contracts but would be virtually assured of handsome profits, even if the projects were run inefficiently.

For such contracts large corporations were willing to invest substantial sums in proposal writing, and it was not at all uncommon for large firms to spend as much as $250,000 to $500,000 (and sometimes even more) in 1950 dollars. (For example, one electronics manufacturer in Philadelphia, which was fairly large but certainly not among the top 10, spent $400,000 to develop a four-volume proposal for a $65 million contract, which it did not win, even then.) Proposals for major contracts can easily run to several thousand pages and require several volumes to present. But in those days some of these proposals were being printed on expensive papers, included costly artwork (even process-color illustrations à la slick magazines), were bound in leather, and delivered in expensive cases that had been custom designed and constructed to contain the several volumes.

The Professional Image.   *That* was considered to be "unnecessarily elaborate" and is the kind of thing against which the RFPs of today enjoin proposers. On the other hand, it is neither necessary nor advisable to become so Spartan in your proposal writing that you sacrifice your image of professionalism. It is possible to produce a proposal on a creaky manual typewriter, bind it with staples, and win contracts, but that is hardly advisable. With what is available today in even the smallest offices that might very well be construed by a customer to be evidence of indifference or carelessness. In today's office you can compose your proposal on electronic typewriters or word processors, make first-class copies, and bind them suitably, to create a thoroughly professional-looking product that does your image justice, and you should do so. You should give substantial evidence that the contract and your own image are important enough to you to work at producing a proper proposal. Certainly it should be neat and clean, properly edited so that it is lucid, and properly illustrated.

Despite the ready availability of these modern methods in most offices today, if you choose to have your proposal typeset, illustrated by professional artists, and produced (printed and bound) by a print shop, that is also perfectly acceptable and is not considered to be "unnecessarily elaborate." Somewhere between those extremes of extravagance and extreme austerity lies a broad middle-ground of opportunity to do the job well and yet within the bounds of good taste and in compliance with that now-familiar injunction against extravagance.

Communication Aids.   The objective of proposal writing is clear and swift communication. Remember that you are competing with others in more than one way, and one of those other ways is in competition for the reader's attention. The customer, faced with the onerous chore of reading many proposals—even when that is only 5 or 6, but especially when that is 20, 30, or more—is going to discard those which are difficult to follow and spend time on those which communicate easily and swiftly.

Unfortunately, many writers, especially those for whom writing is a chore incident to their career work and a chore they do not relish, tend to the assumption that words are their principal, if not sole, tool and that when they are compelled to use an illustration or other aid it is as an adjunct or supplement to the text, which must be introduced and explained thoroughly. That is a misunderstanding of the writing function. The function is to transmit information—facts, ideas, images, and concepts—with unambiguous and crystal clarity, by whatever means are most effective and most efficient. The writer who insists on using words exclusively or nearly exclusively is not likely to ever be as effective a writer as the one who thinks in terms of (1) what is to be conveyed to a reader and (2) what the best means is for conveying that fact, idea, image, or concept.

There are three general methods available to the writer for presenting information and/or arguments on paper:

1. Text descriptions, arguments, narratives
2. Graphic illustrations—drawings, photographs, charts, plots, graphs
3. Tables and/or matrices

The types of information that must be presented also fall into several general classes that must be considered when determining which are the most effective means for presenting the information. Here are just a few such classes:

Images of familiar objects
Images of unfamiliar objects
Abstractions pertaining to familiar ideas
Abstractions pertaining to new and strange ideas
Relationships among or between items

The Specific Kinds of Graphic Aids

It is not a simple matter to sort and classify all graphic aids because there are several different bases on which we might establish classes. Here is one set of rough or general discriminators:

Line drawings
Wash drawings (and similar)
Photographs

"Wash drawings and similar" might include such work as charcoal sketches and everything that is not line work—drawings that tend mostly to the "continuous tone," rather than line drawings. On the other hand, line drawings would include such graphics as the following:

Flowcharts	Pictorials
Graphs	Columns
Plots (simple curve)	Schematics
Plots (multiple curves)	Engineering drawings
Bar charts	CPM/PERT networks
Pie charts	Logic trees

Figures 14-1 through 14-6 illustrate several of these types of drawings. Most are really simple enough to execute and do not necessarily require a professional illustrator, although admittedly a professional illustrator could make these simple drawings a bit more attractive and polished. Still, anyone armed with a template or two and perhaps other simple artist's aids, a pen or pencil, and a bit of patience can do a thoroughly acceptable job of preparing such drawings. (In fact, most of these were prepared by writers, not by illustrators.)

Who Conceives the Illustrations?

It has already been pointed out that it is up to the writer to identify the need for or advisability of using an illustration. Ordinarily, the writer develops the concept for the illustration, also, although it is wise to consult with the illustrator if you are using professional help to create your graphics. The experienced professional illustrator may very well know better ways than you do to present a concept or an analogy graphically.

Tables and Matrices

Another way to aid communication is, as noted, by using tabular or matrix presentations, two methods which are so similar to each other that the terms are often used interchangeably. In fact, we might well use the term *simple table* to refer to the purely tabular presentation, and *matrix* to refer to the more complex tabular presentation. In fact, a table is a simple listing of items, usually with more than one column, used as an efficient means for presenting simple facts about each of a number of items. Usually the leftmost column lists the items and the succeeding columns list data about each item, as in Figure 14-7.

For familiar objects—an orange, a chair, a building, and aircraft— simple textual references and/or descriptions are usually adequate. But when the object is unfamiliar, and especially when it is difficult to describe in ordinary language without using unfamiliar technical terms or jargon, illustrations are a must. Try to describe an apple or an elephant to someone who has never seen one, for example. And trying to describe or discuss relationships among items is similarly easy when only two or three familiar items is involved, but it's another story when many unfamiliar items are involved. For example, one can use simple language to talk about the national production of several different common farm products, but try to explain to a layperson the relationships involved in calculating a flight path among the planets for a NASA explorer vehicle. Even with charts and drawings that isn't easy to do, and without them it's a virtual impossibility.

You may accept as an unvarying principle of all communication aids (illustrations, tables, matrices, and others) that the quality of the aid is inverse to the amount of text required to present and explain it. That is, the perfect communication aid requires no text at all because it explains itself. Let's consider a couple of figures used earlier to examine this proposition.

Table 7-2 was a portion of a typical labor-loading chart. That one simple matrix offers these facts and figures, almost at a glance:

> The phases/tasks/subtasks that make up the project and reflect the project design
> The key people in the project
> The commitments of the key people to the various tasks
> The total effort required for each task
> The total effort required of each key person
> The total effort of all the key people/tasks collectively

Little text is required to support this figure. Quite the contrary, the text used in conjunction with this figure ought to be used to explain the strategies underlying the assignments and estimates shown in the figure.

The milestone chart of Figure 7-3 is another example. Here language is used necessarily in the figure itself, and the effectiveness of the figure lies largely in that language. If the language is accurate and specific enough, no text is required to explain the figure, although text might be used to point out the advantages of the planning shown by the figure.

Compare the figure, the milestone method of presenting the schedule, with the tabular method of presenting the schedule. In the tabular method, since days was the unit, the word had to be qualified with the adjective "working." That was not necessary in the milestone drawing because the unit was weeks, which does not have that ambiguity and so does not have a need for qualifiers. Also, the labels on the lines showing the several functions are unequivocal, as they must be if they are to communicate clearly.

Xerox 5700 Modular Architecture

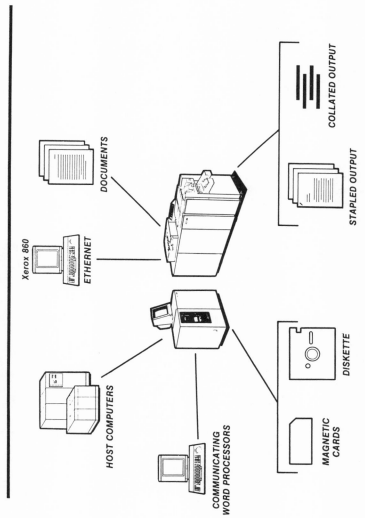

Figure 14-1   Simple pictorial drawing Courtesy Xerox Corporation

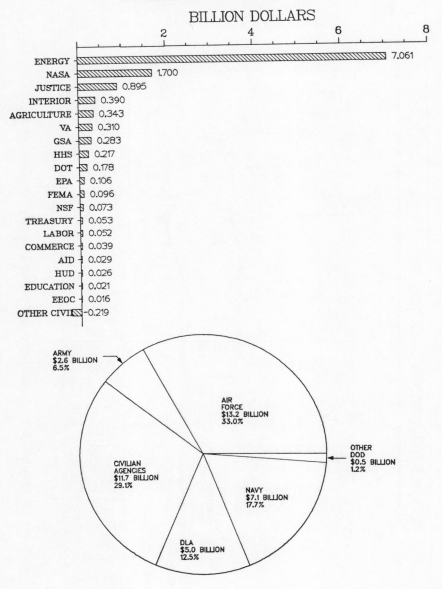

CONTRACT DOLLARS BY EXECUTIVE DEPARTMENTS AND AGENCIES

Actions Reported Individually on SF279

First Quarter Fiscal Year 1984 Year to Date

BILLION DOLLARS

ENERGY — 7.061
NASA — 1.700
JUSTICE — 0.895
INTERIOR — 0.390
AGRICULTURE — 0.343
VA — 0.310
GSA — 0.283
HHS — 0.217
DOT — 0.178
EPA — 0.106
FEMA — 0.096
NSF — 0.073
TREASURY — 0.053
LABOR — 0.052
COMMERCE — 0.039
AID — 0.029
HUD — 0.026
EDUCATION — 0.021
EEOC — 0.016
OTHER CIVIL — -0.219

ARMY
$2.6 BILLION
6.5%

AIR
FORCE
$13.2 BILLION
33.0%

OTHER
DOD
$0.5 BILLION
1.2%

CIVILIAN
AGENCIES
$11.7 BILLION
29.1%

NAVY
$7.1 BILLION
17.7%

DLA
$5.0 BILLION
12.5%

Figure 14-2   Simple bar chart and pie chart

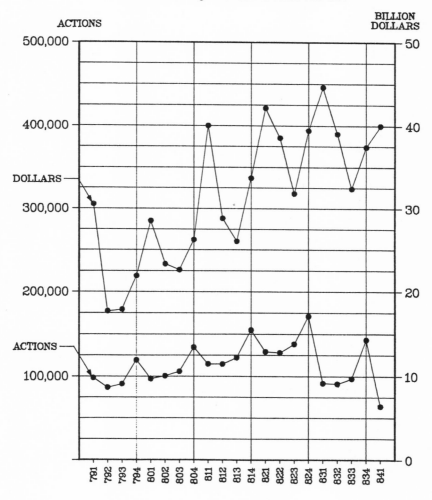

Figure 14-3 Plot (multiple curves)

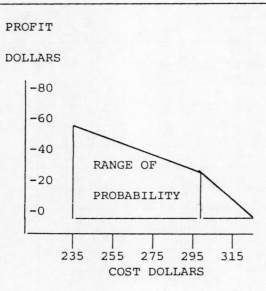

Figure 14-4   Plot (single curve)

DEGREE OF COMPETITION

Actions Reported Individually on SF279

Fourth Quarter Fiscal Year 1983 Year to Date

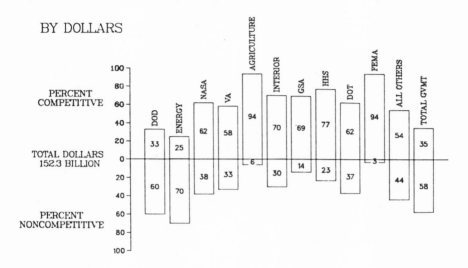

Figure 14-5 Another type of bar chart

SERVICE REQUEST FLOW CHART

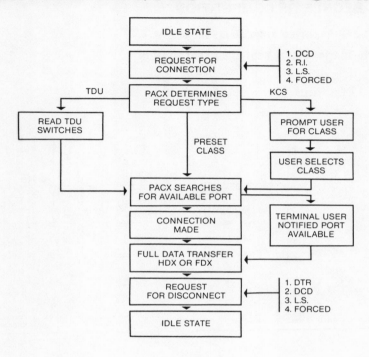

Figure 14-6 Simple functional flowchart. Courtesy Gandalf Technologies, Inc.

PICAS REDUCED TO INCHES

Picas	Inches	Picas	Inches	Picas	Inches	Picas	Inches	Picas	Inches	Picas	Inches
1	0.166	18	2.988	35	5.811	52	8.634	69	11.457	86	14.279
2	.332	19	3.154	36	5.977	53	8.800	70	11.623	87	14.445
3	.498	20	3.320	37	6.143	54	8.966	71	11.789	88	14.611
4	.664	21	3.487	38	6.309	55	9.132	72	11.955	89	14.778
5	.830	22	3.653	39	6.475	56	9.298	73	12.121	90	14.944
6	.996	23	3.819	40	6.641	57	9.464	74	12.287	91	15.110
7	1.162	24	3.985	41	6.807	58	9.630	75	12.453	92	15.276
8	1.328	25	4.151	42	6.973	59	9.796	76	12.619	93	15.442
9	1.494	26	4.317	43	7.139	60	9.962	77	12.785	94	15.608
10	1.660	27	4.483	44	7.306	61	10.128	78	12.951	95	15.774
11	1.826	28	4.649	45	7.472	62	10.294	79	13.117	96	15.940
12	1.992	29	4.815	46	7.638	63	10.460	80	13.283	97	16.106
13	2.158	30	4.981	47	7.804	64	10.626	81	13.449	98	16.272
14	2.324	31	5.147	48	7.970	65	10.792	82	13.615	99	16.438
15	2.490	32	5.313	49	8.136	66	10.959	83	13.781	100	16.604
16	2.656	33	5.479	50	8.302	67	11.125	84	13.947	125	20.750
17	2.822	34	5.645	51	8.468	68	11.291	85	14.113	150	24.900

Common measure	Equivalent	Common measure	Equivalent
Inch	2.54 centimeters.	Dry quart, United States.	1.101 liters.
Foot	0.3048 meter.	Quart, imperial	1.136 liters.
Yard	0.9144 meter.	Gallon, United States	3.785 liters.
Rod	5.029 meters.	Gallon, imperial	4.546 liters.
Mile	1.6093 kilometers.	Peck, United States	8.810 liters.
Square inch	6.452 square centimeters.	Peck, imperial	9.092 liters.
Square foot	0.0929 square meter.	Bushel, United States	35.24 liters.
Square yard	0.836 square meter.	Bushel, imperial	36.37 liters.
Square rod	25.29 square meters.	Ounce, avoirdupois	28.35 grams.
Acre	0.4047 hectare.	Pound, avoirdupois	0.4536 kilogram.
Square mile	259 hectares.	Ton, long	1.0160 metric tons.
Cubic inch	16.39 cubic centimeters.	Ton, short	0.9072 metric ton.
Cubic foot	0.0283 cubic meter.	Grain	0.0648 gram.
Cubic yard	0.7646 cubic meter.	Ounce, troy	31.103 grams.
Cord	3.625 steres.	Pound, troy	0.3732 kilogram.
Liquid quart, United States	0.9463 liter.		

Figure 14-7   Simple tabular presentations.

On the other hand, that table which we often refer to as a matrix is a bit more complex, in that it is generally used to show the correlation of two or more values for any given circumstance or item, and each of the points at which data from the left-hand column coincides with data from an overhead column is called a "cell." An example of this, simple although it appears, is shown in Figure 14-8.

The Word Processor in Proposal Writing

Unfortunately, few organizations have appeared to understand what word processing can do for their writing chores, especially in proposal writing. Far too often the word processor has simply replaced the typewriter. Proposal writers are still working at their desks, scrawling their copy on paper, and turning it over to the typing or secretarial staff, now known by the new euphemism, "word processor operators," but still doing very much the same job that such personnel have always done. Instead of typing the rough drafts, the secretarial people now input the copy for printout, and thus word processing contributes little beyond increasing the efficiency of the typists and secretaries. And while that is, of course, a gain, it is only a fraction of the benefits that could be realized by a more insightful application of word processing.

The true potential of word processing can be achieved only if the writers and editors work at the terminals, inputting their copy directly. To understand this, it is necessary to realize that creating a proposal, or any other document, for that matter, consists of at least three distinct stages of work:

1. First (rough) drafts, after initial planning sessions
2. Reviews, comments, revisions, and succeeding (and final) drafts
3. Production—final editing, art work, composition, printing, and binding

Using the conventional method of having typists input the system ("keyboard" the copy) from handwritten rough drafts results in the chief benefits of word processing deriving primarily in the second and final stages because the system eliminates retyping of any copy that has not been changed. Using conventional systems of the past, as many still do today, unless changes are minor it is often more practical to retype complete pages than to make corrections; ergo, second and succeeding drafts usually require total or near-total retyping of the entire manuscript. And so it is not at all unusual for a proposal, manual, or other such document to go through several complete typing cycles, one for each draft phase, and there might be as many as five or more such cycles, resulting from the following series of events:

1. Editorial reviews of rough drafts
2. First revisions, second draft
3. Technical reviews for technical accuracy and completeness, comments, changes, additions
4. Second revision, third draft
5. Marketing review for salesmanship, related considerations
6. Third revision, fourth draft

PACX COMES IN ALL SIZES TO MEET YOUR NEEDS

Terminal / Port	48	128	256	384	512	640	768	896	1024
32	mini PACX IV								
128		COMPACX IV	PACX IV						
256			Dual COMPACX IV SE		Dual PACX IV SE				
384				Tri COMPACX IV SE			Tri PACX IV SE		
512					Quad COMPACX IV SE				Quad PACX IV SE

NOTE: All combinations of ports and terminals can be supplied. Contact the factory for non-standard configurations.

□ Minimum system: 4 terminals/8 ports
□ Easily upgraded to maximum of 1024 terminals/512
□ Maximum connections: 512 full duplex at 9600 bps

Figure 14-8 Matrix type of tabular presentation. Courtesy Gandalf Technologies, Inc.

7. Management review by top-level (usually corporate) executives, with questions, comments, changes
8. Fourth revision, fifth (and hopefully final) draft

Each of these stages might have iterations, so that at least some portions of the proposal might have an even greater number of revisions and drafts. It is often an inefficient process, and in many cases the major problem becomes one of persuading management to perform their review in time to permit the final changes to be made without the necessity for frantic, last-minute (and often all-night) working sessions to complete the project. (Except for those cases where the government decides to extend the schedule for everyone, there is no such thing as acceptance of late delivery of a proposal: if late, even by minutes, the proposal must be and will be disqualified and rejected.)

Word processing helps this situation to the extent defined, by reducing the amount of retyping (rekeyboarding, that is) required to produce revised manuscript copy.

Word processing can customize "boilerplate" material, which is standardized material that can be used over and over. This includes, for example, such items as résumés of staff members, descriptions of company resources and facilities, accounts of current or recent projects, and other such material. However, there is a hazard in this, too: Usually such material should be customized—modified somewhat—to fit the application. Such customizing can make a vast difference in the contribution to success the material makes. Again, the word processor is an enormously useful resource in its ability to summon up such materials from archive files and creating that modified version that fits the proposal best.

Still another help that can be derived is help with graphics, producing many of them by using programs that produce charts and graphs. Obviously this can be done more rapidly and more efficiently by computer than by pen and template.

The problem with all of this is that unless the writer works at a computer or smart terminal (work station) the benefits in saving labor and time (which latter is often the most precious and least abundant resource in proposal work) are marginal. It is possible for the word processor operator to print out the boilerplate files, have the writer scrawl the changes on the hard copy, and have the operator then make the changes via the keyboard and print out the revised hard copy. But little time or labor are saved by doing this.

On the other hand, when the writer does actual writing at the keyboard the process moves much more rapidly and efficiently. And the writer can summon up those archives on-screen, study the files to find those which are most suitable for adaptation to the current need, and make the changes spontaneously.

The editor, technical reviewers, marketing reviewers, and management reviewers ought also to work at terminals and review copy on-screen, rather than as hard copy. They can, with most programs, make remarks or comments that will not print, but which can be read on-screen by writers charged with making the necessary revisions. Or the reviewers can create a special review file and record their comments, criticisms, and suggestions there.

The common misconception of word processing is that its chief benefit is in the time and labor it saves because it eliminates much of the retyping otherwise necessary. (That is probably the result of understanding word processing as a computer function, rather than as a writing function.) Using it as suggested here, by having all editorial and review functions done directly at the keyboards is only the first step in getting fuller benefits from word processing. (However, this approach does not eliminate the need for word processor operators, for there is still much for them to do in running speller programs and proofreading, in organizing the files, in supervising the printing out of the final hard copy for duplicating, and in attending to sundry other necessary tasks.) But using word processing as suggested here delivers at least one other, highly important benefit: It results in *better* writing, too. Here's why:

A writer's platitude (which is not less true because it is a platitude) has it that all good writing is rewriting, and the professional writer accepts that rewriting is a necessity, just as a knowledge of grammar and punctuation are necessities. Rewriting is hard work and time consuming as well, however, and even the most critical writer self-edits while inevitably weighing the benefits of any given task of rewriting against the time and labor required. Quite often even the painstaking professional reluctantly forgoes some contemplated revision because the need for it is not absolute, and time is pressing.

Word processing has changed that to quite a large extent for the writer who works at the keyboard. Word processing has made revisions, and even major rewriting, so much easier than it ever was before that many if not most writers who have turned to word processing find themselves doing far more rewriting, revision, self-editing, and polishing of their copy than ever before. (The greater efficiency that word processing brings to the process often allows the writer more time to make revisions and polish copy.)

The result is better writing, and that means better proposals and therefore a better chance to emerge as the winner in proposal competitions. That alone, even disregarding all other considerations, should make it worthwhile to seat proposal writers at word processing keyboards.

It's ironic that computer professionals in organizations devoted to computers and their applications appear often to be as slow to recognize this as are those to whom the computer is an awesome mystery.

Procurement Classifications

The columns of the *Commerce Business Daily* that should be of interest to you cover both computer goods and services. The service categories under which you are likely to find relevant requirements include all of the following:

A Experimental, Developmental, Test and Research Work
H Expert and Consultant Services
J Maintenance and/or Repair of Equipment

L Technical Representative Services
M Operation and/or Maintenance of Government Owned Facility
T Photographic, Mapping, Printing and Publication Services
U Training Services
X Miscellaneous

Some of these, such as Category T, may appear inappropriate to computer services. However, if you check Figure 2-1, you will find some examples of computer services called for under that category, as well as others. Sometimes this is human error: the synopsis managed somehow to find its way into the wrong column; it happens with a fair degree of regularity. Sometimes it is deliberate; the agency placing the notice has specifically and deliberately requested that it be in the column where it appears. So unless you keep an eye on all these columns, even though some may appear inappropriate, you are likely to miss a few good opportunities.

Computer goods, as distinct from services, appear under a numbered category, 70. And although some subdivisions of that group were listed earlier, it is helpful to review the entire list, as published by the General Services Administration. These are category numbers used by the General Services Administration's Federal Supply Service, with which you may register and seek listing on the appropriate Federal Supply Schedules. These are term contracts (usually for one year) you can sign with the General Services Administration. (Ask about this at any of the GSA Business Service Centers listed earlier.) There are also some service categories listed, following the numbered supply-group listings.

GROUP 70–GENERAL PURPOSE AUTOMATIC DATA PROCESSING EQUIPMENT, SOFTWARE, SUPPLIES AND SUPPORT EQUIPMENT

7010 ADPE Configuration
7020 ADP central processing unit (CPU, computer) analog
7021 ADP central processing unit (CPU, computer) digital
7022 ADP central processing unit (CPU, computer) hybrid
7025 ADP input/output and storage devices
  Memory—magnetic storage
  Magnetic tape subsystems
  Magnetic disk subsystems
  Printers, high speed (ADP)
  Paper tape devices
  Batch terminal
  Interactive display
  Interactive graphics
  Interactive hard copy
  Other ADP input/output storage devices
7030 ADP software
  Application programs
  Data base management programs
  Systems programs
  Other ADP software
7035 ADP accessorial equipment
  Computer output microfilm equipment

7040 Punched card equipment
7045 ADP supplies and support equipment
   Attachments and features for EDP tape
   Bands, wraparound, tape reel
   Burster, paper forms
   Cassettes, digital, EDP tape
   Reels, empty, glass, porcelain, for EDP tape
   Tape, electronic data processing
7050 ADP components

Despite these categories, requirements of interest may appear under other, more general categories. Following are some of those. (Only those subgroups related to computers are listed here.)

GROUP 69—TRAINING AIDS AND DEVICES

6910 Training aids
   Programmed learning material
6930 Operational training devices
   Computer training devices
   Electricity/electronic training devices

GROUP 71—FURNITURE

7110 Office furniture
   ADP transportation equipment
   Desks and cabinets, card punch and programmers
   Storage and handling equipment for accessories to ADP and EAM systems
   Sound reducing devices for ADP equipment

GROUP 74—OFFICE MACHINES AND VISIBLE RECORD EQUIPMENT

7430 Typewriters and office type composing machines
   Card, magnetic for word processing machines
   Cassette, magnetic tape for word processing machines
   Word processing machines, magnetic surface, card type
   Word processing machines, magnetic surface, disk type
   Word processing machines, magnetic surface, tape type

RELEVANT SERVICE GROUPS LISTED BY GSA

0787 Computer and data processing services
   Computer time
   Engineering
   Keypunch and verifying
   Maintenance, EDP
   Management consulting support, except programming
   Programming services (ADPE)
   Research and development
   Scanning, optical
   Systems design
   Tape magnetic, conversion to microfilm

Tape maintenance, magnetic
Tape service, key
Time sharing
Training
Teleprocessing
Maintenance, PCAM

Glossary

As in every special field, government marketing and contracting has its own special jargon and acronyms. Sometimes the acronym or colloquial term becomes known better and recognized more easily than the formal term or name for which it stands. Moreover, there is no true consistency in the methods employed. The Agriculture Department, for example, is USDA, but the Labor Department is DOL, and the Treasury Department is simply Treasury. The following is a brief glossary of terms you will encounter most commonly in doing business with the federal government.

Advertised bid, advertised procurement; also formally advertised procurement: Procurement requiring sealed bids and public opening on an announced date and time at an announced place, with award normally to the low bidder; usually requires price quotes only and is solicited by IFB (Information for Bid).

ADP: Automated data processing.

ADTS: Automated Data and Telecommunications Service.

AEC: Atomic Energy Commission.

AFB: Air Force Base.

AID: Agency for International Development

ASPR: Armed Services Procurement Regulations; former procurement regulations, replaced by DAR—Defense Acquisition Regulations and, more recently, by FAR—Federal Acquisition Regulations. Below the line: Providing goods or service to customer at cost; sometimes required for certain kinds of items, especially in some cost-plus contracts.

Best and final offer: Invitation often extended to finalists in negotiated procurement to review and adjust their prices before final decision.

BIA: Bureau of Indian Affairs.

Bid set: Package of information and forms required to make bid; same as solicitation package.

Bidder's conference, prebid conference: Conference held in advance of some awards to answer questions and provide more detailed information to bidders and/or proposers.

BLM: Bureau of Land Management.

BLS: Bureau of Labor Statistics.

BOA: Basic Ordering Agreement; contract to supply goods/services at set (contracted) rates, as called for by customer, an indefinite-quantity term contract.

CBD: Commerce Business Daily.

C/E: Corps of Engineers

CO: Contracting Officer.

COB: Close of business, but that time at which the office in question ends its work day, which varies from one office to another; often cited as time bid or proposal is due on given date.

CONUS. Continental United States

COR: Contracting Officer's Representative; also COTR and GTR; government technical manager or project manager.

COTR: Contracting Officer's Technical Representative; see COR.

CPAF: Cost plus award fee, a cost-reimbursement type of contract often used when government wants to furnish incentives to contractor.

CPFF: Cost plus fixed fee; another type of cost-reimbursement contract often used when it is difficult to estimate costs in advance.

DARPA: Defense Advanced Research Projects Agency.

DCA: Defense Communications Agency

DCAA: Defense Contract Audit Agency; DoD contractor auditors, who often audit contractors for other government agencies.

DCASR: Defense Contract Administration Service Region; field office of DoD that carries out many duties for DoD, including security inspections and inspections to approve shipment of contracted-for goods.

D/E: Department of Education

DEA: Drug Enforcement Administration

DIA: Defense Intelligence Administration

DLA: Defense Logistics Agency

DOC: Department of Commerce

DoD: Department of Defense

DOL: Department of Labor

DOT: Department of Transportation

End-product: Item to be delivered; also "deliverable" item. Evaluation criteria: Factors used to evaluate proposals objectively.

FAA: Federal Aviation Administration

FDA: Food and Drug Administration

FmHA: Farmers Home Administration

Form 33: Form usually used as first sheet of solicitation package for both IFB and RFP solicitations.

Form 60: Cost form used by most nonmilitary agencies.

Form DD-633: Cost form used by military agencies.

Form 129: Bidders application form.

FP: Fixed price, as in fixed-price contract.

FPDC: Federal Procurement Data Center

FPR: Federal Procurement Regulations; now replaced by

FAR—Federal Acquisition Regulations.

FRA: Federal Railroad Administration

FTS: Federal Telecommunications System

GAO: General Accounting Office

GSA: General Services Administration

GPO: Government Printing Office

GSA Schedule: Term contract for common-use commmodities.

GTR: Government Technical Representative; same as COR and COTR (which see).

HHS: Department of Health and Human Services

HRA: Health Resources Administration

HSA: Health Services Administration

HUD: Department of Housing and Urban Development

Indefinite quantity: Term contract for goods/services to be supplied as called for and at prices agreed on.

IFB: Information for Bid; see Advertised bid. Labor-hour contract: Type of BOA listing labor rates.

MBDA: Minority Business Development Agency.

NASA: National Aviation and Aeronautics Administration.

Negotiated procurement: Usually solicited via RFP and requiring a proposal competition; contract to be negotiated and not bound by lowest bid.

NHTSA: National Highway Traffic Safety Administration.

NIDA: National Institute of Drug Abuse

NIH: National Institutes of Health

NIMH: National Institutes of Mental Health

NIOSH: National Institute of Safety and Health

NLM: National Library of Medicine

NOAA: National Oceanic and Atmospheric Administration

NOL: Naval Ordnance Laboratory

Nonresponsive: Characteristic of a bid or proposal that fails to respond as requested; also applied to performance of a contractor who fails to respond to the government's direction or requests.

NRL: Naval Research Laboratory

OFPP: Office of Federal Procurement Policy

OMB: Office of Management and Budget

OPM: Office of Personnel Management, new name for Civil Service Commission

OSHA: Occupational Safety and Health Administration

PHS: Public Health Service

Preaward survey: Visit to bidder's facility, prior to contract award, to Inspect and verify that all is as represented by bidder.

Proposal: Response to RFP describing what bidder proposes and pledges to do and at what cost.

Purchase order: Informal type of contract that may be used for smaller purchases (to $10,000 in most agencies, to $25,000 in DoD, under present law).

RFP: Request for Proposals

RFQ: Request for Quotation; often followed by issuing a purchase order to firm submitting lowest quotation.

SBA: Small Business Administration

SOW: Statement of Work, which is specification issued with RFP.

Task order: One of the orders issued under a BOA for services; also used as contracting term, as in Task Order Contract.

T&M: Time and Material, another type if BOA.

TVA: Tennessee Valley Authority
USAF: U.S. Air Force
USA: U.S. Army
USCG: U.S. Coast Guard
USDA: U.S. Department of Agriculture
USN: U.S. Navy
USMC: U.S. Marine Corps
USPS: U.S. Postal Service

INDEX